‘Out of Sight, out of Mind’: Infanticide, Baby Farming and Abortion in South and West Wales, 1870–1922

Shirley A. Smith

First published 2021
by Rowanvale Books Ltd
The Gate
Keppoch Street
Roath
Cardiff
CF24 3JW
www.rowanvalebooks.com

A CIP catalogue record for this book is available from the British Library.

ISBN: 978-1-912655-72-4

Contents

Introduction

Towards the end of the nineteenth century and during the twentieth century, the fear of giving birth to an illegitimate child compelled many women to consider options that were detrimental to infant life rather than face the stark reality of unmarried motherhood. Illegitimate children were frequently born as a consequence of broken relationships; however, a significant number of unwanted pregnancies were the result of sexual harassment and abuse. The ever-present hardship of unmarried motherhood is exposed in the case of a young servant girl, Miriam Jones, who was fifteen years old when she gave birth to an illegitimate child in December 1885. The child's father was reputed to be Miriam's employer, a farmer named William Lewis. Petty session records show that Miriam Jones made three applications to the court to secure maintenance from the child's father, but each attempt failed for 'want of corroborative evidence'.[1] With no financial support, Miriam put her child in the care of a nurse at a cost of two shillings per week, although she earned little more than the cost of childcare. In a state of despair, Miriam abandoned her eighteen-month-old infant in a disused mineshaft at Troedyrhiw, Merthyr. It was reported in the press that when questioned as to the child's whereabouts, Miriam Jones 'invented a story the palpable incredibility of which suggested that her mind must have been somewhat unhinged'. It was claimed that 'the girl's intellect was never considered to be very robust, and she was generally regarded as "rather silly"'.[2] The abandoned child was later discovered in the mineshaft unharmed. Miriam Jones was arrested and appeared at Glamorgan Assizes, Swansea, in May 1887, where she was charged and convicted of the attempted murder of her child and sentenced to eight years' imprisonment.

Many young women and girls like Miriam Jones committed all their resources to raising their illegitimate children, despite the shame and economic constraints of unmarried motherhood. Failure on the man's part to marry the woman once pregnant, or the absence of familial support, forced unmarried mothers to consider the options available. The most likely recourse was to sue the reputed father for the child's maintenance; then again, the process to prove paternity was often humiliating and fraught with difficulties. The workhouse was an option because the place offered shelter, food and a lying-in ward, but the harsh regime meant that most women deemed it to be the last resort. Of course, abandonment of the child to the workhouse was an alternative, although this was a punishable offence if the mother was apprehended by the authorities. Putting the child out to nurse to ease the burden of bringing up an illegitimate infant was another option, yet low wages forced many women to agree to childcare arrangements with nurses who regularly operated as baby farmers. The option also existed for a woman to terminate the pregnancy, though this course of action involved risk since abortion was a criminal offence until it was decriminalised under the Abortion Act in 1967.[3] The illegal operation of abortion was also life-threatening because of the danger of infection after the procedure, although Barbara Brookes points out that 'the level of knowledge possessed by women was apparently high enough to keep the dangers of induced abortion to an acceptable level'.[4] Ultimately, women had 'agency', which Jessica Sheetz-Nguyen explains as 'the ability of individuals to act, to choose one thing and not another, in historical and unique ways'.[5] Unlike Miriam Jones, many women did not consider any other option; they denied their pregnancy to others and determined from the outset to conceal the birth, killed the infant as it was born and secretly disposed of the body.

The objective of this book is to consider the vulnerability of newborn illegitimate infants to the crime of murder at the hands of their mothers. To achieve this aim, consideration is given to the social and economic causes of illegitimacy, and society's reactions to unmarried motherhood and child murder in Wales. Baby farmers, abortionists and other persons were also implicated in the deaths of many infants, either directly or indirectly. Individuals interacted with each other in order to deal with unwanted infants, not only on a personal level but also within the local community as a whole.

Contemporary attitudes concerning mothers who committed newborn child murder were that they were at odds with what was considered to be their natural instinct to protect and nurture. Josephine McDonagh points out that there was 'a strong sense of ambivalence: a fascination with, and a horror of, its violence, but at the same time a seemingly sympathetic tolerance towards it, a willingness to turn a blind eye'.[6] The crime still attracts our attention because of a mother's inability to fulfil her natural role. Indeed, the extreme action taken by a mother in killing her child certainly provides good reason to engage with the subject and to try to understand her motives, because in the majority of cases it was not just a random act of violence. The circumstances and motives associated with cases of newborn child murder expose society's reaction and, crucially, illustrate to what extent social attitudes were a causal factor in the first instance. The crime elicits an important question, and it is also the most obvious one: what led mothers to commit newborn child murder? However, this question does not just relate to single women who murdered their infants, because it is also relevant to other individuals who committed the act or were an accomplice to it.

The motives of other perpetrators of child murder also require explanation. Katherine Watson maintains that 'the historical discourse on new-born child murder has tended to overlook three significant groups: infants who were not neonates; married women; and men'.[7] As this is a group that lacks research, this study also considers the reasons why married mothers killed their infants. Older children were more likely to be the victims of parents who were mentally disturbed at the time the crime was committed; therefore, to provide an overall perspective, the book also examines both maternal and paternal child murder as a consequence of mental illness.

Understandably, the crime is an enduring phenomenon that has generated emotional responses and controversies over time. As Mark Jackson points out, 'there are historical continuities in cases of suspected child murder across many centuries', and 'many of the social, legal, political and cultural concerns related to the supposed murder of new-born children also demonstrate remarkable historical consistency'.[8] Furthermore, studies of individual cases from recent decades inform us that modern-day cases are much the same as those in centuries past, with the focus on single women and the concealment of pregnancy and birth.[9] Michelle Oberman also found that in modern-day cases women reported that they lived with their pregnancies day to day, dealing with their ordinary lives, in the hope that the pregnancy would disappear or that someone would notice and take control of the situation.[10]

As the so-called 'infanticide panic' during the mid-nineteenth century was due mainly to the alarming number of reported infanticide cases in London, cities and larger towns, historians of the Victorian period have studied infanticide as an English phenomenon. This is reflected in earlier studies of infanticide during the late 1970s and 1980s, such as those undertaken by Ann R. Higginbotham, George K. Behlmer and Lionel Rose.[11] Evidence indicates that infanticide also increased in Wales, and social commentators of the day often attributed such cases to the introduction of the New Poor Law and the Bastardy Clause in 1834. McDonagh maintains that there was a division into those 'who saw child murder as a crime committed by sexually deviant, unmarried women', and others who believed 'it to be a crime provoked by archaic or corrupt institutions, which themselves required reform'.[12] The notorious Bastardy Clause, and the dreaded institution known as the workhouse, was to prove injurious to both unmarried mothers and illegitimate children as the new law provided men with the opportunity to evade responsibility for their offspring. Its implementation was to have a significant bearing on cases of infanticide and child desertion as women made desperate attempts to avoid the strict regime of the new purpose-built local workhouse.[13] The situation for women at this point was exacerbated when the Reports of the Commissioners of Inquiry into the State of Education in Wales, published in 1847, attacked the moral character of the lower orders, particularly women, prompting a backlash amongst the Welsh people.[14] As parts of Wales were strongholds of Nonconformity, the religious hard-line approach was to have long-lasting repercussions for women, especially the persistent allegations of immorality levelled at unmarried mothers.[15]

Childcare provision for working-class women was of a variable standard; but it was one option open to unmarried mothers. Alternatively, parents paid baby farmers lump-sum payments to 'adopt' infants on a permanent basis, often fully aware that the infants' chances of survival were low. The practice of baby farming was blamed for an increasing number of infant deaths caused by ignorance, poverty, wilful neglect or cruelty. Baby farming came to public notice largely due to the high-profile criminal case of

Margaret Waters in 1870. Margaret Arnot maintains that Margaret Waters 'became symbolic of the irresponsibility of a section of womanhood who made a trade out of motherhood – child-carers, baby-farmers and midwives were blamed for infanticide as a whole'.[16] As Ruth Homrighaus points out, there were baby farmers of 'different stripes' and they ranged from honest to criminal in nature.[17]

Sherri Broder's study of baby farmers in nineteenth-century Philadelphia reveals that many people at the time were:

> Convinced that the provision of child care for the children of working mothers in poor neighbourhoods was linked to the wholesale murder of infants, working-class and middle-class men and women alike feared that many baby farmers provided child-care services only as a camouflage for the flagrant destruction of unwanted infants.[18]

The *British Medical Journal* (*BMJ*) argued that:

> A child found dead on a doorstep produces a coroner's inquest, and leaders in journals, and indignant sensation with the public; but the laying in the grave of some scores of innocents by the gentle, unobtrusive, and gradual administering of soothing syrups, and other agents productive of infantile quietism, disturbs not the coroner, the press, nor the public.[19]

Simply by treading a fine line it was possible for criminal baby farmers to withhold an infant's basic food and provisions necessary for survival, therefore hastening the child's death and maximising profit. The practice was widely condemned, but not all childminders were baby famers and many genuinely offered childcare to unmarried mothers.

Abortion was one method used to put an end to unwanted pregnancies. Even though women have resorted to the procedure for centuries, Angus McLaren maintains that abortion has not received much attention from historians because 'it has not been viewed as a "respectable" subject of research'.[20] The growing interest in women's history since the 1970s has resulted in a shift in attitude; so the subject is no longer considered inappropriate. Abortion was a criminal act during this period; therefore, the lack of particular interest in the subject is problematical because of the scarcity of primary sources. Despite this, criminal cases of abortion, although very few in number, provide a wealth of information regarding women's lives, unwanted pregnancies, the complicity and role of men and the society in which they lived. As abortion was an illegal practice, Patricia Knight argues that women were 'very reluctant to proclaim that they had attempted abortion which was regarded by respectable opinion with the same horror as infanticide'.[21] Robert Sauer maintains that by the end of the nineteenth century 'infanticide had been largely replaced by abortion as a means of avoiding those burdens'.[22] Even though abortion might have been a preferred option, infanticide cases continued to be brought before the Welsh courts during the years 1870–1922.

While the same issues relating to child murder have remained consistent over time, Anne-Marie Kilday explains that 'The confluence of the fields of medicine and the law in relation to newborn child murder has opened up the study of infanticide to medical and legal historians, and has introduced a further layer of perspectives on this crime, that was simply not in existence 50 years ago.'[23] Considering the position of women as a separate group, Roger Smith highlights their sensitivity to mental illness and discusses infanticide from the 'distinctive social, medical and legal position of women'.[24] Also considering the crime from a medical perspective, Watson found that women who murdered their infants were sometimes labelled as either 'mad' or 'bad' because their behaviour was so unnatural that their actions were deemed pathological in nature. As Watson points out, for the last three decades researchers of infanticide have found that a 'range of emotional, economic and social factors can drive a woman to dispose of an infant; it is not simply a question of 'mad' or 'bad''.[25] Similarly, Anette Ballinger argues that 'the reasons why women kill cannot usually be traced to pathological causes – that is – the majority of these women are neither mad nor bad'.[26]

Infanticide victims were typically illegitimate and newly born. However, married mothers also killed their infants while suffering from mental illness associated with childbirth, which was diagnosed at the time as 'puerperal insanity' or 'lactational insanity', although it is known today as postpartum psychosis.[27] This illness was not the same as the temporary insanity experienced by women during childbirth and utilised as a form of defence in some cases of newborn child murder. Women suffering from puerperal insanity were admitted in increasing numbers to the newly constructed public asylums from the mid-nineteenth century onwards. The asylums, as Joan Busfield points out, 'provided an empire which could be colonised by an emergent breed of medical specialists – psychiatrists – whose power and influence was grounded in the asylums which they tended to dominate'.[28] As mentally ill women provided psychiatrists with a steady flow of patients, Hilary Marland found that 'the nineteenth century represented an optimal environment for puerperal insanity to gain recognition, and to flourish'.[29]

Pamela Michael's significant contribution on the subject of mental illness in Wales highlights the value of asylum records as a source of information, yet puerperal insanity remains a much-neglected subject in Wales.[30] The importance of asylum case files to historians of mental illness cannot be understated, because the records prove to be extremely beneficial to the medical understanding of mental illness as a cause of child murder. Fortunately for researchers, the West London Mental Health NHS Trust has granted public access to the historic records relating to Broadmoor Criminal Lunatic Asylum, currently held at Berkshire Record Office. Access to the Glamorgan County Asylum and Broadmoor Criminal Lunatic Asylum records provides the opportunity to consider the correlation between the condition and child murder. A search of the Glamorgan Asylum casebooks for the years 1874–76, 1886–87, 1895–96 and 1905–06 identified sixty-five cases relating to mothers suffering from puerperal-related mental illness. This particular research is introduced into this study for two reasons. Firstly, an assessment of the causes and diagnoses associated with puerperal-related mental illness aids our understanding of the subject when referring to the case studies of four married mothers confined at Broadmoor for child murder. Secondly, a search of the casebooks helps to determine the incidence of child murder as a consequence of insanity based on data collected from one selected Welsh asylum. The focus is on female insanity, but historians have also studied mental illness as a cause of paternal child murder.[31] As the Broadmoor records reveal a local case of paternal child murder, this provides the opportunity to investigate it from a male perspective.

The subject of infanticide has generated considerable interest from historians over recent years, yet the situation in Wales has largely been overlooked.[32] One study that has brought attention to this subject is Katherine Watson's research relating to the experiences of women as perpetrators of infanticide in Georgian Wales. Watson draws upon records of the Welsh Courts of Great Session dating from 1730 until their abolition in favour of the Courts of Assize in 1830, emphasising the leniency shown by jurors and the relaxation of attitudes during the eighteenth century. This continued into the nineteenth century, when most convictions occurred, following the introduction of the lesser charge of concealment of birth in 1803. It was also the case that the use of medical evidence at infanticide trials continued to produce more acquittals.[33] From another viewpoint, Dana Rabin argues that 'While scholars have pointed to the jury's sympathy with the single women accused of this crime, consideration of the culture of sensibility and its emphasis on experience, emotion and sympathy explains the defences made by the accused and suggests reasons for their acceptance by judges and juries.'[34] Nick Woodward also examined the records for the Welsh Courts of Great Session for the same period and concluded that the number of indictments for infanticide declined in Wales, despite a growth in population and increasing illegitimacy rates. Woodward maintains that one likely explanation for the decline was that 'it was linked to an increase in nuptiality and illegitimacy, which may have reduced the stigma of bastardy and improved the marriage prospects of unmarried mothers'.[35] In contrast to Watson's and Woodward's research on the period prior to 1830, Richard Ireland's study is based on mid-nineteenth-century cases recorded in the Carmarthen Felons' Register between 1844–71. Ireland investigated the legal responses relating to child destruction in Victorian Carmarthen to examine the outcome of those accused in court, which raised questions as to the relationship between the accused, the court and the impact upon communities and 'related jury behaviour to the social conditions and beliefs of south-west Wales'.[36]

While studies of infanticide in Wales have been carried out, one area of this subject that has received little attention is those crimes committed during the late nineteenth and early twentieth centuries. Therefore, as this is a period lacking in research, this book evaluates cases dating from 1870: a suitable point at which to begin an investigation into infanticide in south and west Wales following the 'infanticide panic' of the 1860s. The year 1870 is also an appropriate start date since it was at this point in time that baby farming emerged as an increasing social problem, and it was also during the 1880s that both single and married women were far more inclined to resort to abortion as a form of birth control. The end date of the book coincides with the introduction of the first Infanticide Act in 1922. The Infanticide Act made a provision for a separate offence of manslaughter to be brought against the mother, instead of murder. This removed the mandatory death penalty, which had long been a source of criticism since women found guilty of the crime were forced to endure the torturous ordeal of the threat of impending death by hanging while awaiting a reprieve of the death sentence.

The terminology employed to describe child murder as either newborn child murder or infanticide has changed over time. Mark Jackson explains that during the seventeenth and eighteenth century the term 'newborn child murder' was usually used, but from the early nineteenth century the term 'infanticide' was applied to describe the killing of both newborns and older children. By the early twentieth century, the use of the term 'infanticide' changed once more, which had much to do with the recognition of insanity associated with childbirth as a form of defence. Infanticide 'remains the term most commonly employed by both modern commentators and historians to describe the murder of young children'.[37] Throughout this period Welsh newspapers reported on the crime as both cases of infanticide and child murder; therefore the terms are used interchangeably. The majority of infants were killed at birth or soon afterwards, with most victims under the age of twelve months. However, this book takes into account perpetrators of the crime other than single women. For that reason, the research is not restricted to cases of murder of newborns and includes older infants up to the age of two years. For the purposes of this book, the terminology employed to refer to the murder of infants less than twelve months old is that of infanticide or newborn child murder, although child murder is also used and means the same. The case of the murder of an older child is referred to as child murder.

A diverse range of sources is drawn upon, consisting of petty session court records, Home Office papers, gaol registers, coroners' records, parliamentary reports, pamphlets, medical journals, contemporary journals, periodicals, Glamorgan County Asylum casebooks and case files relating to Broadmoor Criminal Lunatic Asylum. The coroners' inquests for Pembrokeshire and Carmarthenshire have not survived; therefore, in the absence of some records, newspapers have proved to be an excellent source, especially because official documents, where they do exist, are often brief and limited in the amount of information provided. The coroners' inquests are also an important source for locating baby farming cases; a reliance on criminal trials would result in omissions, as many baby farmers often received nothing more than censure from the coroner. This same principle is also applicable in the search for cases of infanticide and abortion that did not proceed to the criminal courts.

Historians recognise the importance of newspapers, not only for the study of infanticide but for crime in general.[38] The publication of letters to the editor and editorials provided commentators and the public with an interesting forum to debate the issues associated with child murder, particularly in cases where women had been convicted of wilful murder. In fact, the press had considerable power to influence the outcome of criminal cases. As David Nash and Anne-Marie Kilday point out, the press could 'construct images and perceptions of the individual criminal and sometimes of an entire criminal class'.[39] One point to consider is that the press had particular political allegiances; therefore, newspapers can be problematic and biased in their opinions. The press were also known for inaccuracies, so potential discrepancies must be borne in mind when scrutinising newspapers, although some official records were not without errors either and could be contradictory at times. Even taking into account any potential errors, newspapers as a source to investigate infanticide do, as Nicola Goc points out, 'provide the rich social and political context that allows us to better understand the motivations of women who killed their babies'.[40] Not surprisingly, given the significance of the local, regional and national press, there is a considerable reliance on newspapers as a source to explore illegitimacy and infanticide within Welsh communities.

The book focuses on a wide range of cases drawn from both rural and urban communities situated in the western rural counties of Pembrokeshire, Carmarthenshire and Cardiganshire and the industrial southern county of Glamorganshire. The issues affecting women cannot be truly understood just by collating data from official records; therefore, a micro-historical approach has been adopted, as few historians have addressed the causes, consequences and impact of infanticide in Welsh communities. Scrutiny of selected cases uncovers and connects a range of significant underlying issues that gave rise to child murder, which can only improve our understanding of the crime.

Chapter One considers the extent of shame and condemnation associated with immorality and illegitimacy to question the perception of unmarried mothers as sexual deviants. The content of the first part of this chapter is pre-1870 because the controversial government reports published in 1844 and 1847 relating solely to Wales expose the prevailing attitudes of the ruling classes directed at women and, therefore, provide the necessary background to the subsequent chapters. The second part of the chapter examines affiliation cases brought before the courts by mothers to establish the paternity of illegitimate children and sue the reputed fathers for maintenance. Breach-of-promise-of-marriage civil court cases have also been introduced into this chapter since a number of illegitimate children were born as a consequence of breach of promise of marriage. The legal actions initiated in the civil courts are fascinating because, as Ginger Frost found from her research, breach of promise cases created scandals, prompting the press to print sensational details, including testimonies, love letters and poetry.[41] These cases form a key source highlighting Welsh courting practices, the breakdown of relationships, gendered attitudes and class divisions. An analysis of cases renders it possible to assess community reactions to illegitimacy and responses by the courts concerning reputed fathers.

Chapter Two explores the activities of individual baby farmers to establish their motives and to what extent the practice existed in Welsh communities. It examines the influence of the issues of gender and class on baby farming, and the reasons why certain individuals took advantage of the baby farmers' services. There is no shortage of reported cases of baby farming in the press; however, this study pays attention to fifteen selected cases in particular, and they are referred to as a source to discriminate between the different types of baby farmers operating in south and west Wales. The chapter also considers the effects of statutory measures and the policing of infant life protection legislation on the reduction of cases, leading to the final elimination of the practice of baby farming.

The third chapter assesses the active role of abortionists in the destruction of infant life, which provided women with the option to terminate an unwanted pregnancy. Although evidence is limited, access to a number of different sources presents the opportunity to investigate the activities of abortionists and midwives during this period. The research sifts through newspaper reports, medical journals, contemporary journals, periodicals and parliamentary reports relating to infant life protection. An assessment of twenty-one criminal abortion cases proves significant because, unlike single women who committed infanticide, abortionists were subjected to the full force of the law if convicted of the criminal offence of abortion. These cases also expose how widely accessible abortionists were within the community. Not surprisingly, this chapter explores the role of gender and class, which was an important factor in the way that it influenced a woman's decision to terminate the pregnancy.

Chapter Four explores the medical condition of puerperal-related mental illness as a cause of child murder, and the legal procedure put in place to manage and detain the criminally insane. The first part assesses the impact the illness had on the lives of affected women and their families. With close scrutiny of contemporary medical journals and the casebooks relating to Glamorgan County Asylum during selected periods, it is possible to categorise women who were admitted with mental conditions connected to pregnancy, childbirth and lactation. These particular women did not commit infanticide, but they represent those suffering from the mental illness and admitted to the asylum by doctors and petitioners. These patient cases provide the necessary medical background to the second part of the chapter, which examines four criminal case studies of married mothers who committed child murder while insane and were later detained indefinitely at Broadmoor Criminal Lunatic Asylum. To address the main issues surrounding insanity and child murder, their cases are examined from the point at which the crime was perpetrated, the arrest on the charge of murder, the use of the insanity plea as part of the judicial procedure and finally the Broadmoor casebooks. Although this part of the chapter is based on the experiences of women and motherhood, a case review of one father, also detained at Broadmoor, exposes the differences in the way that male child-killers, who were understood to be insane, were treated in comparison to female ones. These criminal cases provide the opportunity to consider gender and class disparity in relation to both insanity and child murder. The final part explores the individuals' personal experiences at Broadmoor, and their potential release and reintegration back into the family and community.

The final chapter draws extensively on press reports of criminal trials, periodicals and contemporary journals to assess the causes and the legal consequences of newborn child murder. This chapter is based on seventy cases of concealment of birth and newborn child murder, although it refers to selected indictments to examine the judicial process for women following arrest. It investigates the social and economic issues surrounding the subject of newborn child murder to set in context the causes and consequences relating to the crime. The chapter draws attention to the role of reputed fathers as being indirectly responsible for incidences of the crime to expose gendered attitudes and class divisions. It examines how the law was applied in cases of concealment of birth and newborn child murder, and why single women were treated leniently by the courts. By the 1920s a number of women had achieved recognition in the fields of both politics and criminal justice. Therefore, as gender is of particular concern throughout the book, the final part of the chapter considers the activities of the feminist movement from the 1860s onwards and its influence on the introduction of the Infanticide Act in 1922.

Notes

1 Powys Archives, Cefnllys Petty Session Court Register, R/PS/LW/RG/15.

2 *Western Mail*, 17 May 1887, p. 3.

3 Victoria Greenwood and Jock Young, *Abortion in Demand* (London, 1976).

4 Barbara Brookes, *Abortion in England*, 1900—1967 (Kent, 1988), p. 163.

5 Jessica A. Sheetz-Nguyen, *Victorian Women, Unwed Mothers and the London Foundling Hospital* (London, 2012), p. 6.

6 Josephine McDonagh, *Child Murder & British Culture 1720—1900* (Cambridge, 2003), p. 5.

7 Katherine D. Watson, 'Religion, Community and the Infanticidal Mother: Evidence from 1840s Rural Wiltshire', *Family and Community History,* 11/2 (2008), 116–33 (p. 117).

8 Mark Jackson, 'The trial of Harriet Vooght: continuity and change in the history of infanticide', in Mark Jackson (ed.), *Infanticide: Historical Perspectives on Child Murder and Concealment, 1550–2000* (Aldershot, 2002), 1–17 (p. 3).

9 Julie Wheelwright, '"Nothing in between": modern cases of infanticide', in Mark Jackson (ed.), *Infanticide: Historical Perspectives on Child Murder and Concealment, 1550–2000* (Aldershot, 2002), pp. 270–85; Anne-Marie Kilday, *A History of Infanticide in Britain, c.1600 to the Present* (Basingstoke, 2013), pp. 183–217; Michelle Oberman, 'Understanding Infanticide in Context: Mothers who Kill, 1870–1930 and Today', *The Journal of Criminal Law & Criminology*, 92, 3/4 (2002), 707–38.

10 Oberman, 'Understanding Infanticide in Context', 710.

11 George K. Behlmer, 'Deadly Motherhood: Infanticide and Medical Opinion in Mid-Victorian England', *Journal of the History of Medicine*, 34 (1979), 403–27; Ann R. Higginbotham, '"Sin of the Age": Infanticide and Illegitimacy in Victorian London', *Victorian Studies*, 32/3 (1989), 319–337; Lionel Rose, *Massacre of the Innocents: Infanticide in Great Britain 1800–1939* (London, 1986).

12 McDonagh, *Child Murder & British Culture*, pp. 4–5.

13 Grace Hagen, 'Women and Poverty in south-west Wales, 1834–1914', *Llafur* (1997–98), 21–33; U.Q.R. Henriques, 'Bastardy and the New Poor Law', *Past and Present*, 37 (1967), 103–29.

14 Reports of the Commissioners of Inquiry into the State of Education in Wales (1847), PP, 339 (HMSO, London).

15 Jodie Krieder, '"Degraded and Benighted": Gendered Construction of Wales in the Empire, ca. 1847', *North American Journal of Welsh Studies*, 2/1 (2002), 24–35; Gwyneth Tyson Roberts, *The Language of the Blue Books: Wales and Colonial Prejudice* (Cardiff, 2011).

16 Margaret L. Arnot, 'Infant death, child care and the state: the baby farming scandal and the first infant life protection legislation of 1872', *Continuity and Change* 9/2 (1994), 271–311 (pp. 277–78).

17 Ruth Ellen Homrighaus, 'Baby Farming: The Care of Illegitimate Children in England, 1860–1943' (unpublished PhD thesis, University of North Carolina, Chapel Hill, 2003), 10.

18 Sherri Broder, 'Child Care or Child Neglect? Baby Farming in Late-Nineteenth-Century Philadelphia', *Gender and Society*, 2/2 (1988), 128–48 (p. 129).

19 'Infanticide and Wet Nursing', *The British Medical Journal*, 2/309 (1866), 613–18 (p. 613).

20 Angus McLaren, *Birth Control in Nineteenth-Century England* (London, 1978), p. 231.

21 Patricia Knight, 'Women and abortion in Victorian and Edwardian England', *History Workshop*, 4 (1977), 57–69 (p. 57).

22 R. Sauer, 'Infanticide and abortion in nineteenth-century Britain', *Population Studies*, 32/1 (1978), 81–93 (p. 91).

23 Anne-Marie Kilday, 'Desperate Measures or Cruel Intentions? Infanticide in Britain since 1600' in Anne-Marie Kilday and David Nash (eds), *Histories of Crime: Britain 1600–2000* (Basingstoke, 2010), pp. 60–79 (p. 67).

24 Roger Smith, *Trial by Medicine: Insanity and Responsibility in Victorian Trials* (Edinburgh, 1981), p. 8.

25 Watson, 'Religion, Community and the Infanticidal Mother', 116.

26 Anette Ballinger, *Dead Woman Walking: Executed Women in England and Wales 1900–1955* (Aldershot, 2000), p. 8.

27 Dorothy Sit, MD, Anthony J. Rothschild, MD, Katherine L. Wisner, 'A review of postpartum psychosis', *Journal of Women's Health,* 15/4 (2006), 352–68.
28 Joan Busfield, *Men, Women and Madness: Understanding Gender and Mental Disorder* (Hampshire, 1996), p. 126.
29 Hilary Marland, *Dangerous Motherhood: Insanity and Childbirth in Victorian Britain* (Basingstoke, 2004), pp. 201–2.
30 Pamela Michael, *Care and Treatment of the Mentally Ill in North Wales, 1800–2000* (Cardiff, 2003); Pamela Michael, 'Class, gender and insanity in nineteenth-century Wales', in Jonathan Andrews and Anne Digby (eds), *Sex and Seclusion, Class and Custody: Perspectives on Gender and Class in the History of British and Irish Psychiatry* (Amsterdam-New York, 2004).
31 Daniel J. R. Grey, 'Discourses of Infanticide in England, 1880–1922' (unpublished PhD thesis, Roehampton University, London, 2008); Jade Shepherd, '"One of the Best Fathers until He Went Out of His Mind": Paternal Child-Murder, 1864–1900', *Journal of Victorian Culture,* 18/1 (2013), 17–35.
32 R. W. Ireland, '"Perhaps my mother murdered me": child death and the law in Victorian Carmarthenshire', in C. Brooks and M. Lobban (eds), *Communities and Courts in Britain, 1150–1880* (London, 1997), pp. 229–44; Katherine D. Watson, 'Women, violent crime and criminal justice in Georgian Wales', *Continuity and Change,* 28/2 (2013), 245–72; N. Woodward, 'Infanticide in Wales, 1730–1830', *Welsh History Review,* 23 (2007), 94–125.
33 Watson, 'Women, violent crime and criminal justice', 260.
34 Dana Rabin, 'Bodies of evidence, states of mind: infanticide, emotion and sensibility in eighteenth-century England', in Mark Jackson (ed.), *Infanticide: Historical Perspectives on Child Murder and Concealment, 1550–2000* (Aldershot, 2002), 73–92 (p. 91).
35 Woodward, 'Infanticide in Wales', pp. 124–25.
36 Ireland, '"Perhaps my mother murdered me"', pp. 229–31.
37 Jackson, 'The trial of Harriet Vooght', p. 11.
38 Nicola Goc, *Women, Infanticide and the Press, 1822–1922: News Narratives in England and Australia* (Oxfordshire, 2013); Daniel J. R. Grey, '"Agonised Weeping': Representing femininity, emotion and infanticide in Edwardian newspapers', *Media History,* DOI: 10.1080/13688804.2015.1047332; Peter King, 'Making Crime News: Newspapers, Violent Crime and Selective Reporting of Old Bailey Trials in the late Eighteenth Century', *Crime, History & Societies,* 13/1 (2009), 91–116; Anne Baltz Roderick, '"Only a Newspaper Metaphor": Crime Reports, Class Conflict, and Social Criticism in Two Victorian Newspapers', *Victorian Periodicals Review,* 29/1 (1996), 1–18; Martin Weiner, 'Convicted Murderers and the Victorian Press: Condemnation vs. Sympathy', *Crimes and Misdemeanours,* 1/2 (2007), 110–25.
39 David Nash and Anne-Marie Kilday, 'Introduction', in Anne-Marie Kilday and David Nash (eds), *Histories of Crime: Britain 1600–2000* (Basingstoke, 2010), pp. 1–16, p. 4.
40 Goc, *Women, Infanticide and the Press,* p. 171.
41 Ginger S. Frost, *Promises Broken: Courtship, Class, and Gender in Victorian England* (London, 1995), p. 8.

Chapter One

'He laughs at the law, and he laughs at the poor unfortunate woman'[1]: Unmarried motherhood

The punitive Bastardy Clause, enshrined in the New Poor Law, was introduced in England and Wales in 1834. Its main objective was to lower the number of children born to feckless single women of loose character. The provision for bastardy under the Old Poor Law had been universally condemned as it was considered that want of chastity secured for a woman either a husband or a weekly allowance to support the child. Poor Law Commissioner Mr Walcott complained that bastardy was 'a growing evil in Wales' because of the escalating cost to local parishes to maintain illegitimate children. His remedy was to repeal the existing bastardy laws, following which officials needed only to deal with illegitimate children if they had been orphaned or deserted.[2] The new Bastardy Clause radically transformed the way that unmarried mothers were taken care of, since financial support was restricted in order to reduce the burden on ratepayers. Relief was no longer administered at a parochial level by the parish overseers but centralised under government control, via the newly formed Board of Guardians. As the sole responsibility for illegitimate children was transferred to mothers, both economically and legally, such radical and punitive amendments provoked opposition to the new law in Wales, partly because it would give rise to cases of infanticide and abandonment. Mr Walcott argued that:

> Desertion of children, with infanticide, were objections sometimes urged against the plan; but the great majority of clergymen, magistrates, and others, whom I examined on the subject, thought that the former would not be more frequent than at present; and that abortion and infanticide would be less frequent, not only from there being fewer

> cases to give rise to them, but because the man who in most instances is now the first to suggest these crimes, especially that of abortion, and to assist in their execution, would no longer have an interest in doing so; and the female left to herself, from maternal feelings, and natural timidity, would seldom attempt the destruction of her offspring.[3]

The Bastardy Clause was one of a number of grievances to emerge during the Rebecca Riots in west Wales throughout 1839–43. This popular rebellion has become embedded in Welsh tradition because the discontent, amongst small farmers and labourers in particular, ran far deeper than those associated with the excessive charges extorted at the unpopular toll gates.[4] The toll gates acted as a catalyst for a rural social uprising against the injustice of the New Poor Law, which was aimed directly at punishing society's poor. At a parish vestry meeting at Llangafelach in 1836, it was resolved that the New Poor Law 'will be oppressive and cruel, producing starvation, suicide and infanticide'.[5] Anne Digby points out that as rural protest against the New Poor Law tended to be of a spontaneous and fragmented nature, the rebellions attracted little national publicity.[6] However, in support of the issues raised by the Rebecca Riots, Thomas Campbell Foster, *The Times* newspaper correspondent, published regular updates on the state of south Wales that generated publicity on a national scale.

When the riots finally ceased, the government commissioned an inquiry into the causes of the unrest. The findings, published in the Reports of the Commissioners of Inquiry for South Wales in 1844, provided compelling evidence of the social unrest and economic hardship that gave rise to the rebellion. Just three years later, in 1847, the government appointed commissioners to conduct a second inquiry; its aim was to assess the state of education in Wales. Gareth Elwyn Jones maintains that one commissioner, J. C. Symons, 'made the direct link between lack of education interacting with the volatility of the Welsh character to produce such aberrations as Rebecca'.[7] Undoubtedly, this inquiry went beyond its remit to castigate the lower orders as immoral. In fact, Reverend James Denning commented to the Commissioners of Inquiry that 'From my experience of Ireland, I think there is a great similarity between the lower orders of Welsh and Irish – both are dirty, indolent, bigoted and contented.'[8] In response to the disparaging reports, as Gareth Elwyn Jones points out, 'There was a violent reaction to gratuitous sideswipes, entirely commensurate with contemporary English attitudes, at Wales as a kind of primitive backwater, ignorant and immoral.'[9] As a consequence, the reports became known as *Brad y Llyfrau Gleision* (The Treachery of the Blue Books). The reports criticised the morality of women amidst claims that Welsh peasant girls 'are almost universally unchaste, the wonder would be if they were otherwise'.[10] Indeed, Jodie Krieder highlights the fact that 'Welsh women were identified by both English and Welsh, Anglican and Dissenting middle class men as a source of immorality to be restrained and controlled.'[11] Not surprisingly, the prevailing social and religious attitudes uncovered in the reports were to have long-term implications for unmarried mothers and illegitimate children thereafter.

The evidence presented to the commissioners was indeed controversial, yet the reports offer a rich and informative source of particular value to social historians. Nevertheless, it is important to exercise a degree of caution since the evidence was dependent on the informants' views on immorality, illegitimacy and women. One identifiable source of complaint was that the commissioners were government-appointed, middle-class English men, while those who provided evidence on behalf of the Welsh people were drawn from the ruling middle class, the clergy and magistrates. No men, and certainly no women, from the lower orders provided evidence; hence the inquiries ignored the opinions and experiences of a whole layer of Welsh society.

Under the terms of the Bastardy Clause, unmarried mothers were compelled to provide corroborative evidence at the Court of Petty Sessions in order to sue reputed fathers for child maintenance. This was a difficult process to negotiate; therefore, this chapter focuses on the experiences of women who were left with little alternative but to rear their illegitimate offspring alone, with no financial support. The second part of this chapter examines the affiliation process, as many illegitimate infants were born as a consequence of seduction under the promise of marriage. Breach-of-promise-of-marriage cases are an enlightening source in their own right, revealing details of courtship, seduction, sexual harassment and intimidation of women to procure abortions. Men seldom featured in cases of infanticide. For this reason affiliation applications prove to be extremely useful because they provide evidence of the reputed fathers' social class and expose contemporary male attitudes to illegitimacy. The evidence gleaned goes some way to explain why many women determined that infanticide was the only viable solution to unwanted pregnancies, rather than pursue the reputed fathers through the courts. The press actively reported on these cases; therefore, newspapers are drawn upon as a key source since they provide an ideal opportunity to examine social attitudes regarding illegitimacy, Welsh courting customs, relationships, gender and class. Although controversial at the time, Caradoc Evans's early twentieth-century literary works are also considered in this chapter as a contemporary source. Evans's skilful creation of characters exposed the hypocrisy rife during this period as he challenged the fervent religious mindset of inhabitants living in rural communities of Cardiganshire and Carmarthenshire in particular.[12]

In his evidence to the commissioners of inquiry in 1844, Captain Evans from Llanddowror held that 'The bastardy clause has caused more crime, infanticide, and general demoralisation than was ever known in Wales before, the whole onus being placed on the poor deluded female, and the vile seducer goes scot free, a disgrace to manhood.'[13] This chapter considers Captain Evans's statement, since its aim is to assess a number of issues associated with immorality and unmarried motherhood.

The rural Welsh custom of 'bundling' was understood to be an underlying cause of immoral behaviour, adding to the high incidence of illegitimacy. The custom was defined as 'To sleep on the same bed without undressing; applied to the custom of man and woman, especially lovers, thus sleeping.'[14] 'Bundling' was also known as *caru ar y gwely* (courting on the bed) or 'night courting'.

The chapter takes into account how the shift from the paternalistic Old Poor Law system to the implementation of the hard-hearted Bastardy Clause impacted the lives of women and children long-term. This sets the scene for the remainder of the book as it considers to what extent the Bastardy Clause and the condemnatory Blue Books influenced social attitudes. It also assesses how such radical changes shaped the lives of single women and whether these issues contributed to the rising number of infant deaths in Welsh communities.

'It is a bad time for the girls, Sir, the boys have their own way':[15] Welsh courting customs and illegitimacy

Under the Old Poor Law administration, women were accused of profiting from their offspring since the onus was on putative fathers to pay maintenance, or prison in default of payment, thus rendering the system open to abuse. The authorities alleged that greater numbers of children born to manipulative single women increased the financial support they could claim from fathers. Therefore, the reasoning behind the new punitive Bastardy Clause related back to the theory put forward by Thomas Malthus in his *Essay on the Principle of Population* in 1798. Malthus argued that:

> Breach of chastity was more blameable in a woman than in a man, because the woman had no resources to maintain her own children, because her offence was more conspicuous, and the inconvenience to society greater. The mother could not easily be wrongly identified, the father might. Where the evidence of the offence was most complete, and inconvenience to the society at the same time the greatest, there, it was agreed, the largest share of the blame should fall.[16]

In 1832, as part of the government inquiry into the practical administration of the Old Poor Laws, questionnaires relating to both rural and town communities were dispatched to various parishes across England and Wales. One question put to parish officials referred to the allowance received by a woman for her illegitimate child and whether it repaid her or more than repaid her. It was disclosed that the maintenance paid in the Pembrokeshire parishes of Carew, Llandewy-Velfrey, Narberth South and Llanstadwell amounted to 1s. 6d; this was considered to be 'barely sufficient' for the maintenance of children.[17] In Lampeter fathers generally paid 1s. 4d, an amount also reported to be 'scarcely sufficient' to enable a mother to keep her child.[18] Margaret Lyle found that in order to discourage bastardy, magistrates routinely ordered the paltry allowance of 1s. 6d to be paid to mothers with illegitimate children. This can be seen in Castle Donnington, Leicestershire, where magistrates reduced the allowance paid to 1s. 6d to force women to be more prudent, yet there was little change in the annual return of the number of illegitimate children born during 1828–32.[19] So, contrary to popular belief, women were not profiting in those particular parishes at that point in time.

The threat of punishment was also employed as a deterrent in order to save parishes the expense of maintaining illegitimate children. In the parish of Llandewy-Velfrey, a mother faced possible punishment if she gave birth to a second illegitimate child, or if her conduct was to 'bring her under the denomination of what the Law deems a lewd woman'.[20] At Narberth South, William Hand argued that after the second offence the mother should be sent to the House of Correction and put on the treadwheel for two or three months, as 'this I have known to have had the best effects'.[21] Other suggested remedies included transportation of the woman for seven years for the second offence, or charging the mother and child to the parish in which she became pregnant. The underlying principle was to encourage employers to take an interest in the moral conduct of their servants.[22]

It was common, under the Old Poor Law, that once a woman was pregnant the overseers encouraged the man to marry her by using various means. In default of a maintenance payment, it was not unusual for a parish official to take 'the woman in one hand and a warrant in the other', while the man was given 'the option of going to church, or to gaol'.[23] In 1832, when Thomas Hodge, the overseer for Llangwm, Pembrokeshire, found out that Anne James was pregnant, he informed the court that he called on her, 'and she promised to come with me before a Magistrate, to swear the child of which she was then pregnant. She did not, however, come – nor do I believe she swore it.' The overseer's obvious endeavours to secure maintenance payments from the child's father were futile, because Anne James later gave birth alone in a field and hid the dead infant in a coal pit.[24] Thomas Nutt points out that the commissioners' reports portrayed men as victims of the system: 'False swearing to paternity was presented as rife, often involving the complicity of corrupt parochial officials who would "encourage the woman to pick out a 'good man' who could easily be made to pay."'[25] In his defence of Welsh women, Reverend Davies from Narberth argued in evidence to the commissioners that, 'In England women are so hardened that they will swear children on men that they never saw: but it is not so here; not one woman in ten thousand will take a false oath; and, in the next place, the women are not in that way unless they are deceived by a promise of marriage.'[26]

A successful application to prove paternity was a procedure fraught with difficulty for women after 1834. An amendment to the Bastardy Clause in 1844 weakened a woman's position because she was expected to instigate proceedings without any assistance from the Poor Law guardians. *The Welshman* condemned the amendment arguing that:

> By the new bill the mother is to apply for the summons. At the petty sessions the putative father can have the hearing transferred to the quarter sessions. Now by the bill all the expenses of carrying on these legal proceedings falls upon the mother, who in all probability is an outcast without a shilling in the world to help herself.[27]

The brave attempts of many young women to portray themselves as innocent victims in court resulted in a series of accusations, from both lawyers and witnesses, of alleged immorality with other men. This line of defence was often adopted in court to introduce doubt regarding paternity and to deliberately cast a slur on a woman's character.

Women who failed to provide corroborative evidence at the petty sessions were forced to support their children alone. Henry Leach, a magistrate from Haverfordwest, pointed out that:

> Now being thrown on her own resources, and required to maintain the child, she finds it impossible to maintain it. The magistrates, upon her being brought before them, do nothing. The law only authorises you to arrest not the person but the wages of the man, and the instant that you touch the wages of the man he changes his service and gets out of the way directly; therefore it rests entirely on the mother, and the mother naturally feels what she did not feel before, that the sooner that she can get rid of the child the better.[28]

Colonel Trevor commented that men take every advantage of the new law: 'Men say, "What does it matter? We are scot free" and they take every advantage they can.'[29]

In his evidence to the commissioners' inquiry, Mr James Bellairs, from Haverfordwest, reported that:

> I was talking to my labouring women when this new law came out, and they said, "Ah Sir, it is a fine time for the boys now". Two or three months after I asked one of them, "How do you go on?" She said, "It is a bad time for the girls, Sir, the boys have their own way."[30]

Given the improved employment opportunities in the industrial districts of south Wales during this period, it was of no surprise to find that many reputed fathers fled rural districts to avoid the issue of a paternity summons. However, if south Wales was not distant enough for escaping men, America beckoned; considerable numbers emigrated during this period. Jessica Sheetz-Nguyen's study of the London Foundling Hospital records found that 9.3 per cent of reputed fathers named in petitions had absconded to the United States and Canada.[31]

As outdoor relief ceased under the terms of the New Poor Law, the only means of assistance for desperate unmarried mothers was as workhouse inmates. Despite the harsh environment, the place provided a lying-in ward, food, shelter and clothing. According to the authorities, if conditions were too comfortable then the same abuses would exist as those under the Old Poor Law system. One Haverfordwest Poor Law union official, Mr Bellairs, commented that:

> We have a very nice woman now in the workhouse, a girl of very good character, except that she had the misfortune of having had a child; that girl cannot get £3 wages, and she cannot put out her child under £2 2s. It is a hard case, for wages are exceedingly low.[32]

Abandoned children in England and Wales were often 'boarded out' by Poor Law guardians, rather than be maintained in the local workhouses. Guardians generally paid a small regular payment to women, often elderly, to take in illegitimate and pauper infants from the workhouse, although lack of regulation meant that children were at risk of neglect or abuse. Even though they were under supervision, and despite the apparent risks, infants that had been 'boarded out' by Poor Law guardians probably fared a little better than those 'farmed out' by their parents. In the parish of

Narberth South, officials routinely 'boarded out' infants before the introduction of the New Poor Law. For example, in 1832, William Hand pointed out that an infant was taken away from the mother as soon as it was born and put out to nurse for a payment of 1s. 6d to 2s. per week. He commented that 'The mother is never punished for the first offence, but is occasionally for the second.'[33]

Rachel Ginnis Fuchs found that, conversely, in nineteenth-century France illegitimate infants were left at foundling homes, and they were provided for by the state from the moment of abandonment until the legal age of maturity. In France, abandonment was not a punishable offence, unlike in England and Wales. In fact, Fuchs points out that 'it was the societally approved method mothers had of coping with an unwanted pregnancy or offspring'.[34] Therefore, it proved unnecessary for mothers to abandon infants on doorsteps or adopt any other secretive measures. Infants were homed with state-paid wet nurses, who also acted as their foster parents and were paid by the state to rear children in lieu of the biological parents.[35] The situation of a typical French unmarried mother was similar to that of an unmarried mother in Wales; the woman was in her twenties and worked as a domestic servant, seamstress or a day labourer, and the reason for abandonment was usually for economic reasons.[36]

Cases of infant abandonment reportedly increased after 1834. Reverend Davies, from Narberth, found that:

> It is a common thing that the girls cannot support themselves, and their parents are not able, they come into the union for a month or six weeks, and recover, and they go out then, and say to some woman, 'I am going to service to so-and-so, and I will pay you for the child'. There is a combination between the nurse and the mother; the girl goes away, perhaps to St David's, ten miles off, to service, and the nurse comes to the Board of Guardians, and says, 'Here is a child left with me; I do not know what to do with it'; so we have to take it.[37]

Needless to say, the courts adopted a firm stance regarding infant abandonment because the cost of support was thrown onto the parish ratepayers. One such case involved a single woman, Ann Williams, aged twenty-two years, who was charged at Carmarthenshire Quarter Sessions with 'Deserting her male bastard infant thus endangering its life'. According to the Carmarthen Gaol Felons' Register, she already had one child.[38] Ann Williams had abandoned her infant at Llanfihangel Abercowin and begged for clemency from the court, as she claimed she was very weak when she did it.[39] The young woman was sentenced to four months with hard labour and released from Swansea Gaol on 30 October 1869.[40] Similarly, Hannah Griffiths, a servant from Solva, was sentenced to one month hard labour in Haverfordwest gaol for deserting her illegitimate child.[41] Some unscrupulous childminders were acutely aware that many unmarried mothers were unable to maintain their children without working and recognised the financial benefits of 'fostering' or minding illegitimate children. It was only a matter of course that such arrangements were the precursor to baby farming.

The strict operation of the New Poor Law meant that some Poor Law guardians were accused of hastening the infant's end. One guardian complained to the *Western Mail* that:

> Young girls of sixteen and eighteen enter the workhouse and if they leave to try to maintain themselves the guardians are not allowed to give them an article of clothing, not even to their innocent infants. Widows have illegitimate children, and as soon as they do their allowances for the other children stops. This means that the children must go into the workhouse or starve. Yet, if the illegitimate child dies, outdoor relief is resumed. This is an inducement to allow the illegitimate child to die.[42]

A widow, and mother of two, Hannah Davies from Blaenycoed, Conwil Elfed, was charged in 1866 with concealment of the birth of her child, although she was later discharged. Likewise, Ellen Donoghue was also a widow and a mother of two children. This case in 1869 is discussed further in Chapter Five because she was discharged despite incriminating evidence to support the indictment of concealment of birth.[43] The Carmarthen Gaol Felons' Register recorded eight cases in which single mothers indicted for the wilful murder of their infants, wounding or concealment of birth had other illegitimate children. It is interesting to note that only three women were sentenced to a prison term, with hard labour, whereas five women were discharged without punishment.[44]

The punitive Bastardy Clause and fear of the workhouse were reported to be contributory factors in cases of infant abandonment and infanticide. However, another cause was attributed to the Welsh courting custom of 'bundling', or *caru ar y gwely*, amongst the lower rural classes. Social commentators claimed that it was not a custom practised in England. It was understood to be peculiar to Wales, although that was not actually the case since the custom existed in European countries such as the Netherlands, Scandinavia and Switzerland. The custom was also practised in New England and believed to have been introduced by settlers. An American physician, Henry Reed Stiles, who published his research on the practice of 'bundling' in 1871, traced its beginning to the rural parts of ancient Wales. Stiles held that, in Wales, 'the custom seems to have originated in the scarcity of fuel, and in the unpleasantness of sitting together in the colder part of the year without a fire'.[45] Similarly, in Holland its origin correlated with the thriftiness of its people who believed that fire and candles were an unnecessary luxury during the long winter nights.[46] 'Bundling' was also practised in Ireland and Scotland. Stiles claimed that whatever their national vices, 'the Scotch and the Irish of our day maintain a character of chastity superior to that of many of their more fortunate and more civilised neighbours'. He argued that 'bundling' arose from the ignorance and poverty of the inhabitants, and 'while not salutary in its moral or physical influence is, at all events, less abused than we might reasonably expect'.[47] Clearly 'bundling' served its purpose as a means to keep warm; however, the custom also gave licence for sexual intimacy.

Even in 1893 the Report of the Royal Commission on Labour complained that agricultural labourers participated in the custom of 'night courting': 'Many men "sit up" three or four nights a week, each night with a different girl . . . It is this custom of night courting which is at the very root of all charges of immorality which are so frequently brought against the Welsh people.'[48] 'Bundling' was often frowned upon, yet visitors to Wales were intrigued by the custom. In 1900, one English visitor to Llandysul commented that 'bundling' 'is a custom of the country around here, and is considered quite a venerable institution'.[49] 'Bundling', it was said:

> is carried on chiefly in the counties of Carmarthen, Pembroke (the Welsh portions thereof), Cardigan, Merioneth, Carnarvon and Anglesey. On the whole, it may be said that its greatest strongholds are Cardiganshire and Anglesey, though even in those counties it is gradually dying out.[50]

It was pointed out that:

> There is no doubt that Dissent, especially that form of it known as Welsh Calvinistic Methodism, has done much to bring the custom into bad odour; yet, strange to say, it is in those counties where Welsh Calvinism is strongest the custom chiefly prevails, viz., Cardiganshire and Anglesey.[51]

It is notable that 'bundling' was popular in Cardiganshire, although there were fewer reported cases of infanticide in this county. This suggests that family support networks and local communities accepted 'bundling' as part of normal courtship. Likewise, if the reputed father failed to marry once the woman was pregnant, she was not ostracised within the community to the same extent where the practice was less tolerated and was, therefore, less likely to commit infanticide. In fact, the number of cases of infanticide heard at the Welsh Courts of Great Session during 1800–30 was significantly fewer in the mid and northern counties of Wales, although the lower density of population has to be taken into account when considering the figures. For example, a total of fifty-three cases recorded during the period revealed only one case of infanticide in both Anglesey and Merioneth and two cases in Montgomery. There were three recorded cases of infanticide in Cardigan, Denbigh and Caernarfon, and four cases in Flint. Compare these figures to ten recorded cases of infanticide in Pembrokeshire, nine cases in Glamorgan, eight in Carmarthen, seven in Radnor and four in Brecon.[52] Despite being a rural county, Pembrokeshire had the highest number of recorded cases of infanticide, which also corresponded with the high level of illegitimacy rates recorded in 1842.

It is worth noting that while 'bundling' was blamed for high illegitimacy rates, the number of illegitimate births in 1842 in Wales were lowest in parts of Cardiganshire. Aberystwyth had the lowest rate of 5 per 100 births, whereas the rate for both Cardigan and Aberaeron was 5.6 per 100 births. Haverfordwest, in contrast, appeared to have the highest rate of 9.7 per 100 births, although compared to England this figure was significantly lower than Wigan, which had the highest recorded rate at 18.1 per 100 births.[53] Illegitimacy rates were lower in the urban and industrial areas of south Wales. For example, the rate for Swansea in 1842 was 4 per 100 births, Merthyr Tydfil had 4.7 per 100 births, while the rate for Cardiff, Neath and Bridgend was 5.4 per 100 births.[54] Interestingly, the urban rates for illegitimate births were on a similar level to those in rural Cardiganshire. This similarity could be explained by greater employment opportunities in urban districts, while men in Cardiganshire were probably more inclined to uphold the courting traditions of 'bundling' and marry rather than father illegitimate children. Besides, it was probably less challenging for the authorities to trace reputed fathers within the sparsely populated, close-knit communities of rural Cardiganshire. So, it was not surprising to find that reputed fathers had to abscond if they wished to avoid the issue of a paternity summons.

Stiles reported that marriage was the intended outcome of seduction, and that 'bundling' was an acceptable form of courtship in the lower classes.[55] The arrangement of sleeping quarters for farm servants was a source of complaint because in many instances men and women slept together, therefore encouraging intimacy. The Archdeacon of St David's complained that:

> Bastardy is very common, unchastity, in the youth of both sexes, the rule rather than the exception. This is greatly owing to the conditions under which the farm lads and servant girls are hired (at fairs without character very commonly), and to the excessive liberty allowed them in service.[56]

William Rees, the superintendent of the Church Sunday School at Cayo and Llandingat, found that:

> The general character of the people is honest and industrious. Among farm servants the chastity of women is low, in consequence of farmers conniving at young people's meeting in their houses after the family go to rest; but after seduction the man generally marries the woman.[57]

In Llandissilio, William Morris commented that 'In this district bundling prevails, and is almost insisted on as a necessary condition in hiring servants, who commonly quit a service in which it is forbidden.'[58] Even though social commentators blamed 'bundling' for increased illegitimacy rates, the custom persisted for generations after the publication of the Blue Books in 1847. Catrin Stevens points out that over the centuries Welsh courting customs remained firmly rooted in tradition, despite the social and economic upheavals that had threatened their survival. Stevens maintains that industrialisation and the move away from rural life began a process of erosion, but the questioning of past values in the aftermath of the First World War dealt the final blow to the centuries-old Welsh courting customs.[59]

The controversial Blue Books provoked a concerted effort amongst the ruling classes and religious sectors to redeem the moral integrity of the Welsh people. As John Davies points out, Welsh Nonconformist leaders headed campaigns against 'wantonness, drunkenness and lawlessness, efforts which fully conformed to the moral atmosphere of the Victorian age'.[60] Russell Davies explored the subject of unmarried motherhood against the 'dominant mythology' of Liberal Nonconformist Wales, and rural Wales in particular, as a land of innocence and of pure morals, *Hen Wlad y Menyg Gwynion* (The Land of White Gloves), and questioned its historical validity.[61] A pair of white gloves was traditionally handed to the presiding judge at the Assizes if there were no serious crimes to be heard. For instance, Lord Coleridge was presented with a pair of white gloves at Pembroke Winter Assizes in January 1910. His lordship congratulated the Grand Jury on the absence of serious crime in the county.[62] As Richard Ireland points out, this was not an unusual occurrence in Wales, 'and the self-identification of "*gwlad a menig gwynion*" ("the land of white gloves") became a symbol of Welsh probity'.[63]

Davies referred to the image of Wales as a land of strong morals and little crime, with a quote by Reverend David Davies from Conwyl Gaio to illustrate this belief. Reverend Davies remarked that:

> it is the Protestant Nonconformity of the Welsh people as lived and taught by their religious teachers during the last two centuries that has preserved them from ignorance, lawlessness and irreligion, and made of them one of the most scripturally-enlightened, loyal, moral and religious nations on the face of the earth.[64]

Davies concludes that '"*Hen Wlad y Menyg Gwynion*" had no reality, it was only an image – an image which, if accepted, distorts and blocks out whole layers of life as experienced by ordinary people', and that it 'appears in hindsight, hypocritical'.[65]

During his visits, Thomas Campbell Foster, *The Times* correspondent, found that 'the lower orders in Wales have a considerable degree of religious fanaticism about them, and most of them Dissenters, and are in the constant habit of quoting Scripture for everything which they advance'.[66] As Russell Davies points out, the Welsh were familiar with the scriptures in all walks of life.[67] Religion formed part of everyday existence at a time when most girls were subjected to religious teachings from an early age. Gwyneth Tyson Roberts maintains that religious education was intended to 'teach children to accept legally constituted authority in their spiritual as in their temporal lives'.[68] Subservient female servants would have learnt at an early age that it was their duty to 'submit myself to all my governors, teachers, spiritual pastors and masters; to order myself lowly and reverently to all my betters . . . and to do my duty in that state of life unto which it shall please God to call me, *Book of Common Prayer,* 1830'.[69] Religion also served its purpose as an effective means of social control as families were compelled to adhere to the prevailing ideology of respectability, morality and sobriety.[70] Indeed, Anne-Marie Kilday and Katherine Watson suggest that 'the significance of religious cohesiveness to family and community relations may, in some contexts, have encouraged infanticide to occur, due to a pressure to maintain respectability in religious observant communities'.[71] In fact, it was highly likely that greater perceived respectability in a young woman increased the possibility that the accusation of immorality would be a contributory factor to commit infanticide.

Religious ministers preached against immorality, yet conversely chapels provided meeting places for young people. In 1847 William Morris stated that, 'The great number of nightly prayer meetings leads to immorality; there are places at which lovers agree to meet, and from which they return together at late hours.'[72] It is difficult to determine contemporary attitudes amongst chapel members because Nonconformist records were either non-existent, have not survived, or are now in private hands, rendering them inaccessible. If records do exist then any mention of exclusion of members would, most likely, be brief.[73]

The author Caradoc Evans grew up in a strong Nonconformist community at Rhydlewis, a short distance from Newcastle Emlyn. Evans presented a contentious image of Nonconformist west Wales in his volumes of short stories *My People* (1915), *Capel Sion* (1916) and *My Neighbours* (1919). As John Harries points out in his introduction to *My People,* Evans wrote about incendiary issues from within the fictitious village of Manteg, such as money worship, social hypocrisy, endemic brutality and the abuse of women.[74] Harries maintains that 'For years Evans had been storing local characters and incidents, many gathered on summer holidays at Rhydlewis.'[75] Although Evans's work provoked a hostile response from the Welsh people, cases of affiliation prove that the stories represented real life in west Wales far more than was admitted, or even accepted, at the time of publication.

Evans broached the subject of illegitimacy in *My People*. His portrayal of Lissi in 'The Redeemer' reflected the strong religious zeal with which preachers railed against illegitimacy. In this short story Evans portrays a servant girl, originally taken from the workhouse at Castellbryn (Newcastle Emlyn) to work for a widow, Ellen the weaver. Bern-Davydd was the minister of Capel Sion, although for the purpose of the story Evans refers to him as the ruler, denoting his perceived upstanding position within the chapel and the wider community. Lissi forms a relationship with Bern-Davydd's son, Adam, and becomes pregnant. The very idea that Lissi, a 'poorhouse brat', is expecting Adam's illegitimate child means that Bern-Davydd, his son Lamech and his wife Puah conspire to end the relationship.[76] The intention is to force Lissi to admit that she had been with other men. One night Puah drapes herself in a bedsheet, forming a ghost-like silhouette, and appears in front of Lissi in the darkness. Overcome with fright, she runs away as fast as she can, but she is 'overtaken by unfamiliar pains . . . The child she delivered – a man child – was dead, and from her travail Lissi passed into madness'.[77] Puah's malicious behaviour was not out of the ordinary since women could be very unforgiving to their own sex. Actually, such hostile behaviour could have benevolent roots, and was often adopted as a deterrent against immoral behaviour amongst single women, acting as a form of social control. Lissi's character was fictional; however, her experience of religious hypocrisy is uncovered in real-life cases of illegitimacy.

Caradoc Evans wrote of the subjugation of women in another short story, 'Greater Than Love'. In this story, Sam asks Esther to accompany him on a seaside trip to Morfa, but she refuses, accusing him of courting Catrin. Here, Evans made reference to the custom of *caru ar y gwely* when Esther says, 'Is there not loud speakings that you have courted Catrin in bed? Very full is her belly.'[78] At Morfa, Esther is approached by Hws Morris, a young minister of religion in training, who flatters her. She cannot see through his deception, and Morris seduces her. Afterwards, when Esther says, 'Let me stay with you,' Morris replies, 'Shut your throat, you temptress. For why did you flaunt your body before my religious eyes?' Esther replies, 'Did you not make fair speeches to me?' Morris is shown to discard responsibility for his actions, placing the onus on Esther for his transgression. 'Terrible is your sin,' says Morris. 'Little Big Man bach, forgive me for eating of the wench's fruit.'[79] Here, Evans confronts religious hypocrisy, drawing attention to the issues of gender and double standards of sexual morality. Indeed, when Evans's stories are considered alongside other primary sources, the portrayal of his key characters provides a contemporary understanding of strong, religiously held beliefs in many west Wales communities.

Religious ministers preached against the evils of immorality, yet some were not without sin. Ministers, not normally associated with scandalous behaviour, were pursued through the courts to accept liability for their illegitimate offspring. A scandal occurred in Cardiganshire when Reverend Jenkin Rees, a Congregational minister from Cilcennin, Cardiganshire, was summoned to court at Aberaeron in 1895. This paternity case offers a glimpse of one community's reaction to the alleged immoral behaviour of a Nonconformist minister who, despite his position, was not above ridicule. Reverend Rees was reputed to be the father of the third illegitimate child of an unmarried mother, Jane Davies. Her other two children had previously been affiliated to their respective fathers. The *Western Mail* reported that for days prior to the hearing, it had been the general topic of conversation locally and the courtroom was filled with a 'mixed and excited audience'. The newspaper's report suggested that local interest was focused far more on Reverend Rees, as a religious minister, than on Jane Davies in her quest to affiliate yet another illegitimate child.

When Jane Davies described the first time they had sexual relations, it caused great laughter, which was followed by cries of 'order' in the packed courtroom. Many onlookers were clearly amused as the drama unfolded. The magistrate pointed out: 'Laughter on the part of any of you shows a want of taste. It is a serious case and it reflects greatly on your morals to laugh and seem to glory in such a distressing case.' The solicitors for both parties requested that all respectable women leave the court, especially if they had some self-respect. This led to some movement in court, but only a few women left the room. It is interesting to note that, despite having their standards of respectability called into question, the majority of women remained in court regardless. When Jane Davies informed Reverend Rees of her condition, he asked her to ‘sign a paper that he was free, and to put it on somebody else’, but she refused his request. Interestingly, the false swearing of a child onto another man was an accusation normally levelled at women, not men. Again, double standards of sexual morality prevailed in court. Evidently, only Reverend Rees had much to lose if he was named as the father. The man was described as a bachelor, yet Jane Davies was ‘a woman who had, unfortunately, fallen twice before’. The fact that the woman had given birth to three illegitimate infants was obviously a slur on her character. It was pointed out to the Bench by her own representative, ‘That there was no doubt that the defendant knew the girl’s character, and he asked why, in the name of all conscience, should a man in his position go continually to her house, knowing the character of the woman he was visiting.’ Reverend Rees’s defence argued that ‘if an order was granted it not only meant social degradation, but the blasting forever of the good name and reputation which he had maintained for 40 years or more’. Jane Davies had ‘fallen twice before’; therefore it was impossible to damage her reputation any further. Reverend Rees was ordered to pay the weekly sum of 1s. 6d. The Bench pointed out that, ‘We only make it small because the woman has had two children previously.’[80] Not only was this a paltry sum, but it was the same amount reportedly paid in 1834, and described at the time as ‘barely sufficient’ to maintain a child. Even though some reputed fathers were ministers of the gospel, their behaviour was no different to that of other men in the same situation, and members of the community treated them as such.

The introduction of the New Poor Law had a universal impact on all poorer members of society in need of financial support – men, women and children – yet the Bastardy Clause singled out unmarried mothers in particular. Lisa Forman Cody points out that the New Poor Law revealed ‘a fundamental shift in thinking about poverty and welfare from paternalism to Liberalism’, and those proponents ‘imagined both men and women as free agents economically responsible for themselves’.[81] Forman Cody also found that a few wealthier individuals perceived unmarried mothers as victims of seduction who were 'unable to provide for themselves in a modern capitalistic marketplace unless they were given traditional, protectionist forms of charity'.[82] Many unmarried mothers invoked sympathy amongst members of the ruling classes, such as Henry Leach and Captain Evans, because circumstances dictated that it was impossible for them to be economically independent.

'Why don't you marry the girl?'[83]: Illegitimacy and broken promises

Affiliation applications and cases of breach of promise of marriage reveal that many illegitimate infants were born as a result of failed relationships. Some couples had been courting for a considerable time before women consented to intimacy. Ginger Frost maintains that 'women used their sexuality in courtship' and that 'they must have realised the risks of pregnancy and desertion, but they entered sexual relationships because of affection and hopes of marriage'.[84] Evidence reveals that a high percentage of women living in rural communities were pregnant when they married. The rector of Begelly, Pembrokeshire, reported that 'Out of 70 marriages, in six only had the brides not been visibly *enceintes*.' The rector also pointed out that seduction is 'generally followed by marriage if the woman conceives, not otherwise'.[85] Proof of this practice is visible in parish baptism and marriage registers where the date of marriage was closely followed by the baptism of the first child. As an incentive to refrain from sexual relationships before marriage, the Reverend L. H. Davies, from Troed y Raur, Cardigan, promised to return the marriage fee to all couples should their first child be born after nine months of marriage, and only one in six couples proved to be entitled to claim it.[86] The situation in rural Wales was comparable to the Scottish agricultural labouring class. In 1868 Dr Strachan, a Scottish physician, observed that a high proportion of women also gave birth within eight months of marriage. Strachan found that nine out of ten women either had illegitimate children, or were pregnant at the time of marriage.[87] It is notable that Scottish courtship practices were akin to courting customs in Wales, and that marriage was the intended outcome if a woman was pregnant as a consequence of 'bundling'.

Evidence indicates that a number of illegitimate children were conceived on the understanding that marriage would ensue.

Likewise, Michael Mason points out that in many parts of England between a third and a half of all brides were pregnant. Mason found 'a close affinity between the behaviour which led to marriage and that which led to non-marital conceptions and births; they seem to be two aspects of the same thing, always varying together and in the same direction'. While the rate of pregnant brides was higher in some rural districts of Wales and Scotland, Mason indicates that as part of courtship, pregnancy would lead to marriage, or it was understood to be the outcome.[88] Women might well have consented to intimacy under the promise of marriage as a means to secure economic stability or to provide an improved standard of living at least. Many women feared being 'left on the shelf', with no prospect of marriage. In fact the inability to secure a husband was viewed as social failure on the woman's part, and they were often economically disadvantaged if they remained single. An article in the *Western Mail* reported that 'Marriage is necessary to the fullness of the life of either sex, and any scheme of life for the average man or woman which excludes marriage or discourages it is a crime against nature – a conspiracy against the well-being of mankind.' It was understood that 'Women, like men, are meant by nature to marry. Celibacy is, in either sex, an exceptional, abnormal, unnatural condition.'[89] To remain single was considered at the time to be an unnatural state; hence some women consented to intimacy for fear of being 'left on the shelf'.

A commonly held perception was that unmarried mothers were victims of inter-class seduction and later abandoned by their seducers. There is evidence to support such cases because women, who were mainly servants, sued Nonconformist ministers,[90] solicitors,[91] a town councillor,[92] a gentleman farmer,[93] a police constable[94] and a publican,[95] to name just a few reputed fathers pursued through the courts. The fact that servants sued middle-class men implied that illegitimate children were often born as a result of inter-class seduction, or sexual harassment. Female servants were subservient to their masters; therefore, being naturally acquiescent and fearful of losing their post, it was not surprising to find that many were susceptible to sexual harassment.

While many women struggled to cope once pregnant, not all were dismissed by their employers. One reputed father, Edward Abse from Bridgend, appealed against an affiliation order to contribute towards the illegitimate infant of his servant, Susan

Jones. Edward Abse had urged her to travel to Neath and abandon the infant at the workhouse door. He was quick to point out to Susan Jones that there were many cases of abandonment where mothers had not been traced by the authorities. Indeed, men often coerced women to get rid of unwanted infants one way or another. Edward Abse had paid for drugs to induce a miscarriage since abortion was an option often seized upon by men. However, when the attempt failed, his wife also coerced the young woman to terminate the pregnancy. It was interesting to note that Susan Jones's sister provided evidence in Edward Abse's defence. She informed the court that Susan Jones had told her that another man was responsible and not Edward Abse; this was confirmed by two other witnesses. Despite evidence to support his case, the man's appeal was dismissed and granted in favour of Susan Jones.[96]

Evidently, Edward Abse had had sexual relations with his servant, and handing over money and items to pawn implied that the child was his. Françoise Barret-Ducrocq maintains that men like Edward Abse, 'when forced to acknowledge what had happened, they offered compensation in money, showing at least that domestic service and sexual services had become confused in the master's mind'.[97] The use of working-class girls by middle-class men, as Barret-Ducrocq points out, meant that 'the professional duties of maids sometimes extended, unofficially, to the sexual servicing of another class'.[98] It was plausible that Edward Abse's wife had prior knowledge of his relationship with Susan Jones since, as Barret-Ducrocq found, 'some wives saw their partner's ancillary love affairs as a means of lightening their own conjugal burden'.[99] Consequently, many wives like Mrs Abse turned a blind eye to their husbands' philandering and extra-marital affairs, especially as it reduced their own risk of pregnancy and its associated health risks.

Instigating court proceedings against putative fathers was less daunting for women after the introduction of the Bastardy Laws Amendments Act in 1872. Women were now in a position to seek assistance from Poor Law guardians to pursue putative fathers through the courts; but this did not mean that the process was any less humiliating. The amendment probably explains why the number of affiliation applications taken out against middle-class men increased after 1872. Servants summoned employers to answer charges of paternity, although there were fewer cases of this nature due to the difficulties in seeking redress in court. The case of Hannah Jones, a domestic servant, and a 'buxom country girl' from New Quay, provides an example of how difficult it was for servants to pursue employers for maintenance. The plaintiff was involved in a paternity case against her former employer, a Cardiganshire squire named John Jordan Jones, and encountered difficulties even with assistance from Poor Law guardians.[100] Clearly, the case generated considerable interest locally owing to John Jones's prominent position. Evidence indicated that Hannah Jones was not his first victim, either, given that John Jones admitted that he paid maintenance for another illegitimate child by his former servant.[101] It was reported that the man first made sexual advances two weeks after Hannah Jones began working for him. It was alleged that she had been unable to lock her bedroom door because John Jones had cut up a matchbox and filled the keyhole with the pieces. Hannah Jones was employed by John Jones for six months, until she left in July 1897. The baby was born in February 1898, although the woman's first attempt to affiliate the child was not made until April 1898, while she was in Aberaeron workhouse. Hannah Jones had written to the squire to inform him that he was going to be named as the father. Apparently John Jones asked if she would put the paternity onto someone else, and in return he would pay for the child privately. As Hannah Jones was chargeable to the union, the summons had been issued under the instruction of the Poor Law guardians. John Jones's solicitor objected to this course of action because the guardians should be parties to the action, and not the woman. He remarked that, 'The guardians had put the woman forward for a very unworthy reason, and backed a pauper with a solicitor, instead of coming out to face the music themselves, as was their duty.' As in so many cases, Hannah Jones was accused by the squire of having had relationships with other men in order to cast doubt over paternity. Her position was weakened further since she had given birth to a stillborn baby in the past. In fact, Hannah Jones's mistress at that time had known nothing about her pregnancy until the day that she gave birth. It was reported that John Jones was determined to defend himself, and that he would spend his last shilling in doing so. However, he incriminated himself by asking Hannah Jones to meet him after dark in lonely places because he did not want to be seen in her company. The woman appeared to be a credible witness, especially as her evidence was supported by a number of John Jones's letters. Despite this, the case was dismissed for want of corroborative evidence.[102]

Hannah Jones did not relent, because another summons was issued in November 1898. Apparently, while Hannah Jones was in his employment, John Jones's wife had warned her about her husband and that she needed to 'watch him'. It was also reported that John Jones and his wife slept in separate rooms. The evidence put forward was detailed, as it was in the first application. Again after the Bench deliberated in private, the summons was dismissed for want of corroborative evidence.[103] In January 1899 Hannah Jones summoned the squire for a third time. In this instance, her solicitor was in possession of another letter from John Jones agreeing to settle and pay four shillings per week, together with all costs, including expenses relating to the birth of the child.[104]

The case revealed that John Jones had abused his position to influence the outcome in dismissing former applications even though evidence indicated otherwise. He finally incriminated himself in a letter submitted to the court on the third attempt; otherwise the squire would, no doubt, have won the case. In fact, there were many cases where an employer's social prominence determined whether a summons was even issued in the first instance, let alone the child successfully affiliated. Undoubtedly, without the union's financial contribution to legal costs, it was unlikely that Hannah Jones would have been in the position to sue a man of John Jones's social standing. In addition, it was in the union's interest to pursue him to save the long-term expense of supporting Hannah Jones and her illegitimate child in the workhouse.

In the majority of affiliation applications, mothers summoned the reputed fathers and successfully pursued them for maintenance. However, in some cases, because a woman's reputation was called into question, it was rendered difficult for the court to determine the correct identity of the child's father. For example, at Swansea Police Court, a paternity summons was issued by Beatrice Maud Theophilus against Richard Watson. Under cross-examination, the woman admitted that 'she had paid a visit to Mrs Rees at Morriston for the purpose of getting rid of a child'. It seems almost certain that Mrs Rees was the infamous abortionist discussed in Chapter Three. Further disclosures caused a sensation in court when Beatrice Theophilus confessed to having previously had a child, and that the father was her brother. Richard Watson, the alleged father in this particular affiliation case, stated that he had met her when 'he went to the shop where the plaintiff was to buy tobacco, and she would not take his money, but laughingly suggested immorality, and at subsequent meetings this occurred'.[105] In this case the summons was dismissed; although it was heard on a few other occasions but repeatedly dismissed for want of corroborative evidence. It was reported that, despite her disreputable character, sufficient evidence was put forward to allow the case to proceed once more. On this occasion, the case was successfully concluded, with an order duly made against Richard Watson for 3s. 6d per week until the child was fourteen years of age.[106]

In another similar case, Elizabeth Lewis applied for a paternity order against John Davies, an 'agent' from Swansea. In court, she was accused of going to places of work to meet men coming out at the end of their shifts, implying that she was promiscuous. Humiliated, Elizabeth Lewis strenuously denied the accusation. Apparently, she was nicknamed 'Six o'clock' because she was in the habit of going to workplaces to meet men about that time.[107] As the press reports make clear, an appearance in court remained a degrading experience, regardless of a woman's character.

The Victorians thrived on the notion of respectability, which was a recurrent theme throughout this period. Respectability, argues K. Theodore Hoppen, 'had always been a slippery affair, easier to recognise than describe'.[108] According to *Bow Bells*, respectability was not about money or social position: 'To be respectable is to be worthy of respect: and he deserves respect who has most virtue.'[109] Hoppen maintains that 'mid-Victorian working people, like mid-Victorians generally, found it easy to sustain a variety of overlapping identities determined by age, gender, earnings, respectability, size of family, level of skill, intelligence, religion and health'.[110] The idea of respectability was not exclusive to a particular class, as *Bow Bells* pointed out: 'While those who live honestly, and strive to do what they can, constitutes in reality the respectable class, irrespective of the fact whether they eat with silver forks or steel ones.'[111] The evidence in a number of cases indicates that a woman was worthy of respect provided that she was of good character, although the prevailing double standards and deliberate character assassinations meant that this was often difficult to achieve.

Sarah Davies, a servant from Loughor, successfully obtained a maintenance order against William Rees for their illegitimate child, but not before questions were raised about her respectability. Like many other men, William Rees appealed against the order. It was alleged that the 'improprieties' took place while 'night courting' at the farmhouse where Sarah Davies was employed, after the family had gone to bed. One witness understood the couple would be married, as William Rees professed to be courting her and regularly escorted her to and from chapel. In court, like a number of women, Sarah Davies firmly denied 'certain improprieties' with other men. Eventually the court confirmed the order with costs.[112] Sarah Davies's case was typical: William Rees challenged a previous maintenance order and tarnished her character in the process.

In defence of friends or family, it was not uncommon for witnesses to commit perjury, which was frequently detrimental to a woman's character. At Kilgerran Petty Sessions, Martha Evans sought an affiliation order against Benjamin Phillips. When he appeared before the magistrates, Benjamin Phillips called as a witness James Jenkins, who 'deposed to certain acts' which would exonerate Benjamin Phillips from maintaining the child in future. In this case, James Jenkins swore that he had been at Kilgerran, but the prosecution proved that on the alleged dates he was employed at Llandore Steel Works in Swansea. James Jenkins was convicted of perjury and sentenced to twelve months with hard labour. The judge commented that perjury 'is too common, not only in the Principality but all over England'. James Jenkins was told by the judge that his punishment 'will be a warning to others who endeavour to serve their friends for a moment at the expense of truth and at the expense of another person's character'.[113] The two men had conspired to enable the reputed father to avoid maintenance payments, but the lies destroyed the woman's reputation. For some reason, the *Pembrokeshire Herald* reported that facts of the case were not fit for publication.

Witnesses conspired to assist either unmarried mothers or reputed fathers in affiliation cases. Naturally, living in close-knit communities meant that local gossip ensured that intimate details pertaining to individuals were common knowledge long before cases were heard in court. The lively reactions from the public gallery were a telling indication of whether witnesses were lying under oath or not. Mary Jane Mathias, a 'genteel-looking girl' from

Pembroke Dock, summoned George Lifton to pay maintenance for his illegitimate child. She had known him for three years and he was recognised to be her sweetheart, yet the young man abandoned her when she told him that she was pregnant. When the Bench asked George Lifton if he had any connection with her, he replied, 'No, sir, never in my life.' This caused a sensation in court since the local community was well aware of their relationship, as were her parents. The enthusiastic responses from the public gallery could certainly influence the Bench as to the extent of the relationship, and question the credibility of witnesses on oath. The Bench ignored George Lifton's testimony and he was ordered to pay Mary Jane Mathias 2s. 6d per week, which was received with applause from the public gallery, but the acclamation was promptly suppressed.[114]

Not all men were determined to absolve themselves from further responsibilities. At Roose Petty Sessions, Haverfordwest, farm servant Samuel Williams admitted paternity and wanted to marry the mother of his illegitimate child. The account of the court proceedings in the *Western Mail* reveals a humorous exchange between the magistrate and father. Samuel Williams was asked by the magistrate, 'Why don't you marry the girl?'

He replied, 'The parson can't marry one, sir.'

The magistrate asked, 'Why, won't she have you?'

'No, I don't think she will,' he replied.

The court was clearly amused by the comments. The Bench agreed that Samuel Williams had acted fairly in offering to marry Elizabeth Hughes, and he was ordered to pay 1s. 6d per week.[115]

Even with corroborative evidence, proving paternity was a process fraught with difficulties, and it was understandable why women were worried, embarrassed or discouraged from doing so. Miriam Jones, the young servant girl mentioned previously, had made three attempts to sue her former employer for child maintenance before she abandoned her eighteen-month-old daughter in a disused mineshaft.[116] Margaret Evans, a servant, charged eighty-year-old Reverend William Powell from Llanpumsaint, Carmarthen, with being the father of her illegitimate child. She had been in his service for seven years and alleged that sexual relations took place while she was living there. Reverend Powell eventually admitted paternity after the third application to the court. On each occasion, a medical certificate was produced stating that the elderly man was too weak to appear. In his absence, Reverend Powell was ordered to pay Margaret Evans three shillings per week, plus costs.[117] Putative fathers took measures not only to safeguard their own reputations but also to evade the long-term maintenance payments. Yet, in cases where men could reasonably question a woman's character, it was understandable that this led them to challenge affiliation proceedings brought against them.

The punitive Bastardy Clause did not deter women from giving birth to illegitimate children, but it did have a devastating impact on their ability to maintain them alone. Arguably, evidence indicates that illegitimate infants were born to women who had been sexually harassed or abused, but more often than not, cases revealed that they were seduced under the promise of marriage. Whether pregnant or not, some women were not deterred from bringing about a civil action against men for breach of promise of marriage. Breach-of-promise-of-marriage cases were more likely to be the preserve of the middle and upper classes. However, from the 1870s onwards, working-class women sought redress and sued for damages in court. Ginger Frost maintains that the Evidence Amendment Act in 1869 permitted working-class women to sue for breach of promise. The law reform directly contributed to the increase in breach-of-promise cases because women could now provide evidence on their own behalf.[118] For instance, nineteen randomly selected cases dated between 1871 and 1893 revealed that seven working-class women, six middle-class women, and one man sued for breach of promise of marriage. Another five civil actions were instigated by servants. Breach-of-promise lawsuits were not necessarily the preserve of women, but the plaintiff in the sole case involving a man was ridiculed and provided a great deal of entertainment in court. The defence counsel contended that 'an action of this kind, brought by a man, was not one ought to meet with any encouragement'.[119] Farmers appeared to be the worst offenders in breach-of-promise cases, as many servants and housekeepers lived in. It was not surprising to find that the women's constant close proximity to their masters made them more susceptible to seduction and more likely to have illegitimate children fathered by the defendants. In many cases letters, written by both parties, proved to be incriminating, although such correspondence was largely presented as evidence in middle-class actions. It was a humiliating process for women to proceed with affiliation orders, yet it appeared to be equally embarrassing to sue for breach of promise of marriage.

Breach-of-promise cases attracted a great deal of attention, with crowded courts and many female onlookers in attendance. The most intimate details were laid bare in the form of love letters that were read out in court and later published in the press. In some cases, lawyers seemed to play to the audience to cause amusement at the couple's expense. Witness testimonies often caused outbursts of laughter too. Women were often accused of having 'improper relations' with other men in paternity cases, although the Bench generally ruled in the women's favour. Even so, the opportunity to degrade women in the process was not overlooked. However, in breach-of-promise cases, the balance of power shifted in favour of women. Men were more likely to be ridiculed because their behaviour was described in detail, often through the reading of bundles of love letters, and their actions were later exposed via the press. And to make matters worse, men usually had to settle on substantial damages. It was interesting to note that by the time most cases came to court, women had often recovered from the breakdown of the relationships. Cases prove that women primarily engaged in legal action to claim compensation; but pursuit of men through the courts was also a way of redeeming their character, especially if broken relationships had resulted in the birth of illegitimate children.

In 1873 Miss Margaret Williams, the daughter of a respectable farmer from Tregynon, brought an action against a Baptist minister, the Reverend T. M. Thomas. He was also the son of a respectable farmer from Newport, Pembrokeshire. The evidence revealed the 'grossest conduct' on Reverend Thomas's part, although he was not present in court. Not only had he deceived Margaret Williams, but she was also pregnant after he had seduced her under the promise of marriage. It was reported that Reverend Thomas had accepted a pastorate of a church at £100 per year.[120] Margaret Williams's counsel summed up in court that in the assessment for damages the jury would have to take into account 'her outraged feelings and wounded pride'. A number of personal letters were read out in court and later published in the press. The correspondence proved that Reverend Thomas was writing to Margaret Williams on very affectionate terms within days of marrying another woman. Her counsel's comments in court encapsulated men's attitudes towards women and marriage at that time. His remarks also emphasised women's reliance on men and the need to secure a husband, particularly a man of means. He contended that 'when a woman loses the position she had expected by the prospect of having a home of her own, which she regarded as her empire, she lost her all'. He went on to assert that, 'Love is a woman's whole existence' and that Margaret Williams, 'no doubt looked, as other women do, to some share in his glory'. The counsel then addressed her seduction, declaring that having yielded to the man she loved, 'she goes back to the society of her friends humiliated and disgraced'. He felt that 'nothing can be suggested that will mitigate her sorrow' and argued that 'The only means a woman has to set herself right is that of resorting to a jury to give her compensation.'[121] Margaret Williams was awarded £300 in damages.[122]

In 1893 Mary Davies, who could not 'be said to be prepossessing', sought to recover £100 damages from David Jones, an aged farmer, for breach of promise of marriage. She had been employed by him while his wife was still alive but left when she gave birth to his illegitimate child. Mary Davies took another post on a nearby farm and while at that place was visited by David Jones, who 'went there at night and courted her in bed, after the custom of the country'. The owner of the nearby farm, her employer, testified that he heard David Jones say to Mary Davies that he was going to marry her. It transpired that there was only a partition between the beds of the farmer and Mary Davies. Apparently, the farmer had been asked to listen to the conversation. David Jones denied all the evidence against him, which was so conflicting that the jury could not decide upon a verdict.[123] Mary Davies's case proved that not all actions resulted in compensation. In some cases women failed to achieve the desired outcome and subjected themselves to ridicule and embarrassment in pursuit of a claim. Then again, perhaps women also sought redress via the courts as a way to seek revenge; therefore men justifiably defended their interests.

Conclusion

The punitive Bastardy Clause was introduced to discourage feckless single women from giving birth to illegitimate children and, therefore, relieve ratepayers from the unnecessary expense of maintaining them in the community. However, the deterrent effect of the new law did not prevent illegitimacy, because it permitted too many men to act with impunity. As a consequence, the Bastardy Clause had a long-term detrimental effect since unmarried mothers undoubtedly endured the financial burden, and the social stigma, of rearing illegitimate children, while the new law provided men with greater freedom to evade responsibility. The impact of gender and class were clearly exposed in the commissioners' reports into the operation of the Poor Law, which were heavily weighted in favour of men, while injurious to women. A woman shouldered the blame and was denied financial support because she had 'voluntarily become a mother, without procuring to herself and her child the assistance of a husband and a father'. It was argued at the time that 'There can be no reason for giving to vice privileges which we deny to misfortune.'[124] The strict regime of the workhouse as the only means of assistance punished unmarried mothers even further, and many made determined efforts to avoid admission. The pursuit of putative fathers through the courts was without doubt a degrading experience for women; but in the majority of cases the courts ruled in the mother's favour, often in spite of the man's social class.

The fear of religious condemnation did not appear to deter courting couples from intimacy, although abandoned pregnant young women no doubt feared the wrath of God, so often preached of from the pulpits as a means to uphold standards of morality. The disparaging nature of the Blue Books published in 1847 resonated amongst the ruling classes and religious communities for decades, although, for the most part, life for the lower rural orders carried on much as normal.

The rural Welsh custom of 'bundling' or *caru ar y gwely* was blamed for immoral behaviour, although a man engaging in such relations usually married once the woman was pregnant. It seemed that a woman consented to intimacy in the knowledge that marriage would take place prior to the birth and the child would therefore be legitimised. Yet the male freedoms associated with the Bastardy Clause disrupted the time-honoured courting custom of 'bundling'; therefore, it gave men the opportunity to evade both marriage and the responsibility of maintaining their illegitimate offspring.

The scene has been set for the subsequent chapters, since the underlying causes that led to increased cases of infant deaths can be seen to have originated, partly, from the introduction of the New Poor Law and the Bastardy Clause. Without familial support, the new law forced women to make stark choices that were detrimental to infant life. Abandonment of the child was an option, but infant survival rates within the workhouse were also low. Demand for childcare, as a means to avoid the workhouse, led to baby farming and premature infant deaths at the hands of someone else. Abortion was another option available to women to avoid unwanted pregnancies and was often actively encouraged by men. Obviously, cases of abandonment, abortion and infanticide occurred long before the introduction of the Bastardy Clause. However, rather than rushed marriages or the issue of affiliation orders against reputed fathers, common under the Old Poor Law, the punitive new clause forced a number of women to commit infanticide.

In 1834, Mr Walcott commented that, 'We believe that in no civilised country, and scarcely in any barbarous country, has such a thing ever been heard of as a mother's killing her child in order to save the expense of feeding it.'[125] Indeed, Mr Walcott had a valid point until the underlying causes are taken into consideration. In England and Wales a woman was usually dismissed by her employer because she was pregnant, and was often left with no other alternative but the workhouse. Poverty and shame, men's lack of accountability, and the humiliating procedure to secure maintenance payments led a woman to commit infanticide and not, as according to Mr Walcott, the desire to save the expense of feeding a child.

Notes

1 Reports of the Commissioners of Inquiry for South Wales (1844), PP, 16 (HMSO, London), p. 107.

2 Report from His Majesty's Commissioners of Inquiry into the Administration and Practical Operation of the Poor Laws (1834), PP (HMSO, London), p. 97.

3 Report from His Majesty's Commissioners, p. 175.

4 Pat Malloy, *And They Blessed Rebecca: An account of the Welsh Toll-gate Riots 1839–44* (Llandysul, 1983); David Williams, *The Rebecca Riots* (Cardiff, 2011).

5 'Poor Law Act', *The Times,* 12 September 1836, p. 3, *Times* Digital Archive, https://www.gale.com, accessed 23/02/2007.

6 Anne Digby, 'The Rural Poor Law', in D. Fraser (ed.), *The New Poor Law in the Nineteenth Century* (Basingstoke, 1976), pp. 149–70 (p. 152).

7 Gareth Elwyn Jones, *The Education of a Nation* (Cardiff, 1997), p. 17.

8 Reports of the Commissioners of Inquiry into the State of Education in Wales (1847), PP, 339 (HMSO, London), Part II, Brecknock, Cardigan and Radnor, p. 99.
9 Gareth Elwyn Jones, *Modern Wales: A Concise History* (Cambridge, 1999), p. 289.
10 Reports of the Commissioners of Inquiry into the State of Education, p. 254.
11 Jodie Krieder, '"Degraded and Benighted": Gendered Constructions of Wales in the Empire, ca. 1847', *North American Journal of Welsh Studies*, 2/1 (2002), 24–35 (p. 30).
12 Caradoc Evans, *My People* (1915, reprinted Bridgend, 2014).
13 Reports of the Commissioners of Inquiry for South Wales, p. 75.
14 Henry Reed Stiles, *Bundling: Its Origins, Progress, & Decline in America* (Boston, 1872, reproduced Massachusetts, 2004), p. 13.
15 Reports of the Commissioners of Inquiry for South Wales, p. 177.
16 Quoted in U. Henriques, 'Bastardy and the New Poor Law', *Past & Present,* 37 (1967), 103–29 (p. 109).
17 Report from His Majesty's Commissioners, Appendix B, Answers to Rural Questions, pp. 657–58.
18 Report from His Majesty's Commissioners, p. 638.
19 Margaret A. Lyle, 'Regionality in the late Old Poor Law: The treatment of chargeable bastards from Rural Queries', *The Agricultural History Review*, 53/2 (2005), 141–57 (p. 156).
20 Report from His Majesty's Commissioners, p. 658.
21 Report from His Majesty's Commissioners, p. 660.
22 Report from His Majesty's Commissioners, p. 180a.
23 Report from His Majesty's Commissioners, p. 174.
24 *The Cambrian*, 24 March 1832, p. 3.
25 Thomas Nutt, 'Illegitimacy, paternal financial responsibility, and the 1834 Poor Law Commission Report: the myth of the old poor law and the making of the new', *The Economic History Review*, 63/2 (2010), 335–61 (p. 338).
26 Report of the Commissioners of Inquiry for South Wales, p. 203.
27 *The Welshman*, 31 May 1844, p. 4.
28 Reports of the Commissioners of Inquiry for South Wales, p. 168.
29 Reports of the Commissioners of Inquiry for South Wales, p. 107.
30 Reports of the Commissioners of Inquiry for South Wales, p. 177.
31 Jessica A. Sheetz-Nguyen, *Victorian Women, Unwed Mothers and the London Foundling Hospital* (London, 2012), p. 99.
32 Reports of Commissioners of Inquiry for South Wales, p. 177.
33 Report from His Majesty's Commissioners, p. 660.
34 Rachel Ginnis Fuchs, 'Crimes against Children in Nineteenth-Century France: Child Abuse', *Law and Human Behaviour*, 6, 3/4 (1982), 237–59 (p. 240).
35 Fuchs, 'Crimes against Children', 241.
36 Fuchs, 'Crimes against Children', 242.
37 Reports of Commissioners of Inquiry for South Wales, p. 203.
38 Carmarthenshire Archives (hereafter CA), Felons' Register Carmarthen Gaol, ACC 4916, No. 1297.
39 *Western Mail,* 5 July 1869.
40 CA, Felons' Register, No. 1297.

41 Pembrokeshire Archives (hereafter PA) Register of Prisoners, Summary Convictions, 1850, PQ/AG 10.

42 *Western Mail*, 21 October 1870, p. 4.

43 CA, Felons' Register, 1158, 1306.

44 CA, Felons' Register, 188, 206, 302, 366, 731, 994, 1271, 1297.

45 Stiles, *Bundling*, p. 30.

46 Stiles, *Bundling*, p. 36.

47 Stiles, *Bundling*, p. 23.

48 Report of Royal Commission on Labour, *The Agricultural Labourer,* Vol. II, Wales, 1893, C 36 (HMSO, London), p. 63.

49 *Evening Express*, 28 July 1900, p. 2.

50 *Evening Express*, 5 June 1900, p. 2.

51 *Evening Express*, 7 June 1900, p. 2.

52 National Library of Wales, Court of Great Sessions, Wales 1730–1830, https://crimeandpunishment.library.wales, accessed 15/11/2019.

53 Proportion per Cent of Illegitimate Children to the Births Registered in 1842, Sixth annual report of the Registrar-General (1842) BPP 1844 XIX (540) xxxii, www.histpop.org, accessed 26/05/2018.

54 Sixth annual report of the Registrar-General, p. xxxiii.

55 Stiles, *Bundling*, p. 30.

56 Commission on the Employment of Children, Young Persons, and Women in Agriculture 1867, (1870), PP, 13 (HMSO, London), p. 42.

57 Report of Commissioners of Inquiry into the State of Education, p. 34.

58 Report of Commissioners of Inquiry into the State of Education, Part I, Carmarthen, Glamorgan, and Pembroke, p. 254.

59 Catrin Stevens, *Welsh Courting Customs* (Llandysul, 1993), p. 8.

60 John Davies, *A History of Wales* (London, 1994), p. 392.

61 Russell Davies, "In a Broken Dream': Some aspects of sexual behaviour and the dilemmas of the unmarried mother in south west Wales, 1887–1914', *Llafur,* III (1983), 24–33 (p. 24).

62 *Pembrokeshire Herald and General Advertiser*, 14 January 1910, p. 3.

63 Richard W. Ireland, *Land of White Gloves? A history of crime and punishment in Wales* (Oxfordshire, 2016), p. 8.

64 Davies, 'In a Broken Dream', 24–5.

65 Davies, 'In a Broken Dream', 30.

66 *The Times,* 3 July 1843, p. 6, *Times* Digital Archive, https://www.gale.com, accessed 31/08/2006.

67 Russell Davies, *Hope and Heartbreak: A Social History of Wales and the Welsh, 1776–1871* (Cardiff, 2005), pp. 324–375 (p. 324).

68 Gwyneth Tyson Roberts, *The Language of the Blue Books: Wales and Colonial Prejudice* (Cardiff, 2011), p. 179.

69 Roberts, *The Language of the Blue Books*, p. 179.

70 For an overview on religion in Welsh society see Davies, *Hope and Heartbreak*, pp. 324–375; Russell Davies, *Secret Sins: Sex, Violence & Society in Carmarthenshire 1870–1920* (Cardiff, 1996), pp. 186–230.

71 Anne-Marie Kilday and Katherine D. Watson, 'Infanticide, religion and community in the British Isles, 1720–1920: Introduction', *Family and Community History,* 11/2 (2008), 84–99 (p. 84).
72 Report of Commissioners of Inquiry into the State of Education in Wales, p. 254.
73 Bert J. Rawlins, *The Parish Churches and Nonconformist Chapels of Wales: Their Records and Where to Find Them*, Volume One, Cardigan-Carmarthen-Pembroke (Salt Lake City, 1987).
74 Caradoc Evans, 'The Redeemer', *My People*, (1915, reprinted Bridgend, 2014), p. 20.
75 Evans, 'The Redeemer', p. 11.
76 Evans, 'The Redeemer', p. 128.
77 Evans, 'The Redeemer', p. 132.
78 Caradoc Evans, 'Greater than Love', *My People* (1915, reprinted Bridgend, 2014), p. 151.
79 Evans, 'Greater than Love', p. 156.
80 *Western Mail*, 28 November 1895, p. 6.
81 Lisa Forman Cody, 'The Politics of Illegitimacy in an Age of Reform: Women, Reproduction, and Political Economy in England's New Poor Law of 1834', *Journal of Women's History*, 11/4 (2000), 131–56 (p. 131).
82 Forman Cody, 'The Politics of Illegitimacy in an Age of Reform', 131.
83 *Western Mail*, 21 June 1869, p. 2.
84 Ginger S. Frost, *Promises Broken: Courtship, Class, and Gender in Victorian England* (Charlottesville and London, 1995), p. 98.
85 Reports of the Commissioners of Inquiry into the State of Education, p. 421.
86 Reports of the Commissioners of Inquiry into the State of Education, p. 60.
87 Stiles, *Bundling*, pp. 135—42.
88 Michael Mason, *The Making of Victorian Sexuality* (Oxford, 1994), p. 67.
89 *Western Mail*, 28 August 1869, p. 4.
90 *Western Mail*, 4 May 1882, p. 3; 30 June 1884, p. 3; 28 November 1895, p. 6; 13 February 1899, p. 6; *The Pembrokeshire Herald & General Advertiser*, p. 4.
91 *Western Mail*, 10 April 1878, p. 4; 5 September 1882, p. 4.
92 *Western Mail*, 23 June 1894, p. 5.
93 *Western Mail*, 5 January 1899, p. 7.
94 *South Wales Daily Post*, 20 September 1900, p. 4.
95 *Western Mail*, 6 February 1882, p. 4.
96 *Western Mail*, 5 January 1899, p. 7.
97 Françoise Barret-Ducrocq, *Love in the Time of Victoria* (London, 1991), p. 49.
98 Barret-Ducrocq, *Love in the Time of Victoria,* p. 49.
99 Barret-Ducrocq, *Love in the Time of Victoria*, p. 48.
100 *Evening Express*, 29 April 1898, p. 2.
101 *South Wales Daily News*, 25 November 1898, p. 6.
102 *Evening Express*, 29 April 1898, p. 2.
103 *Aberystwyth Observer*, 1 December 1898, p. 4.
104 *Aberystwyth Observer*, 5 January 1899, p. 2.
105 *Western Mail*, 24 February 1899, p. 6.
106 *The Cambrian*, 7 April 1899, p. 5.
107 *Evening Express*, 31 December 1903, p. 3.

108 K. Theodore Hoppen, *The Mid-Victorian Generation 1846–1886* (Oxford, 1998), p. 46.
109 'What Constitutes Respectability?' *Bow Bells* (1882), p. 500.
110 Hoppen, *The Mid-Victorian Generation*, p. 65.
111 'What Constitutes Respectability?' *Bow Bells*, p. 500.
112 *Western Mail*, 18 October 1876, p. 6.
113 *Pembrokeshire Herald and General Advertiser*, 28 February 1873, p. 2.
114 *Western Mail*, 31 January 1871, p. 2.
115 *Western Mail*, 21 June 1869, p. 2.
116 Powys Archives, Cefnllys Petty Session Court Register, R/PS/LW/RG/15.
117 *Western Mail*, 5 February 1877, p. 7.
118 Frost, *Promises Broken*, p. 135.
119 *Western Mail*, 24 February 1871, p. 2.
120 *South Wales Daily News*, 20 August 1873, p. 3.
121 *The Welshman*, 22 August 1873, p. 6.
122 *South Wales Daily News*, 20 August 1873, p. 3.
123 *Western Mail*, 23 October 1893, p. 6.
124 Report from His Majesty's Commissioners, p. 347.
125 Report from His Majesty's Commissioners, p. 198.

Chapter Two

'She who lurks within': The baby farmer and the community network

It was widely acknowledged that the Bastardy Clause contributed to the increased cases of infanticide and infant abandonment. Evidence to support this claim was visible in contemporary sources, newspapers and the relevant government Commissioners' reports published in 1834, 1844 and 1847. Despite the hardship many unmarried mothers managed to survive on their paltry wages by employing childminders to care for their children, whereas others found it increasingly difficult to manage financially and looked for support elsewhere. As demand for childcare increased, minders realised that potential profits could be gained from 'adopting' or nursing illegitimate infants. Therefore, this form of childcare degenerated into what became known as baby farming. Baby farming was particularly prevalent from the 1870s until the early decades of the twentieth century and existed in a society where most unwanted children were a burden, both in economic and social terms. Infants died at the hands of baby farmers in increasing numbers; but baby farmers did not act alone, as the practice was facilitated by others. Putative fathers, family members, neighbours, midwives and nurses aided the removal of unwanted infants via community networks located amongst the working classes, where baby farming thrived.

'Adopting' or nursing infants for financial rewards presented baby farmers with an income; hence, a few well-chosen words in an advertisement had the potential to convince parents that a '"respectable woman" who wishes to "adopt" an infant, promising "a mother's love and care" for a small premium of five pounds'[1] could be relied upon. Such an offer was mutually beneficial since baby farmers provided both parents with the opportunity to conceal their unwanted infants by permanently 'adopting' an infant for a lump-sum premium, as opposed to minding infants for weekly or regular payments. However, behind the facade often lay a more disturbing objective, because the worst abuses of children usually occurred in cases of lump-sum 'adoptions'. The prime objective of baby farmers with criminal intent was to systematically withdraw support and provisions for an infant's basic needs for survival, therefore hastening its death. This allowed baby farmers to retain a higher proportion of the payment ostensibly made for the infant's upkeep.

The practice of baby farming is undoubtedly a disturbing subject to approach, but it does highlight significant issues relevant to Welsh women and children, whose history has often been overlooked. Shurlee Swain maintains that 'Nineteenth-century baby farming has been a difficult topic for historians, its existence assumed or denied, but rarely questioned. Such reactions suggest a sensitivity surviving much longer than the practice itself.'[2] In recent years historians have tended to focus their research on high-profile criminal cases to expose the complexities of the practice, particularly as an English urban phenomenon.[3] Yet the practice of baby farming was of international concern. The Welsh press actively reported on baby farming in both England and Wales; moreover, newspapers also provided accounts from other countries—for example, Australia,[4] Germany,[5] Russia[6], Austria,[7] Belgium[8] and Ireland[9]—proving that it was practised on an international scale.

Ruth Homrighaus argues that historians have paid too much attention to criminal baby farming due to the interest in sensational cases, making it easy to misinterpret the meaning of baby farming in English society. Consequently, 'historians have left important questions of baby farming unresolved', and 'made little effort to discriminate between baby farmers of different stripes'.[10] The practice was prevalent in England, particularly in large towns and cities, but how widespread was baby farming in Wales? In order to understand baby farming in Welsh communities, the cases presented in this chapter offer a glimpse of a diverse group of baby farmers of 'different stripes'. The details uncovered by the press in some cases are not perceptible in other primary sources; therefore, newspapers are referred to as a key source since the extensive reporting on the realities of life at a local level exposed the baby farmers' social class, background and methods of operation.

Baby farming highlights significant issues relating to gender, class and the prevailing double standards pertinent to both baby farmers and parents, and inherent in the majority of cases. The first part of the chapter makes a distinction between criminal baby farmers, whose deliberate neglect caused untimely infant deaths, and non-criminal baby farmers who offered paid childcare on a regular basis. The influence of gender and class is examined in the second part of the chapter to explain why certain individuals employed the services of baby farmers. The common perception of the poverty-stricken baby farmer who 'adopted' a poor servant girl's illegitimate infant is palpable; however, as this chapter will make evident, baby farming permeated several different sections of society. The emerging infant life protection groups, feminist campaigners and medical experts called for state intervention as baby farming threatened the lives of infants due to neglect, malice or ignorance. Therefore, the final part of the chapter assesses the body of laws relating to infant life protection legislation introduced as a result of government inquiries, to consider how effective the new laws were in bringing about an end to baby farming.

The practice of baby farming in Welsh communities

Baby farming was referred to at the time as a profession, although as Homrighaus argues, 'No respectable woman would have called herself a baby farmer. "Baby Farming" was an accusation, not a profession.'[11] Similarly, Anette Ballinger maintains that 'Baby farming as a profession was both despised and stigmatised, since its existence emphasised the contradictions between dominant images of idealised motherhood, and its reality for those women whose circumstances did not fit this image.'[12] From another perspective, Margaret Arnot points out that 'from the mid 1860s "baby-farming" took over from "infanticide"', and that 'the discovery of "baby-farming" provided a scapegoat, something apparently easier to deal with because it was characterised by a cash relation between the infant and its nurturer'.[13] Certainly, it could be argued that in some cases the financial transactions sanctioned other individuals to commit infanticide as unwanted infants were assigned to their fate. Although, as Anne-Marie Kilday found, 'The extent to which this kind of maternal devolution was in effect infanticide by proxy is difficult to ascertain.'[14] Many infant deaths were effectively hidden by poverty; therefore, a low standard of living amongst the lower classes with attendant high infant mortality makes it difficult to identify this form of infanticide. An illustrative case is that of Mrs Martha White, a baby farmer from Milford Haven, who reportedly buried nine or ten children in her care without suspicion.[15] Mrs White was allowed to bury significant numbers of children; therefore, it is not unreasonable to suggest that in some cases infants might well have been killed by their own mothers at birth had the responsibility for their welfare not been premeditated beforehand and devolved to minders like Mrs White.

From the late 1860s onwards, the public's attention was drawn to the widespread social commentary pertaining to baby farming as an alternative to child murder perpetrated by the mother. Even assuming a certain degree of naivety, parents must have had grave doubts whether infants 'adopted' for lump sums would be well cared for after handover. During this period there was no formal legal process for the adoption of children in England and Wales. Lionel Rose points out that 'It was perfectly proper and legal to hand over or sell one's child to another – though the "adoption", so-called, had no force in law and could be revoked.'[16] Not surprisingly, as this form of adoption had no regulatory laws, it had the capacity to degenerate into baby farming. As it was a relatively complex practice, a brief outline is necessary to differentiate between criminal baby farmers, likely to 'adopt' infants for lump-sum payments, and other providers of childcare.

In 1871 the government appointed the Select Committee on the Protection of Infant Life (SCPIL) after significant pressure from infant life campaigners for state intervention. Its remit was to inquire as to the best means of preventing the destruction of the lives of infants put out to hired nurses by their parents. The outcome of the inquiry was published in the Report from the Select Committee on Protection of Infant Life (RSCPIL). According to the SCPIL, criminal baby farming was the adoption of children with 'an utter disregard of what will become of them, and possibly with the intention that their lives should be criminally soon brought to an end'.[17] Whether death was intentional or not, evidence suggests that in some cases arrangements were agreed whereby infants were not expected to survive.

Baby farmers were also known to act as midwives or to operate as part of a network trading in unwanted infants. Midwives of questionable character recorded stillborn births after attending the delivery of infants born alive and murdered at birth. Dr Winter, a former editor of the *British Medical Journal* (*BMJ*), pointed out that 'Midwives wickedly inclined know well what it is to produce a stillbirth, or in the horrible language of their craft, a "quiet 'un".'[18] The *BMJ* complained that 'The reckless indifference to child life which leaves stillborn children buried in the back garden or cast out upon the dust heap, and their births left unregistered is purely English, and would not be tolerated in any other civilised country.'[19] In fact, it was reported that every country in Europe registered stillborn children, apart from Russia.[20]

Benjamin Waugh's article published in the *Contemporary Review* amounted to a severe condemnation of the practice of baby farming in England.[21] Waugh, a Congregational minister and director of the National Society for the Prevention of Cruelty to Children (NSPCC), divided baby farmers into two groups: those who took in infants to earn a living and those he classed as criminals. He divided the latter group into procurers and receivers. The procurer's 'business is to snare; her receiver's is to slay'.[22] Waugh found that procurers were often present at the births of illegitimate infants; they were namely low-class monthly nurses (nurses who attended the mother for a month after childbirth), midwives, workhouse nurses and keepers of lying-in establishments. He argued that most were 'probably helping the mother out of her "trouble", not for gain, yet sending to houses which exist for gain'.[23] As we will see later in this chapter, Waugh's findings were mirrored in the stark reality of baby farming in Welsh communities.

The situation was similar in Australia, as Shurlee Swain's research identified a clustering of infant deaths in the vicinity of Melbourne's Women's Hospital. Swain discovered that the hospital was surrounded by boarding houses providing accommodation for single women awaiting confinement, midwives known to perform abortions and small lying-in hospitals where attendants were willing to ask no questions. The nurses formed part of a chain in which infants passed through several hands before reaching their eventual 'home'. Infants provided a market for baby farmers, and the babies did not travel far before they died. Swain points out that 'the steps in the chain are clearly identified: the "ladies' nurse" with premises in a major street passed the infant over to a licensed or unlicensed nurse in one of the smaller streets or lanes, and money changed hands at every point'.[24]

Similar to Swain's findings in Melbourne, the case of Mrs Hannah Price, a midwife from Newport, provides evidence of a procurer who passed infants from one person to another, while money changed hands at each stage. In 1871 the death of a fourteen-day-old unknown infant occurred after the mother, described as being of respectable appearance and with a manner that showed she was well-to-do, arrived at Mrs Price's house unannounced and close to giving birth. Mrs Price's evasiveness at the coroner's inquest meant that, despite detailed enquiries, the jury failed to establish the mother's identity or where the money was to come from to support the infant had it lived. The mother stayed for more than a week, and paid Mrs Price accordingly. Mrs Price agreed to keep the infant, allegedly for eight shillings, but then persuaded a local woman to 'adopt' it for four shillings per week. The baby subsequently died in her care, which the coroner recorded as death by natural causes. Mrs Price admitted that she had been involved in two similar cases of infant death in the past. The press reported that Mrs Price had claimed the instances occurred by total chance, 'The mothers being perfect strangers to her, and coming quite accidentally to her house in pains of labour!'[25] These two cases, if indeed there were only two, do not confirm that she was running a lying-in establishment for secret confinements. It was evident that the well-to-do mother received a complete service of assistance in labour and the discreet removal and 'adoption' of the child in return for payment, therefore confirming Mrs Price's role as both a procurer and a midwife. No doubt Mrs Price advertised her services, since it was highly unlikely that an expectant mother would arrive on her doorstep by accident. Mrs Price's methods were noticeably comparable to those adopted by baby farmers in Melbourne.

Baby farmers often relied on classified advertisements to ply their trade, although it was unlikely that this was a feasible option for those from poor backgrounds because the cost was prohibitive. The use of classified advertisements by some baby farmers was central to their operations since access to cheaper newspapers provided opportunities to attract infants nationwide. A typical advertisement in the *Evening Express* read: 'Wanted, by respectable person, child to adopt or nurse, small premium; good home; good references.

Apply Roberts, 97 Woodville Road, Cardiff.'[26] In 1891, at a House of Commons sitting, Mr Channing MP asked Mr Matthews, the Home Secretary, whether he would consider legislating to control or prevent the use of such advertisements. Mr Matthews replied, 'I do not see my way to legislative interference with these advertisements, which do not invite to anything necessarily illegal.' Furthermore, Mr Matthews claimed that the police found the advertisements provided useful clues as to the whereabouts of baby-farming establishments.[27] Eventually, the majority of newspapers refused to print such advertisements. Homrighaus points out that by 1932 it was against the law to either place or print an adoption advertisement under a bogus name or address, and by 1943 all personal adoption advertisements were banned.[28] The response to advertisements exposed the perceived willingness of unmarried mothers desperate enough to trust complete strangers to supposedly bring up their children.

The popular use of advertisements by women to locate carers for their children is partly explained by the need for secrecy, and not necessarily due to the desire to destroy their children by leaving them in the hands of unscrupulous childminders. Dr A. Wiltshire commented that:

> Secresy [*sic*] is the thing needful. If you give them opportunities for putting their children away quietly where they can be well taken care of, I think it would be a gross injustice to these poor women to say that they have no maternal affection or instinct. On the contrary, I have good reason for knowing that they have that affection, but the burden is so great for them that they do violent deeds. [29]

In fact, mothers often tried to maintain contact after handover of their children. Françoise Barret-Ducrocq found that where infants had been left at private institutions, 'some mothers wrote letters year after year asking again and again for news of the child's welfare. A woman might get a baby "off her hands" only to find that the emotional mortgage was for life.'[30] Certainly, the handover of infants did not necessarily mean that mothers were not concerned about their welfare, because many women had no other way of providing for their illegitimate offspring.

Not all childcare providers were baby farmers, yet carers tended to be labelled in the same manner and baby farming was associated with disreputable practices. Homrighaus maintains that 'the *BMJ* used the term "baby-farmer" to refer to proprietresses of lying-in establishments and midwives as well as childcare providers, thereby blurring the distinction between these roles and associating all three with criminal practices'.[31] The case of Mrs Helen Kendall, a labourer's wife from Cardiff, provides a distinction between criminal and non-criminal baby farmers, proving that a bona fide carer could be accused of baby farming. In this case, the mother had left her fourteen-month-old infant in Mrs Kendall's care while she searched for her husband in America. The press reported the case as one of baby farming, although the evidence could not be substantiated. Mrs Kendall was charged following allegations that the infant had died from starvation because he only weighed half the expected weight for an infant of his age. The woman maintained that he was a hungry baby and that she fed him well but he remained very thin. Two neighbours confirmed that the infant was well fed and cared for, but he was sickly and failed to thrive. The infant was admitted to the Cardiff infirmary because he was covered in sores. However, Mrs Kendall was later instructed to remove the child from the infirmary. When the childminder's young daughter collected the infant, he had only been dressed in a nightdress and shawl at the infirmary, exposing his bare legs and feet to the cold.[32] The coroner concluded that the lack of clothing when the infant left the infirmary contributed to his death and did not attach blame to anyone.[33] Mrs Kendall's case provides evidence of how the boundary between baby farmers and bona fide carers was indistinct because the term was readily applied to those who practised all forms of paid-for childcare.

A number of baby farmers were particularly cruel to infants in their care once the children were acquired, but why? Deprivation could reasonably explain an infant's poor diet, but could it justify cruelty and systematic neglect? It was argued in *The Times* that once an infant was transferred to the baby farmer and the transaction concluded, her attitude changed. 'It is not surprising that the other party to the bargain is inclined to grudge the cost and trouble of the responsibility she has been paid to undertake; and, as use hardens her to cruelty and carelessness, neglect rapidly ripens to crime.'[34] Then again, as Sherri Broder found in Philadelphia, mothers could leave children with baby farmers and disappear without paying boarding fees. By doing so, baby farmers 'served as unwitting and unwilling agents in the process of abandonment'.[35] Mrs Martha White, from Milford Haven, was one baby farmer whose behaviour was consistent with the observations put forward in *The Times*, and a comparable example to support Broder's findings. In 1871 two servants, Elizabeth Griffiths and Lettice Rees, entrusted their illegitimate infants to Mrs White's care. Both infants subsequently died of neglect and abuse. Lettice Rees had been an inmate at the Pembroke Union workhouse for four months before she placed her one-month-old infant in Mrs White's care. It was alleged that the woman starved the babies and allowed them to cry for hours, and that she beat the infants in bed and called them 'dirty little devils'. A neighbour reported that she had only ever seen Mrs White feed Elizabeth Griffiths's infant cold tea with no milk. One day the baby was found lying face-down on a pile of rags. The neighbour asked Mrs White to nurse the infant, but she refused, claiming that the mother had left it with her without payment.[36] She argued that non-payment justified neglect. It was reported that Elizabeth Griffiths regularly paid the baby farmer two shillings per week, so it seemed that Mrs White was lying. She was eventually charged at the Pembrokeshire Spring Assizes in February 1872 with killing the infant belonging to Lettice Rees. In this case, the woman was acquitted, despite the shameful neglect.[37]

At a meeting of the SCPIL, Mr A. Gernon pointed out that while many children were disposed of criminally, it was difficult to bring criminal charges. Neglect was compounded with the kind of food babies were fed, because the infants wasted away due to their inadequate diet.[38] Owing to the mother's paltry wages, insufficient money was paid to the baby farmer or minder to sustain the infant and allow enough profit to defray her living expenses. Dr A. Wiltshire found that children needed as much as a quart of milk per day, at an approximate cost of 5d. Therefore, it would be impossible for a person to rear an infant without adequate recompense for the cost of milk.[39] In 1871 the approximate cost to feed an infant the correct amount of milk was two to three shillings per week. Yet, in some cases referred to in this chapter, baby farmers were paid as little as two shillings; five shillings per week was the average amount paid. Dr Lankaster maintained that a child could not be properly cared for and fed for less than five shillings per week.[40] Evidence indicates that infants were fed cold tea, flour and water, and other unsuitable farinaceous foods in order to cut costs.

Evidently, there was a fine line between causing infant deaths without arousing suspicion and being convicted of committing a criminal offence. Hence, deliberate infant neglect required careful management to avoid detection. Cases revealed that baby farmers usually resorted to one of two methods. One method, for those with criminal intent, was to acquire sickly infants under two or three months old, preferably with lump-sum payments for their care. The reasoning behind this method was that newborn infants had a much greater risk of dying quickly without giving rise to suspicion, therefore maximising profits. At an inquest, a baby farmer frequently claimed that the infant was sickly when she took charge of it, implying that she was in no way to blame for its death. Working-class women, mostly servants, usually employed the services of baby farmers on a weekly basis, whereas putative fathers were more inclined to arrange lump-sum adoptions to absolve themselves of any long-term responsibilities. When unscrupulous baby farmers adopted infants in return for weekly payments, it was in their interest to obtain strong, healthy infants. This meant that the infant could withstand being fed the minimum amount of food, which left more of its mother's hard-earned maintenance for the baby farmer's own purposes. As Waugh pointed out, baby farmers 'eke out their own living by eking out a baby's dying'.[41] In many cases the mother often visited and noticed the infant losing weight, yet the baby farmer insisted that she was doing her best. Elizabeth Griffiths visited her infant while in Mrs White's care fortnightly, sometimes more often. She noticed the infant's weight loss, but Mrs White told her it was due to teething. It was reported that the infant had been with Mrs White for three months and was a fine baby when she arrived, but just a skeleton when she died.[42]

Lump-sum payments ranged between £5 and £10 in the majority of cases. However, twenty-month-old Richard Davies was 'adopted' by Isaac and Mary Thomas from Red Roses, near Whitland, for a payment of £30. The infant was the illegitimate child of Mary Davies from Swansea, although the child was born at Llanddewi Velfrey, Narberth. William Owens, the father, also from Llanddewi Velfrey, was ordered to pay three shillings per week, but Mary Davies accepted his offer of a lump-sum payment of £30 in discharge of the magistrate's order and passed the child on to Mrs Thomas. It was reported by the jury in this case that:

> they emphatically disapproved of their conduct living as they do in a two-roomed cottage with five young children of their own, and undertaking for the sum of £30 paid down to bring up and educate an illegitimate child of another person free from any further claim on the mother and putative father.[43]

In William Owens's case it was obviously cost-effective to offer a lump sum rather than pay the child's weekly maintenance order. A calculation based on twenty shillings to £1 meant that the infant's costs were approximately £1 every six weeks or so. Therefore, if the basic cost of rearing the infant was approximately £8 per year, then the payment of £30 would cover costs for about three to four years. Even £30 was nowhere near enough to raise a child, so with cases where the lump sum was as little as £5, the money would be expended after just eight months, even if it was genuinely spent on care for the child.

Neighbours and the authorities were not ignorant of the existence of baby farming in some local communities. Even when charged with an offence, many baby farmers received no more than condemnation and continued to elude the authorities. *The Examiner* argued that 'magistrates and the police – whether cognisant or not of the existence of the "farms" – want either the power or the will to proceed against them, except in the most flagrant of cases'.[44] Moreover, Waugh noted that:

> Only the baby farmer can supply the coroner's inquest with the material for its judgement. Its criminal verdict, too, is restricted to manslaughter, and on the evidence produced that is almost never possible. Failing manslaughter, her conduct is nothing criminal.[45]

In fact, baby farmers continued to practise even after a run-in with the authorities. Sarah Talbot, a widow, alias Mrs Ward, had managed to evade the authorities at Neath until it was too late to protect the infant that she had in her care. Mrs Ward agreed to 'adopt' the illegitimate child belonging to Mary Thomas for £10. It was alleged that the child's grandfather was to contribute £5 towards the premium. The putative father, John Williams, had absconded to America, thus escaping any responsibility for the child's upbringing. Mrs Ward was known to the local police because she had made a habit of taking in children to nurse.

Apparently, when questioned by Superintendent Phillips, Mrs Ward informed him that while she was out of the house, the baby had been put down on the bed with 3s. 6d placed underneath it, and that she knew nothing of its parents or where it had come from. Superintendent Phillips was told by the magistrates not to interfere when he reported that Mrs Ward now had Mary Thomas's child in her care.[46] The infant died while in Mrs Ward's care, and she subsequently appeared in court in December 1874 charged with causing its death. The police superintendent had expressed concern because Mrs Ward had been charged two years earlier following the death of another infant while in her care.[47] As Rose explains, 'the police were legally shackled in the matter of surveillance' as baby farming was not an illegal activity. It was also the case that prior to 1897 the authorities could not enter a property without a magistrate's warrant and some evidence of criminality.[48]

There was a dispute in Pembrokeshire as to whose responsibility, and under which authority, it was to intervene in a suspected case of baby farming. It was alleged that three or four babies were confined in a 'pestilential abode' at Prendergast, Haverfordwest. The *Haverfordwest & Milford Haven Telegraph* reported that it may not have been known that such an establishment existed, and that 'readers have little or no knowledge of the strange things going on in the diminutive world immediately surrounding them'.[49] The alleged case generated heated exchanges in the local press after a charge was levelled against the Medical Officer of Health and the Inspector of Nuisances that it was their duty to become initiators in the prosecution of a criminal case. It was argued that the interference of the Health Officer would be an invasion of a territory that was not his, but clearly belonged to the borough police.[50] One reader commented that:

> The duties of the Medical Officer of Health are surely sufficiently multifarious already, without expecting them to overstep those lines laid down by law, and to become Public Prosecutors of Baby Farmers to gratify the "inveterate" prurience of "inveterate gossips".[51]

Baby farming at Prendergast had continued unabated until it came under the notice of concerned individuals, although the response of the authorities was deemed to be inadequate in this case.

Cases where the authorities failed to act jointly occurred in both rural and urban communities. For instance, the coroner for Neath complained to the Secretary of State after procedures adopted by the borough police were found lacking in connection with the discovery of a dead infant in a box. The police superintendent had authorised the infant's burial without informing the coroner of the facts or conducting any further investigations. The coroner was concerned that if this matter was not brought to the Secretary of State's attention, then it might lead to 'grievous and serious abuses'.[52] The Board of Guardians at Lampeter clashed with the Chief Constable of Carmarthenshire concerning unsolved infanticide cases in the district.[53] In Carmarthen the coroner complained that the perpetrator, who had committed infanticide, should have been traced by the police.[54] In reality, the financial implications to local authorities to conduct such investigations might have been one reason for this lax attitude.

It was evident that members of the community had to be vigilant, rather than rely on the authorities to intervene in baby farming cases. Lack of intervention on the neighbours' part inadvertently condoned the activities of baby farmers. Neighbours were often reluctant to interfere in how parents, or adoptive parents, reared their children. Waugh confirmed that this attitude was not uncommon. He stated, 'the police are not informed; and the neighbours, when they know a little, do not interfere. One woman commented that "You get no thanks for interfering for them sort of children".'[55] This was the case when Isaac and Mary Thomas took Richard Davies into their care. The neighbours were aware that the child was not being properly cared for. William Dalton stated that the child did not thrive, and that he was conscious of the ill-treatment when he visited blacksmith Isaac Thomas. It was reported in the press that the infant's death was caused by a haemorrhage between the outer membrane and the brain on the crown of the head.[56] The editor of the *Western Mail* commented that 'baby farming is always a gruesome subject but when anything approaching it is found in that remote corner of Wales which lies around Whitland it is especially distressing'.[57] Some neighbours were hesitant to interfere, yet others reported baby farmers who contravened what they considered socially acceptable behaviour. Mrs Martha Jenkins was so concerned about the deaths of the two infants in Mrs White's care that she reported the woman to the police. Mrs Jenkins asked, 'Is it in your power to interfere in this Baby Farming that is now going on in this town? If so, I hope you will do your best to have justice done for the sake of the dear innocent children.'[58] Another neighbour spoke of how she had always been on good terms with Mrs White until a child died in her care, and she told the woman that there ought to be an inquest. Neighbours interfered in this particular case; however, one reason for lack of intervention in many cases was because individuals who lived in close proximity to each other preferred not to provoke trouble amongst their neighbours.

For the most part, baby farmers were socially accepted within the community, but not all operated without some form of surveillance. Baby farmers took in infants as a source of income, although there was nothing unusual in this arrangement as women had provided paid childcare long before baby farming developed into an issue of social concern. Equally, mothers entrusted their infants to others because, more often than not, they could not afford to maintain themselves without working. As a consequence, the economic constraints experienced by both parties were a primary cause of baby farming. Furthermore, unmarried mothers and illegitimate children were also viewed as a financial burden to society, not to mention the social stigma associated with illegitimacy. Therefore, it was not surprising to find that the baby farmer was a viable option for unmarried mothers in particular.

Baby farming: the influence of gender and class

The practice of baby farming was defined by social and economic factors, but also central to understanding the complexities are the issues of gender and class inherent in the majority of cases. Arnot maintains that 'the overall controversy about baby-farming and responsibility for children needs to be understood in the context of the nineteenth-century negotiation of gender relations'.[59] Medical experts were critical of the apparent lack of maternal care amongst working mothers and referred to high-profile baby farming scandals in England to support the claims made against childcare providers. Again, Arnot points out that 'by charging fees for wet- or dry-nursing children, women were bringing relations between women and children out of the enclosed, privatised space defined as "natural", into the economic and public world'.[60]

Similarly, Homrighaus found that the opinions of nineteenth-century medical experts were based on class and gender bias, and that they blamed baby farming on the corruption of working-class women.[61]

The intrusion of men, especially those in the medical profession, into the women's sphere of child-rearing attracted the attention of feminist groups. The National Society for Women's Suffrage resented the attack on working-class women and formed the Committee for Amending the Law in Points wherein it is Injurious to Women (CALPIW) in protest. The CALPIW were influential in the campaign for the protection of infant life in the wake of the case of Brixton baby farmer Margaret Waters. In 1871 W. T. Charley, MP for Salford, introduced the Bill for the Better Protection of Infant Life on behalf of the Infant Life Protection Society (ILPS).[62] Despite the best intentions, the bill, aimed at licensing hired nurses, had the effect of antagonising women's groups, the CALPIW in particular. In response to the bill, the CALPIW published a disapproving critique in the form of the pamphlet, *Infant Mortality: Its Causes and Remedies*,[63] which was co-written by leading feminist campaigner Elizabeth Wolstenholme and her close friend Rosamund Hervey.[64] The CALPIW objected to the bill because, firstly, 'it confounds together the women who take entire responsibility of a child off the shoulders of its natural guardians, and those who only share that responsibility with one or both parents'.[65] Secondly, 'by increasing officialism, police interference, and espionage, it tends to add to the already oppressive burden which the rate payers have to bear'.[66] Thirdly, the bill 'merely aims at removing the apparent and proximate causes of the fearful mortality prevailing among nurse children, whilst it leaves the real and ultimate causes untouched'.[67] The CALPIW argued that the existence of baby farming was often due to ignorance and poverty, and it was wrong to condemn all women providing childcare arrangements.

The CALPIW also addressed another major concern: the role of fathers. Rather than criticise childcare providers, the CALPIW argued that, 'Should an illegitimate child die, or suffer bodily harm, from starvation, desertion or neglect, indict the father for manslaughter, or cruelty.'[68] In a meeting, the SCPIL realised the difficulties of enforcement and commented that, 'You cannot get at the father, in many instances, but you could in almost all instances get at the baby farmer.' Dr Wiltshire responded, 'I think it is desirable that the baby farmer should be got at.'[69] This confirmed the CALPIW's frustration since the focus remained on the providers of all childcare rather than on the father's participation in the child's upbringing. Ernest Hart argued that even if 'the bastardy laws were made much more stringent and the whole burden were laid on the father, I see no reason to suspect that would either diminish baby farming, or make it less necessary to protect children'.[70] Even though the SCPIL acknowledged the father's lack of responsibility, a man remained in a strong position; therefore, targeting all forms of childcare providers became the main objective.

Baby farming did not exist solely for the benefit of the lower and working classes. Middle-class and upper-class parents also employed baby farmers to remove unwanted infants, although this chosen method was more likely due to social factors, and the need to conform to the ideology of respectability. An article in *John Bull* pointed out that 'children are abandoned by the higher as well as the lower classes, social position not concurring with secret shame'.[71] Not surprisingly, baby farmers could demand substantial amounts of money from wealthier parents since cost was not an issue. Maintaining secrecy and respectability was far more crucial, although this was also essential for many working-class mothers and of equal importance to some fathers. Cases revealed that a number of infants from middle-class backgrounds travelled long distances to be placed with baby farmers. The long-distance arrangement was obviously preferable if anonymity was the prime objective. More often than not this was achieved via a response to an advertisement, and it frequently entailed a lump-sum payment with no further contact with the child. With an 'out of sight, out of mind' approach, parents rarely discovered if the infant had died. This was not universal, however: when a middle-class mother from Reading entrusted her infant to the care of Mrs Ann Rees from Bassaleg, she asked if an advertisement could be placed in the *Christian World* should the infant die. In fact, the mother had responded to Rees's advertisement of her services as a childminder in the same publication in the first instance.[72] Rees took advantage of advertising in a nationwide publication because she could attract the attention of middle-class parents and, therefore, demand higher premiums for unwanted infants. In this case, Rees travelled by rail to collect the child from Reading. Distance did not interfere with Rees's operations, because she 'adopted' infants from England as well as from within her own locality. This more lucrative method of baby farming probably grew due to railway expansion as infants could be transported around the country with relative ease. Not only did all parties travel considerable distances to hand over infants, but they also took advantage of railway stations as meeting places. Baby farmers and parents were unlikely to be recognised if secrecy was an issue. The trafficking of infants is notable because evidence revealed that some infants from rural communities were removed to places such as Neath and Swansea. Likewise, infants from urban areas sometimes found their new 'home' in rural communities.

Reputed fathers were often determined to keep secret liaisons hidden, particularly as secrecy was considered a crucial factor in smaller and rural communities. This was the case for Sarah Owen, a widow and mother of two, from Llanddeusant in Carmarthenshire. Sarah Owen had placed her seven-month-old infant in the care of her sister-in-law, Mrs Ann Small, for three shillings per week. The infant died later at Mrs Small's home at Neath. The post-mortem revealed that the body was in a most extreme condition of emaciation and weighed only 7 lbs, the weight of a newly born child. Sarah Owen declined to reveal the father's identity at the inquest until the coroner threatened to commit her for not answering his question. She admitted that the father was John Hopkins, who had allowed her eight shillings per week for maintenance of the child.[73] It appeared that he was not without the means to pay for the child and, in comparison to the majority of other maintenance payments, eight shillings was a reasonable amount, yet Mrs Small alleged that she had only received three shillings, which was less than half the allowance provided by the father. Sarah Owen and John Hopkins were neighbours and they lived in a small rural community; so the need for secrecy was probably relevant to both parties.[74] This might explain why Sarah Owen gave birth at her sister-in-law's home and intended to leave the baby at Neath. Mrs Small was charged with manslaughter at the inquest, and the coroner made out his warrant accordingly.[75] In this case, the Grand Jury ignored the Bill at Glamorgan Assizes; therefore, Mrs Small did not face trial and she was discharged from custody.[76] The evidence suggests that John Hopkins wished to remain anonymous, even though Sarah Owen was not afforded the same opportunity to conceal her identity in court, thus reflecting gender bias in the father's favour.

The issues of gender and class were apparent in another case concerning Sarah Talbot, mentioned previously, or Mrs Ward as she was better known. This particular transaction relied on a network of individuals; therefore, it provides an illustrative case of baby farming within the community. The case concerned putative father Morgan Jones, single woman Mary Reynolds and Mrs Ward, but this was not just an arrangement between three people. In fact, seven individuals were implicated, all of whom contributed to the infant's death in one way or another. Morgan Jones, a married man, arranged for his illegitimate child to be removed from its mother, Mary Reynolds, immediately after the birth, via a community network that consisted of a midwife, family and friends. The twelve-day-old infant died under suspicious circumstances after being put out to nurse with Mrs Ward. It was reported that 'a large amount of excitement was occasioned in the neighbourhood, it being generally believed that the deceased died in consequence of gross neglect on the part of the woman Talbot'. At the coroner's inquest Mary Reynolds, from Neath Abbey, denied knowing the father's identity or where he lived. Eventually she admitted that she thought his name was Morgan Jones. Mary Reynolds claimed to have met the man only three times, twice by appointment and once by chance. The issue of class occurred when the coroner asked Mary Reynolds if the father was a gentleman or a working man. She replied that, 'He was more like a gentleman than anything else when I saw him – he was like one of you.' Mary Reynolds appeared to play no part in the transaction with Mrs Ward, although she admitted knowing the childminder's name and address. It was reported that Mary Reynolds had not seen the infant, and made no further enquiries about its care after the birth. When the infant was handed to Mrs Ward, she already had three infants in her care, although one had just died. Mrs Ward told the coroner that, 'I have reared altogether about 25 children and only one has died out of the lot before. I should not have had any of these children if it had not been for begging and praying me to have them; but I shall never be happy without children.' The foreman of the coroner's jury stated that, 'they had seen the place where the child was nursed, and their censure was not without foundation'.[77]

Mrs Ward was probably being disingenuous in her statement, but certain cases revealed that a number of baby farmers operated because they were approached by desperate parents, rather than seeking out infants for themselves.

As a single woman without financial support, Mary Reynolds probably had little option but to comply with Morgan Jones's instructions, especially as her own father would not let her keep the child, and she may well have been relieved by the arrangement. It could be argued that Morgan Jones eased the economic burden by accepting responsibility, even if it was to hide his indiscretions. The verdict in Mrs Ward's case was condemnation of the practice of taking in infants to nurse. However, this experience did not prevent Mrs Ward from baby farming in the future, as she was brought before the coroner again in 1874 charged with manslaughter following the death of another infant in her care. In that particular case Mrs Ward was acquitted at the Glamorgan Assizes and released from custody.[78]

In some cases putative fathers absconded to the popular destination of America. Emigration permitted fathers to avoid service of a paternity summons. For instance, in Elizabeth Griffiths's case the father had emigrated to America, leaving her to maintain the child on her own.[79] Similarly, Mrs Helen Kendall took care of her lodger's baby so that the mother could search for her husband in America.[80] Mary Thomas from Neath handed over her five-month-old illegitimate infant to Mrs Ward because the father, John Williams, a coachman, had also emigrated to America.[81] America offered people numerous employment opportunities and prospects for a new life, as well as being a convenient way to escape parental responsibilities. Indeed, if twelve months had lapsed since the birth of the child, the father no longer had to accept responsibility, unless he had contributed to its maintenance within the first twelve months following birth.[82] According to the Bastardy Laws Amendment Act 1872, the putative father could be summoned within twelve months following his return to England upon proof that he had ceased to reside in England within twelve months following the birth.[83]

By way of contrast, some mothers also found America a convenient destination to avoid parental responsibilities. A mother from Cayo in Carmarthenshire deserted her three illegitimate children and supposedly emigrated to America.[84] In a complete role reversal, Ebenezer Morgan, a Swansea tin-plate worker, hired Mrs

Hughes to nurse his daughter from the age of ten weeks because her mother, Ann Jones, had emigrated to America. When the child was two years old, her grandmother went before the Board of Guardians with a request that the child be handed over to her in accordance with her son's wishes. Mrs Hughes was instructed by the guardians to hand the child over, but she forcibly tried to snatch her back. It was reported that several guardians believed they had no right to decide who had custody and handed the child back to a delighted Mrs Hughes. She was reported as saying she did not want 'anything for the keep of the child', and that she 'wouldn't part with it for the world'. The woman left the Union 'greatly rejoicing'.[85] It appears that Mrs Hughes had formed an affectionate attachment to the child, providing evidence that not all hired nurses were negligent or financially motivated. This particular case confirmed the CALPIW's protests that it was wrong to assume that all childcare providers practised along the same lines as baby farmers.

Mrs Mary Ann Kendall, from Swansea, conformed to the middle-class perspective of a drunken baby farmer when she neglected a ten-month-old infant in her care. Mrs Kendall was found lying helplessly drunk on the floor with the emaciated body of the infant lying a little distance away. The infant was the daughter of Catherine Carlson, the wife of a sailor, although the child was understood to be illegitimate. Mrs Kendall was paid 3s. 6d per week to take care of the child.[86] Mrs Ann Morgan, a concerned neighbour, found the infant covered with vermin while in Mrs Kendall's care. It was reported that 'its head was that of a skeleton, the skin hanging like parchment about it. The thighs were no thicker than a man's thumb, and every bone in the body might literally be counted and almost seen'. Conversely, the infant was 'a splendid baby, healthy, strong and well' before Mrs Kendall took charge four months before.[87] The doctor stated that 'the emaciation of the child arose from constitutional disease, and he had prescribed for it from its birth'. As there was no charge of actual abandonment in this case, the woman was discharged. The *Western Mail* expressed disapproval and reported that 'she escaped the punishment she richly deserved'.[88] The personal circumstances and predilections of baby farmers determined whether they were prone to drink or not.

Unlike married mothers who worked and managed to obtain childcare, albeit of varying quality, unmarried mothers often lacked a support network. Married working mothers usually left their children with relatives, the local childminder or older children. Landladies and neighbours also helped with childcare arrangements. Anna Davin points out that at the turn of the twentieth century a report found that half of the working mothers in London regularly left children with relatives. Davin also found that sometimes children were locked indoors for the day when adults were absent, or if older were locked outdoors.[89] In some cases baby farmers worked while children were in their care, and left the infants alone for hours at a time. The press reported that when Mrs Small had Sarah Owen's infant in her care, a witness had heard the baby crying bitterly when the door of the baby farmer's house was closed and padlocked from the outside.[90] Jane Williams also left the infant in her care alone and crying, sometimes for three hours at a time, leaving neighbours to care for it.[91]

It could be argued to a certain extent that baby farmers were also victims of the practice because they too struggled against the constraints of poverty and economic difficulties, often through no fault of their own. Indeed, some women were forced to provide a meagre living by whatever means, and they were only involved in baby farming because of their husbands' failure to provide on the grounds of unemployment, disability and/or drunkenness. Waugh argued that:

> there were professional nurses who made a living, together with their husbands and children, out of the proceeds of the trade of baby-farming. In this class of cases, very often the husbands spent idle lives, spending the money paid for the maintenance of the children.[92]

This was the situation for Mrs White and her husband, William White. The man was considered a 'harmless lunatic' and was often seen begging. Mrs White sometimes took in lodgers as another means of adding to the household income. It was reported that she had sixteen persons living at the house in two small rooms upstairs and two small rooms downstairs, although it was never registered as a common lodging house. It was known to have been a refuge for prostitutes and thieves.[93] John Ward, Mrs Ward's cohabitee, was known to drink. John Ward informed the court, in the case relating to Mary Reynolds's infant, that he told the police superintendent 'one little rat was dead, and expected the other would be dead by morning'. John Ward blamed his callous comments regarding the infants on having 'had a drop to drink'.[94]

Most baby farmers operated as receivers of children from the poorer sections of society. However, the case concerning middle-class baby farmer Henrietta Hunter is a complete contrast in the way that she conducted her operations. Mrs Hunter was known to have had a superior education and originated from a very respectable family, yet she was a procurer of unwanted infants. In his initial definitions, Waugh described the typical procurer as 'mostly of clean, genteel, respectable clothing and manners. She often professes that she has been married three, five, or seven years, has had "no child", and is "anxious to adopt one from the birth".'[95] Mrs Hunter's advertisement seeking a new influx of children was consistent with Waugh's own findings; it read: 'Married couple, without children, residing in Glasgow, would like to take baby as own; no after claim, small premium required.'[96] Women like Mrs Hunter looked, dressed and spoke in a respectable manner, and those handing over infants could well have been deceived into thinking that the children would be cared for. A baby farmer, in communications with those outside her own locality, was in an ideal position to fabricate the truth regarding personal circumstances or dramatically enhance her status if necessary. This was an acceptable method assumed by procurers who had once lived a respectable life but whose financial circumstances had changed for the worse.

In September 1905 Henrietta Hunter was charged with the attempted murder by suffocation of Edna Lilian Thomas, aged three months, and also with abandoning and exposing the child so as to endanger her life at Llangyfelach, Swansea.[97] The press reported that Mrs Hunter had abandoned the infant in a water-filled ditch, but the baby was rescued by passers-by when they heard the sound of crying. The infant died in the workhouse a month later, but not as a direct result of Mrs Hunter's actions. This case is worthy of further explanation not only because of her social class, but because she had been held in high esteem and placed in a position of trust with children. Investigations revealed that the woman was an incredibly shrewd character and, not surprisingly, the press provided extensive coverage of the sensational case. Mrs Hunter operated under assumed names, and her behaviour was typical of the 'respectable procurer'. In early

1905 she was employed for a short time at Briton Ferry, and during this period Mrs Hunter received a number of letters. The letters addressed to Mrs Hunter were from women who had adopted, or wished to adopt, advertised infants, which led the police to the theory that the woman acted as the agent for some 'babies home'.[98] According to her employer, Mrs Hunter proved to be of excellent service. She was reported to have been 'a most cultured lady, an excellent pianist, and exceedingly affectionate to the children'. Yet she was procuring infants and passing them on to receivers for financial gain. Mrs Hunter claimed to have spent a year in Calcutta. Amongst the letters found in her possession was one written by J. M. C. of Western Buildings, Calcutta, dated April 1904, which implied she was some form of musical tutor or governess.[99] It is not evident why Mrs Hunter should have resorted to baby farming, since she was obviously a very accomplished woman held in high esteem and capable of earning a respectable living.

In August 1905, while Mrs Hunter was employed as a housekeeper in Swansea, it was alleged that she visited Scotland under the pretext that her father had died. While absent, she placed an advertisement in the *Western Daily Press* under the name of Mrs David Hunter. The advertisement was answered by Mrs Burnsell from Somerset, who met Mrs Hunter at Cardiff Station to hand over the infant. It was alleged that Mrs Burnsell had received the child from Dr Edwards of Wincanton in reply to an advertisement, and she had received the sum of £33 for doing so. Mrs Hunter had previously arranged to pass the infant to a woman at Landore Station near Swansea, but she failed to arrive. It was at this point that Mrs Hunter decided to abandon the infant in the ditch.[100] In this case the chain was obvious. The infant was only three months old, yet she had already been passed between three individuals, and arrangements had been made for a fourth person to receive the child. Mrs Hunter was convicted at Glamorgan Assizes for the crime and sentenced to ten years' penal servitude.

Henrietta Hunter's decision in 1905 to abandon the infant finally put an end to her lucrative business. The press reported that the previous year, Mrs Hunter had left Llanelli in a hurry. While living there she operated under the assumed name of Dora Johnstone; her real name was Hannah E. Johnson. The woman was understood to be the daughter of an army captain, while her husband, a lieutenant, had reportedly been killed in the South African war. In

1904 Dora Johnstone was employed as a housekeeper for a well-known commercial traveller residing in Llanelli, during which time she received 'streams of letters'. The woman was frequently absent from her post, visiting Edinburgh, London and Oxford under the pretext of sorting out her investments. On one occasion Dora Johnstone returned from Edinburgh with an infant, whom she successfully passed on to a fellow employee's mother with an arranged payment of £1 per month. This was paid for the first month but ceased when she disappeared. In October 1904, while living in one of the best suburbs in Bristol, she was arrested for selling goods obtained on the hire system. Dora Johnstone was charged at the Bristol Sessions under her real name of Hannah E. Johnson for fraudulently selling goods in order to settle her debts. She was sentenced to four months in prison for fraud. Surprisingly, Hannah E. Johnson had also been imprisoned for six weeks in 1901 for obtaining goods by signing her name as a clergyman.

It was during this trial for fraud in 1904 that details of Dora Johnstone's baby farming business in Llanelli came to light. Long after the woman had left her post at Llanelli, the mail continued to arrive. Her employer opened the post and found that the letters were from persons enquiring about the welfare of a number of infants. One infant was traced to Mrs Esther Davies at Llanelli, who had received a twelve-month-old 'chubby baby' from Dora Johnstone with an arranged fee of £1 per month that was never paid. Despite this, the baby was well cared for. Esther Davies alleged that she knew nothing of the baby's parentage or where it had come from, but it arrived at Llanelli 'dressed in the most expensive clothes, and looking as if it had come from a luxurious home'. Even though Esther Davies had only received one sovereign for the child's keep, she said that 'I would rather bring her up for nothing than part with her now.' Another recipient, Mrs Baker from Cardiff, came forward to say that she also had a baby left in her care. Mrs Baker claimed that Dora Johnstone had asked her at the time if 'I would like to have a lump sum down, say, £70 or £100', which was not paid. The infant was eighteen months old, and had been in Mrs Baker's care for ten months. It was alleged that the father was a gentleman. Mrs Baker was now worried that 'Dolly would be sent for', but said that she had no intention of being parted from the child. It would appear that under different aliases, and via a number of advertisements, Dora Johnstone had received infants from various parts of the country, including Scotland and England, for sums as much as £70 or more. If this information is correct, then it provides evidence that children were being given up by well-off parents. The fact that Dora Johnstone was an educated middle-class lady obviously meant that she came into contact with men and women who were in a position to pay considerable sums to maintain secrecy and conceal the child's identity. The authorities managed to trace twelve infants back to Dora Johnstone, but as she had disappeared, many children were admitted to the workhouse.[101] It is interesting to note that even though the two infants had been 'farmed out', they appeared to be well cared for by their adoptive mothers, who were rearing the children at their own expense, and they were not prepared to be separated from them either. Not all childminders had criminal intentions, because in these particular cases the children were adopted by women who genuinely cared for them.

Hannah E. Johnson, under the known aliases of Mrs Henrietta Hunter and Dora Johnstone, failed to conform to the middle-class ideology of femininity and respectability. Her situation was exacerbated because she already had a criminal record, again conflicting with the expected standards of middle-class values, which, no doubt, contributed to her lengthy prison sentence. As Lucia Zedner argues, 'a criminal woman offended against her very social role; her whole character repudiated the revered qualities of femininity'.[102] During her trial in 1905 it emerged that Mrs Hunter had tied the infant's bonnet in such a way as to aid suffocation, while exposure to the night air in a ditch only pointed to its imminent death. Therefore, abandonment of an infant in this manner was, as Kilday points out, a form of 'delayed infanticide'.[103] Mrs Hunter had to relieve herself of the infant, yet she appeared to lack foresight in this case and failed to act within the boundaries of the law. Mrs Hunter could have abandoned the infant at the railway station unharmed; therefore, she would have been charged with abandonment, assuming that the woman was apprehended of course, rather than attempted murder. Kilday found that 'Strenuous efforts to track a suspect down were only made if the child had not survived its desertion.'[104] In fact, as in other cases, it was unlikely that Mrs Hunter would have been detected. In terms of class, the diverse methods of operation adopted by middle-class Mrs Hunter and poverty-stricken Mrs White provide evidence that these women could be described as baby farmers of 'different stripes'. Evidence of Mrs White's practices were typical of an impoverished baby farmer, and she appeared to represent the worst of her kind. Her motivation to farm infants was obvious, while at the same time she embodied the 'evils' of baby farming so complained about by the social commentators of the day. Nevertheless, the woman managed to escape punishment even though infants continued to die of starvation and neglect while entrusted to her care.

The high-profile case in 1907 of baby farmer Rhoda Willis, alias Leslie James, generated a great deal of public attention because she was tried and convicted of murder. Rhoda Willis had assumed the name of Leslie James from the man she was cohabiting with in 1905.[105] In this case Leslie James did not cause the infant's death by neglect, like most other baby farmers, but by wilful murder, which meant that she was subjected to the full force of the law laid down for the crime. She was not the biological mother; therefore she could claim no mitigating circumstances inherent in the case of an infanticidal mother. The trial of Leslie James was held on 23 July 1907 at Glamorgan Assizes, Swansea, where she was charged with 'feloniously, wilfully, and of malice aforethought having killed and murdered the infant female child of Maud Treasure at Cardiff on 3 June 1907'.[106] It was reported that Maud Treasure of Fleur-de-Lis, Pengam, was a single woman who already had one illegitimate child, aged seven years.[107]

The charge referred to the murder of Maud Treasure's infant, but the extraneous evidence relating to two other infants introduced by the prosecution prejudiced Leslie James's defence from the outset. Records show that she had received two other infants for a premium some weeks before 'adopting' Maud Treasure's infant. However, the two infants had not been 'farmed out' by desperate single mothers, because Mrs Emily Stroud, from Abertillery, was the mother of one infant and there appears to be no evidence to suggest she was a widow. Moreover, it was not made clear why the child was 'farmed out'. Mrs Stroud had given birth a month earlier and had paid Leslie James £6 for the 'adoption'.[108] The other case concerned the illegitimate infant belonging to Stanley Rees from Salford, Manchester.[109]

At this point in time, Leslie James was employed in Pontypool as a housekeeper to bootmaker David Evans. Shortly after the acquisition of Mrs Stroud's infant, she told him that she was going to Birmingham to collect money bequeathed to her by her uncle. When she departed, she took Mrs Stroud's infant with her, but on that same evening it was found on the doorstep of the Salvation Army Home in Cardiff with a note attached. The infant was apparently six weeks old, fairly nourished, clean and healthy. Having abandoned the child, Leslie James did not return to David Evans, but took up new lodgings with landlady Mrs Wilson. Some baby farmers preferred to remain mobile and lodge in different locations, therefore aiding their operations. This method made it easier to procure infants and change residence at the same time without arousing suspicion. It was reported in the press that when Leslie James arrived at Mrs Wilson's, she had another infant in her care. The three-day-old infant was Stanley Rees's illegitimate child, although she told Mrs Wilson that it was her own. Leslie James then persuaded Mrs Wilson to adopt this infant for a premium of £1. Evidence revealed that landladies were sometimes involved in the adoption of infants, but not necessarily by choice. The following day Leslie James left her lodgings and returned later in a drunken state. The next morning, Mrs Wilson heard something fall upstairs, only to find that she had fallen out of bed. Her attention was drawn to a bundle lying at the foot of the bed under the mattress. Inside the parcel was the naked body of a dead infant wrapped in newspaper and a towel.[110] This was Maud Treasure's infant, received from the woman's mother, Mrs Mary Treasure, and her sister, Mrs Lydia English. Leslie James admitted to the coroner that she had been too frightened to show the dead baby to Mrs Wilson.[111] She was subsequently arrested and charged with wilful murder.

Leslie James had once been a respectable woman, who came from a well-off background and was described as 'being of superior education and a fine handsome woman with fair hair, a good musician and clever at needlework'.[112] The death of her husband, Thomas Willis, triggered a chain of events that had a detrimental effect on her life thereafter. In 1896 Rhoda Willis, as she was then, cohabited with marine engineer Stewart MacPherson until 1901. They had three children together during their relationship, although their first child died. In his statement to the police, Stewart MacPherson also referred to Rhoda's child from her marriage to Thomas Willis as his adopted daughter.[113]

He stated in his evidence that Rhoda was attentive to the house and their children.[114] Up to this point her character was good, and she appeared to have complied with the middle-class ideology of motherhood and domesticity, although by 1907 her two youngest daughters were living with relatives and not with their mother. Stewart MacPherson did not divulge why she was unable or incapable of looking after her children. Ginger Frost points out that 'an issue peculiar to cohabitees was the question of children; because they were illegitimate, fathers had no legal rights to them'.[115] Unlike married parents, mothers of illegitimate children were the sole legal guardians.[116] It is noteworthy that Leslie James did not have custody of the children, although the evidence suggests that she only began to drink after her relationship with Stewart MacPherson ended. Not surprisingly, a combination of the relationship breakdown and her inability to fulfil her role as a mother could well have been a contributory factor to her reliance on alcohol. Added to this, it was reported that twelve months previously 'Mrs James was knocked down by a bicycle on Cowbridge Road, Canton, and for twelve weeks she was under treatment at the workhouse infirmary. There she underwent another operation, this time for an injury to her head sustained in the bicycle accident.'[117]

Leslie James was convicted of wilful murder and sentenced to death, but the jury did not make a recommendation for mercy in her case; hence, the decision to carry out her execution by hanging fell to the Home Secretary, Herbert Gladstone. He asked the presiding trial judge to clarify a few crucial points before he made his decision:

> Firstly, in a petition to me the prisoner admits her guilt but says she was 'completely in the hands of unscrupulous people'. Presumably she means Mrs English and Mrs Treasure, the former of whom I gather you considered as truthful witnesses. Is there any likelihood they suggested or encouraged her to kill the child? Secondly, when the prisoner reached home she appeared to be helplessly drunk. She was of drunken habits. Is it a reasonable supposition that when she was given the baby she was plied with liquor under the influence of which she committed the crime? Thirdly, the exposure on a doorstep of another infant shows reckless cruelty. Do

> you consider that in killing the child she was beginning a practice of child murder? Fourthly, may it be said that there was no deliberate premeditation proved? By her own story when Mrs Wilson discovered the body James said "I am not going to stand all the blame, someone else is in it as well as me". The baby had been put into a parcel. Where was this parcel made up? Was it at Mrs English's house? Or where? If there was a deliberate intention to murder it was very badly planned. The woman received the baby to the knowledge of two women, then apparently before going home and after 6 p.m. killed the child and wrapped it in paper. And according to Mrs Wilson's evidence she came home on June 3rd "helplessly drunk". All this shows that James' character was very bad, but is it not likely that there was something wrong on the part of Mrs English, and that the crime committed under the influence of drink was not designed in cold blood?[118]

These vital questions should have been asked and clarified during the trial.

Leslie James might have successfully secured a reprieve if the crime had been committed the following year, in 1908. It was after Leslie James's trial that the Criminal Appeal Act of 1907 was introduced to provide for a criminal appeal court. This court was created for those tried on indictment and convicted of the offence. Jill Pellow points out that, 'This did not affect the prerogative of mercy exercised by the Home Secretary because it enabled him to refer cases, if necessary, for retrial to the new court.'[119] Had Leslie James's case been heard at the criminal appeal court, the crucial questions raised by the Home Secretary at such a critical stage should have been answered in court.

Home Office minutes dated 8 August 1907 recorded that 'This was a clear case of murder, but it was not a premeditated and thought out murder, and it was the murder of a child which had not reached the stage of conscious existence. It is a crime more against society than against the murdered individual.'[120] Therefore, the crime was not considered as serious as the murder of an individual already established as a person. Ellen Ross maintains that 'according to medical people, and in the practice of the law, newborns were not officially viewed as persons'.[121] Similarly, Colin Heywood raises the point that the 'the death of a newly born baby was always less distressing for parents than that of a child they had experienced several years of bonding'.[122] In this case, Maud Treasure's infant was illegitimate and seemingly unwanted; so no parental bonds had been broken.

It had long been argued that those involved in baby farming should be indicted and implicated in the crime. Even though Mrs English and Mrs Treasure were referred to as 'respectable and truthful' members of society, the fact remained that they were active participants leading up to the infant's death, yet they remained within the boundaries of the law. Mrs Treasure attended her daughter, Maud Treasure, during the birth, although it was not established whether she was a regular attendant at the births of illegitimate infants. However, four years later the 1911 Census revealed that Mary Treasure, aged seventy-two, was a maternity nurse.[123] The same census return revealed that Lydia English was aged thirty-eight and lived in Swansea. She had been married to a coal miner for eighteen years and given birth to eleven children, although five had died. Maud Treasure, by then aged twenty-seven, was also living with the English family.[124]

Interestingly, the Women's Purity League (WPL) Cardiff appealed to the Home Secretary for the condemned woman's reprieve, believing that 'she is a victim of an infamous system which requires legal suppression'.[125] Despite all efforts, the Home Secretary stated that:

> Having regard to the widespread laxity which exists as regards infant life, the extent to which the abominable system of baby farming prevails, and the difficulty which usually exists of proving intention to kill, it appears to me of the utmost importance to do nothing to weaken Home Office practice in connection with baby farming cases. I think remission in this case would tend to weaken that practice. Under all the circumstances I much regret that I find myself unable to interfere with the course of the law.[126]

The decision to execute Leslie James caused considerable public interest, while debates opposed to capital punishment circulated in the press as to whether the death penalty should be inflicted upon women. Anne Logan maintains that 'narratives of the twentieth-century campaign against the death penalty seldom make much mention of its gendered aspects, perhaps because the overwhelming majority of capital convicts were male'.[127] Just before Leslie James's impending execution, she confessed, 'I killed the child on the train. I would like those who tried me, particularly the judge, to know this. I would not like them to have anything on their minds or think that they had made a mistake.'[128] The evidence and the circumstances surrounding the case indicated that this could have been a case of 'infanticide for hire', but this was not pursued in court. Whatever the case may have been, the infant was discovered wrapped in a towel and newspaper inside a parcel and handed over to a total stranger for a premium without any further responsibility for the infant's welfare. Irrespective of the witnesses' involvement, Leslie James committed the crime, and she was executed on 14 August 1907 at Cardiff Gaol.[129]

Henrietta Hunter and Leslie James did not exactly fit the profiles of other baby farmers such as Mrs Ward, Mrs White or Mrs Small. When all the baby farming cases referred to in this chapter are considered collectively, Leslie James was among those who caused the least amount of suffering, yet she paid the highest price. Leslie James's case draws attention to the fine line that separated the actions of one baby farmer from another, even though the infant's death was the end result. Moreover, baby farming was not illegal; therefore, it was essential that baby farmers operated within the boundaries of the law, particularly as it was difficult to prove malicious intent. When the operational activities undertaken by Leslie James are compared to those of Mrs White or Henrietta Hunter, it is obvious that there were definitely different levels of abuse, which in turn places her execution in context. Some respectable middle-class women, who had fallen on hard times, realised that trafficking infants was a useful method to obtain considerable sums of money with relative ease. Evidence indicates that Leslie James and Henrietta Hunter obtained infants to pass on promptly, and they were unlikely to subject infants to systematic abuse, unlike other baby farmers. However, their actions were extremely high-risk. The difficulty of establishing culpability, and the choice of safer methods to bring about infant deaths, meant that the majority of baby farmers managed to evade the law and escape the extreme punishment meted out to Leslie James.

The criminal cases of Leslie James and Henrietta Hunter revealed a number of similarities. Both women chose to rid themselves of the infants shortly after acquisition, therefore establishing themselves as procurers. They cohabited with men and later assumed their surnames. When the relationships ended both women found it was convenient to take posts as housekeepers, a suitable arrangement that provided them with a home. The women were also known to fabricate the truth, especially in Mrs Hunter's case. They left their places of employment for a short time, allegedly due to family bereavements, which also coincided with the acquisition of infants. The two women operated in a similar manner and took advantage of the railway and classified advertisements to aid procurement. Leslie James had previously been convicted and served a short prison sentence for theft in 1906.[130] Mrs Hunter was also imprisoned for fraud in 1901 and 1904, while living in one of the best suburbs of Bristol.[131] Leslie James failed to escape the gallows, and Henrietta Hunter was imprisoned for ten years because they both committed a deliberate act to wilfully end a child's life.

The trial of Leslie James and her subsequent petition for a reprieve reveal significant issues relating to gender and class. Her complicated personal life exposed a vulnerable woman, which had a detrimental effect on her plea for clemency. The searching enquiries into Leslie James's past made the Home Office's decision to carry out her execution less difficult. As far as senior officials were concerned, Leslie James already had a criminal record, she was a woman of low morals, and she was a bad mother and a drunkard.[132] It was apparent that the Home Office's assessment of her character did not take into account the fact that Rhoda Willis, as she was known then, had been a good mother, and she had previously conformed to the required standards of middle-class feminine ideology and respectability. It could be argued that Leslie James was a victim of a system that permitted the legal trade in infants for a premium. Yet the practice would not have existed without parents, and family members, willing to part with infants for financial reward. Leslie James's trial revealed how the role of other active participants added to the incidence of infanticide. It was evident that while Leslie James's trial was flawed in parts, the Home Secretary allowed the law to take its course, despite his searching questions regarding her case.[133]

Unlike other baby farmers in this chapter, Leslie James was held up by the Home Secretary and Home Office civil servants as an example to be a deterrent to other baby farmers with criminal intentions, although the practice remained legal and the abuses continued. It was evident that baby farmers were financially motivated for different reasons, and baby farmers, infants and parents were drawn from working-class and middle-class backgrounds. Putative fathers also employed the services of baby farmers, although there were far fewer of these cases. Baby farmers exploited the existence of unwanted infants to their own advantage in the same way as parents, in some cases, took advantage of the privations and vulnerability of baby farmers. It was evident in all cases that there was a desperate need for legislation to protect infants while entrusted to all childcare providers, not just those with criminal intent.

The effectiveness of infant life protection in the community

In 1870 the high-profile case of Margaret Waters, the Brixton baby farmer, provided campaigners with the impetus to call on the government to introduce legislation to protect infant life. As a result of a government inquiry, conducted by the Select Committee on the Protection of Infant Life (SCPLI) in 1871, the Infant Life Protection Act was implemented in 1872. This was the first of a series of acts introduced between the years 1872 and 1908 to legally protect children from neglect and cruelty. The first Infant Life Protection Act was a significant piece of legislation, although Harry Hendrick argues that it 'was a failure both in conception and practice'.[134] Likewise, Anette Ballinger maintains that 'The licensing and regulation of baby-farmers did nothing to enhance the chances of infant survival, but did much to ensure an increase in prosecutions of poor working-class women whose financial position remained unchanged.'[135] This was evident in Mrs Ward's case, and others, because their economic circumstances and attitude did not alter as a result of prosecution. The lax policing of the Act, as Hendrick points out, meant that 'few local authorities pursued even their limited powers with any enthusiasm so that by the end of the 1870s very little had been achieved'.[136] This lack of enthusiasm was an issue in Welsh communities prior to the 1872 Act and afterwards.

The 1872 Act stated that a childminder who cared for 'more than one' infant, less than one year old, must register with the local authority. Childminders were required to record infants received into their care and report any deaths directly to the coroner. However, the Act failed to take into account minders caring for only one infant less than twelve months old since they were not required to register with the authorities. Rose maintains that the exemption of one-baby foster homes from registration was a significant failing: 'So long as a nurse had only one infant under 12 months, she could cram in as many as she saw fit above that age without having to register; and she could allow a rapid succession of lone infants to die off without having to register.'[137]

The ineffectiveness of the 1872 Act was evident in the case of an infant belonging to Elizabeth Thomas from St David's. In 1873 she placed her ten-week-old infant with Martha Morris at St David's, who agreed to care for it for two guineas per quarter with £1 paid in advance. The child was healthy when it was handed to Martha Morris, but when the mother visited shortly afterwards, she found the infant dying in a filthy state covered in vermin. The mother took the child to the doctor immediately, but it died that same day. At the inquest, the 'respectable jury' returned an open verdict, though one of them held out for a verdict of manslaughter. Martha Morris had flouted the 1872 Act because she had two infants less than twelve months old in her care without registering with the authorities. The police followed up the matter of her contravening the 1872 Act.[138] Elizabeth Thomas found her baby near death, and there appeared to be no evidence to indicate that Martha Morris had taken the infant to the doctor. It was common practice for a baby farmer to seek medical advice as the sick infant weakened, often when it was too late to save its life. This method provided evidence in the event of future legal proceedings of the baby farmer's apparent concern for the infant's health, while knowing that it was unlikely to survive. As Waugh succinctly put it, 'It is as easy to get a baby's life out of it as it is to rub off the dust from a butterfly's wing.' The susceptibility of nurse children meant that it was not difficult to weaken the infant's health. Waugh found, 'Insufficient clothing on bitter nights will bring on ailments; ailments neglected will end in death.'[139]

It was obvious that once a baby farmer had acquired a certificate to bury the infant, evading the law was straightforward. In fact, as soon as one infant died, the baby farmer accepted another. Elizabeth Griffiths's infant was incredibly emaciated when it died; however, Mrs White buried it without suspicion at the time. A registrar's burial certificate was required, although the burial could still take place as long as the person conducting it notified the registrar within seven days. When Lettice Rees's infant died while in Mrs White's care, the body of Elizabeth Griffiths's infant was exhumed as part of the investigation into malpractice.[140] In Mrs White's case, current regulations had permitted the two burials to take place without suspicion. There was also the dubious practice of burying infants that had been born alive but were reported to the authorities as stillborns. This was discussed during the meeting of the SCPIL when Ernest Hart put forward the need for compulsory registration of stillborn children.[141] Yet the registration of stillbirths was still omitted from the 1874 Registration Act. Two decades later, the Report from the Select Committee on Midwives' Registration (RSCMR) pointed out that 30,412 illegitimate infants were registered in 1890, or one in every 22 births. It was recorded that the proportion of 'one in eight, to one in 10 of illegitimate children are stillborn, whereas of legitimate children the proportion is one in 18 to one in 20 only'.[142] These figures confirmed that many illegitimate infants were probably born alive, but no effort was made to ensure that the infants breathed, or they were killed at birth.

An inquest was held on the death of Mrs Fitzgerald's illegitimate infant. Details reported in the press reveal that Mrs Fitzgerald was lodging at Dowlais with Mr and Mrs Welch at the time since her husband had emigrated to America five years earlier. Mrs Sarah Herbert, a midwife, was called to attend the birth, but she was sent away on arrival as the infant had already been delivered. The midwife was informed later that the baby had died, and acting on the information provided, Mrs Herbert registered the death as that of the child belonging to Mr and Mrs Welch. The midwife declared that the infant was stillborn and that she had been present at the birth, even though that was not the case. It was alleged that Mrs Herbert had made a false declaration to the Dowlais Burial Board. On exhumation of the body, the post-mortem indicated that the infant had been born alive but had died from suffocation.[143] Mrs Herbert pleaded that 'she thought what the people told her when she arrived at the house was true'. The midwife was fined fifty shillings, including costs, or imprisonment for one month on default.[144] When questioned on the issue of stillbirths, Dr Farquharson stated, 'I am always having cuttings from papers about the misdoings of midwives on the subject, and if it is found out everybody is down upon her.'[145] The circumstances surrounding the death of Mrs Fitzgerald's infant were suspicious. Graham Mooney points out that there was 'an economic incentive to have a dead infant buried as stillborn, particularly for the poorer classes'. For example, Mooney found that St Pancras Burial Board charged 7s. 8d for a burial of an infant born alive compared to 2s. for one that had been stillborn.[146] Based on the evidence put forward, it appeared that Mr and Mrs Welch lied to the midwife, or perhaps it was agreed that Mrs Herbert would register the infant as stillborn to save on the expense of burial.

Undoubtedly, the activities of some midwives were dubious; however, ignorance also contributed to maternal mortality. Mrs Elizabeth Morgan, a charwoman, was charged with the manslaughter of Mrs Fanny Lodge, from Llantwit Fardre. Not surprisingly, Mrs Morgan was undefended in court. The woman had been called in to act as midwife, but complications set in during the birth. It was reported that Mr Lodge realised his wife was in danger, but Mrs Morgan repeatedly said, 'have patience, it will be alright presently'. Mrs Lodge died of excessive haemorrhage because the afterbirth had been neglected, and too much time had lapsed before calling for medical assistance. Mrs Morgan was convicted of the offence and sentenced to two months' imprisonment with hard labour.[147] In 1892, it was pointed out in the RSCMR that the training and registration of midwives would lead to increased medical knowledge. Competent and qualified midwives would also know when it was appropriate to send for medical assistance. Trained midwives also understood the term 'moral responsibility', and were aware of the dangers of continuing without medical assistance when required.[148] Finally, the Midwives Act was introduced in 1902; therefore, any person new to the profession had to be qualified and registered with the Central Midwives Board, although currently practising midwives were allowed to continue until 1910.

In 1896 the case of Amelia Dyer, the notorious Reading baby farmer, resulted in the passing of the Infant Life Protection Act in 1897. Again, this Act failed to amend the number of children received by paid childminders to 'one or more infants' less than twelve months old, although the protected age was raised to five years. Under the new legislation, any minder keeping more than one child up to the age of five years had to register with the local authority. In theory, the Act was straightforward for child carers who were compliant with the regulations. A person who received payment for looking after children for a period longer than forty-eight hours was required to give notice to the Board of Guardians within forty-eight hours. The notice requested information with regard to names, age and sex of the infants and also the abode of both the persons placing and receiving the infants. Notice and full particulars were required if an infant was transferred. Any person who received a child less than two years old for a lump sum not exceeding £20 without any agreement for further payment was required to provide notice within forty-eight hours. If not, the sum was liable to be forfeited. A person was required to inform the district coroner if an infant died while in their care, within twenty-four hours of the time of death. No infant could be received by a person who had been convicted of any offence under the 1897 Act, or who had been deprived of the care of a child. Any person disobeying the law was liable to a fine not exceeding £5 or imprisonment for not more than six months.[149] The 1897 Act was still flawed because of the £20 ruling, and the number of children taken in for reward remained at 'more than one infant', despite pressure to amend it to 'one or more infants'. Rose maintains that the most ill-conceived provision in the Act was the £20 rule: 'The thinking behind this was that only in cheap, low-class "adoptions" was the child really at risk, but the scope for connivance to hoodwink the authorities was obvious.'[150] Most infants referred to in this chapter died after they had been adopted for lump-sum amounts of £5 or £10.

In 1899 Mrs Ellen Barry, a widow from Cardiff, was charged under the Infant Life Protection Act 1897 with neglecting two illegitimate infants while in her care. Mrs Barry earned her living by letting out lodgings while she was also in receipt of parish relief, but in this case the relief ceased when she took in the two infants. The fact that Mrs Barry was no longer in receipt of parish relief probably meant she was compliant with the 1897 Act, and she had registered the children with the Board of Guardians. Mrs Barry had come under the notice of the NSPCC Inspector, and under the current legislation it was permissible for the inspector to enter her home to observe the children himself. Homes receiving more than one child were liable to inspection, without obstruction, by the inspector or person appointed by the Boards of Guardians. If the premises, or the person, were found to be unfit, the children could be removed to a place of safety or the workhouse.[151] The 1897 Act proved successful in this case. Mrs Barry was prosecuted for neglect and imprisoned for two months with hard labour, although a longer sentence could have been handed down under the terms of the Act. In spite of her wrongdoing, it could be argued that her imprisonment was disproportionate in comparison to baby farmers who committed worse acts of cruelty, neglect and death with impunity.

At the turn of the twentieth century, imperialism and the future protection of the country were interlinked with infant life protection and welfare legislation. Ross argues that 'The infant welfare movement belonged to the decade of imperialist agitation preceding World War I in which women's reproductive capacity and men's fighting capability became matters of government interest and activity as never before.'[152] Likewise, Ivy Pinchbeck and Margaret Hewitt point out that, '"We must begin with the children" became the recurring theme of the increasing number of people only recently made aware of the importance of maintaining the health of even the most lowly of the population.'[153] This sentiment was reflected at a meeting between the rector of Prendergast, Haverfordwest, and the NSPCC. It was mentioned that 'every child saved through the agency of the society means an addition to the assets of the Empire', and that 'the nation's wealth consists of sound minds and healthy bodies . . . a continuous succession of healthy sons, trained to maintain and extend the empire'.[154] It was at this same meeting that an agreement was reached to form the Ladies' Committee acting for Haverfordwest and district, as a local auxiliary of the NSPCC, to assist in achieving this aim.

Further amendments to legislation were introduced in 1908 in the form of the Children Act, which finally revised the number of children taken in for reward to 'one or more infants'.[155] The following cases provide examples of the effectiveness of the legislation in curbing some of the excesses of baby farming. In 1908 an inquest was held on the death of a servant girl's three-month-old illegitimate infant who had been adopted by Mrs Eliza King, from Newport, for thirty shillings. It was reported in the press that the baby weighed just six and a half pounds when he died. It became apparent that other illegitimate infants who had previously died while in her care had been insured. It seemed that

Mrs King deliberately neglected infants to cause death and, therefore, claim on the insurance policy. The woman admitted that she did not advertise, but replied to advertisements in a Newport newspaper. All eight of Mrs King's own children had died. It was reported that she then made the extraordinary claim to the coroner that six of her children had breathed, but they had been buried by the midwife, who was in violation of the law. Mrs King was summoned because she had received an infant under the age of two years for the sum of thirty shillings, without any agreement for any further payments, and she had also neglected to give notice to the local authority within forty-eight hours of its arrival. As this was her first offence, Mrs King was fined ten shillings or seven days' imprisonment.[156] Mrs King behaved in much the same way as other baby farmers did when she denied knowing the name of the woman from whom she took the child, or why the child was brought to her house. This was an extremely unlikely situation because, as Broder found in Philadelphia, 'baby farmers were unlikely to accept charge of an infant without being certain of who would pay the fee'.[157]

In 1910 Matilda Eden, from Haverfordwest, was summoned for unlawfully neglecting an infant in a manner likely to cause unnecessary suffering under Section 12 of the 1908 Children Act. If convicted, a person was liable to a £20 fine or up to six months' imprisonment. It was reported that the infant belonged to a theatrical couple and had been in Mrs Eden's care for two years. The couple paid five shillings per week maintenance, although the childminder claimed that she had not been paid for several months. Mrs Eden had seven children of her own, who appeared to be properly nourished and cared for. The infant weighed less than 13 lbs at just over two years old, compared to the usual weight of 25 lbs for a child of her age. The infant was admitted to Haverfordwest workhouse, where she soon gained more than 3 lbs in weight; however, Mrs Eden claimed, 'They are forcing things to fatten her to bring a case against me.' Matilda Eden was fined £3, including costs, or in default imprisonment for twenty-eight days. The woman was granted seven days to pay.[158]

The 1908 Children Act did not deter married couple Walter and Lydia Elms from baby farming. In 1917, the couple from Pembrey were charged with the wilful neglect and murder of an unknown female child. The couple had received five illegitimate children for £10 each, and £15 for one other.[159] The 1874 Registration Act required registration of infants within forty-two days of birth, but in this case only one child had been registered.[160] Lydia Elms said that, 'I know we should have registered them, but we did not want the people about here to know.' The infant was only two weeks old when it died, and it was unregistered. As far as the records were concerned this infant did not exist; therefore, its death could not be registered. Even with compulsory registration it was still possible to evade the law and skew the number of illegitimate births and deaths. The post-mortem revealed that the primary cause of death was starvation and the secondary cause was pneumonia, but the defence claimed that death was due to the child's inherited inability to digest food. The couple had been constantly moving from one district to another as a means to avoid detection. Their deliberate failure to register the children meant that they were able to continue baby farming without interference from the authorities; they were able to flout the law. Three years earlier Lydia Elms had been charged at Hereford County Police Court for keeping a child without registering it. That child subsequently died, and another child from Worcester also died some months before from malnutrition and bronchitis while in her care. Walter and Lydia Elms were each sentenced to five years' penal servitude. However, the judge pointed out to them that, 'They had stood in great peril of being found guilty of murder and hanged.' He regarded it as 'a very serious and dangerous offence, especially at a time when human life was so precious to the country'.[161] Not only did the judge reflect on the loss of life on the battlefields during the First World War, but he also demonstrated that he considered the life of an illegitimate child in the same context as that of a legitimate child.

Two weeks later, the *Cambria Daily Leader* reported that the Carmarthenshire baby farming case had come to the attention of Lord Henry Cavendish-Bentink. It was reported that Cavendish-Bentink intended to ask the secretary of the Local Government Board to inquire into 'which part of the Children Act dealing with infant life protection is administered in that district; and if there be no woman visitor, whether he will recommend to the local board of guardians that one be immediately appointed'.[162] The neighbours seemed reluctant to intervene and report the Elms to the authorities for infant neglect, despite the fact that 'there was a bit of dissatisfaction in the neighbourhood as to the way they had treated it'.[163] In this case, the couple were able to breach the statutory legal requirements of the

1908 Children Act. Therefore, without cooperation and intervention from members of the local community, it was difficult for the authorities to enforce the law.

If the value of infant life was mounting before the First World War, then the severe loss of life during 1914–18 was a significant factor in the move towards formalising the practice of adoption. Pinchbeck and Hewitt point out that the social consequences of the First World War made legislation inevitable:

> The publicity given to the unhappy lot of war orphans on the one hand and of unwanted "war babies" on the other prompted an increased concern regarding the dangers of unregulated, *de facto* adoptions and to demands of the institution of legal adoption as practised in other countries.[164]

Fortunately, the end of the First World War marked the beginning of a formal approach to genuine adoptions of unwanted infants.

By the interwar years, infant protection and welfare had progressed considerably since the formation of the ILPS in 1870. For decades, a series of child protection legislation had been implemented, but the formal Adoption of Children Act was not introduced until 1926. Adopted children were now subject to a court order and could not be reclaimed by the natural mothers. While lump-sum adoptions were no longer an issue, the abuses lay elsewhere. Rose argues that 'abuses arose from the unsuitability of some adoptive parents and the failure of certain adoption societies, and more commonly private intermediaries, to check the applicant's circumstances and motives, sometimes with appalling consequences'.[165] Rose points out that in 1937 the Horsborough Committee investigated the working practices of the 1926 Adoption Act due to consistent abuses and failings, because some adoption societies and private intermediaries still failed to home children with suitable adoptive parents. Rose maintains that 'the ensuing Adoption of Children (Regulation) Act 1939 closed the loopholes and made baby farming truly a thing of the past'.[166]

Conclusion

Baby farming was perceived as an urban phenomenon; however, the practice was present in rural west Wales, although there were significantly fewer cases than in the urbanised districts of south

Wales. This is understandable given the density of population and the disparity between social and economic structures of rural and urban societies. Baby farming developed as an economic exchange between baby farmers and parents as a means of coping with society's unwanted infants, no matter what class they were born into. In the case of unmarried mothers, baby farming tended to ease the social and economic burden of bringing up illegitimate children on scanty wages, and it was, to a certain extent, an alternative to infanticide. In some cases, the financial transaction agreed between baby farmers and parents could well be interpreted as 'infanticide for hire'. Unquestionably, a fine line existed between the unintentional death of a child due to poverty and that of malicious intent to cause death on the part of the carer.

Close scrutiny of the selected cases renders it possible to differentiate between the different types of baby farmers who practised openly within Welsh communities. It is evident that some childcare providers were labelled as baby farmers (and therefore associated with unscrupulous practices harmful to the children in their care), such as Mrs Helen Kendall, even though the evidence did not support the charge. Mrs White, Mrs Ward and Mrs Small represented poverty-stricken baby farmers who earned a meagre living by receiving or 'adopting' infants for a premium, or spending the mothers' hard-earned maintenance payments while the infants in their care were neglected and died. Mrs Price operated as a midwife and a procurer; therefore, she had the potential to earn increased premiums. Leslie James was also a procurer of infants; yet, it could be argued that, in comparison to other baby farmers, she was as much a victim of baby farming as Maud Treasure's infant. Without doubt, procurer Hannah Johnson, alias Henrietta Hunter and Dora Johnstone, operated a viable business earning considerable sums of money trafficking infants nationwide. The evidence suggests that Hannah Johnson was the worst of her kind; she was a middle-class, accomplished woman who had always been gainfully employed and capable of earning a very respectable living, unlike the other baby farmers referred to in this chapter. Hannah Johnson's case also reveals that not all receivers of children were neglectful, because the two trafficked infants traced back to her were reported to have found suitable adoptive parents. Furthermore, this evidence regarding the adoptive parents would have remained uncovered without the additional investigations of newspaper journalists. Hence, with the aid of the press as a key source, it is possible to discriminate between baby farmers of 'different stripes', proving that the lines between genuine childcare and both criminal and non-criminal baby farmers were undeniably blurred.

The numerous debates concerning illegitimate children and infant life protection were dominated by nineteenth-century attitudes to the issues of gender and class: issues that are central to understanding the complexities of baby farming. For the most part, baby farmers were perceived to be women from the poorer sections of society who provided a service for the sole benefit of lower- and working-class women. However, evidence reveals that the practice was facilitated by others, and it permeated different sections of society. Men were active participants in baby farming, and this was particularly noticeable with married or cohabiting couples. Some baby farmers also originated from the middle classes, but for one reason or another, the individuals concerned no longer held the position in society that they had once been accustomed to. It appears that middle-class women, like Henrietta Hunter, procured infants to pass on to receivers promptly as a means to generate income without lowering their status too far. The employment of baby farmers was not confined to the poorer classes, since middle-class parents also entrusted their unwanted infants to the care of both working- and middle-class baby farmers. There was no geographical boundary to the trafficking of infants either. Infants were procured locally or from England, and Scotland in some cases. In reality, many infants reached their final 'home' many miles from their place of birth.

On the whole, women employed the services of baby farmers, while some men acted independently to make arrangements to have their unwanted infants 'adopted'. Yet, in many cases brought before the courts, reputed fathers were conspicuous by their absence. For instance, there appeared to be no record as to the father of Maud Treasure's baby, or that of Mrs Stroud's baby in Leslie James's case. Stanley Rees, a married man, was keen to hand over his illegitimate infant, despite the seemingly devastating effect it had on the mother. In fact, the mother travelled to Cardiff and retrieved the infant herself.[167] Morgan Jones also acted independently to organise the 'adoption' of Mary

Reynolds's baby, while many other reputed fathers absconded to far-off destinations to avoid any future liabilities.

Evidence proves that it was possible for baby farmers to exploit loopholes in the relevant legislation, or the regulations were ignored entirely in some cases. The legislation was put in place to regulate childcare providers and protect children, yet many children continued to die of neglect. This was often a result of ineffective policing of legislation by the local authorities. Moreover, baby farmers like Mrs Ward did not refrain from 'adopting' infants even after an appearance in court. Baby farming persisted because the underlying causes remained unresolved; reputed fathers continued to evade their responsibilities whenever possible, while women's scanty wages meant that better quality childcare was unaffordable. Equally, as a consequence of the Bastardy Clause, poverty-stricken baby farmers recognised the economic vulnerability of unmarried mothers and the profitability of 'caring' for unwanted infants. The campaign to protect infants and eradicate baby farming began in earnest in 1870, but it was not until the 1930s that the practice finally disappeared. The decades in between were interspersed with the execution of the occasional convicted baby farmer as a stark reminder that the trade in unwanted infants for financial gain was morally wrong, yet it still remained a legal practice.

Notes

1 *The Times*, 4 July 1870, p. 9, *Times* Digital Archive, https://www.gale.com, accessed 23/02/2007.

2 Shurlee Swain, 'Toward a social geography of baby farming', *History of the Family*, 10 (2005), 151–59 (p. 152).

3 Margaret L. Arnot, 'Infant death, child care and the state: the baby farming scandal and the first infant life protection legislation of 1872', *Continuity and Change*, 9/2 (1994), 271–311; Anette Ballinger, *Dead Woman Walking: Executed Women in England and Wales 1900–1955* (Aldershot, 2000); Daniel Grey, '"More ignorant and stupid than wilfully cruel": Homicide trials and 'Baby-Farming' in England and Wales in the wake of the Children Act. 1908', *Crimes and Misdemeanours*, 3/2 (2009), 60–77; Daniel Grey, 'Discourses of Infanticide in England, 1880–1922' (unpublished PhD thesis, Roehampton University, London, 2008); Ruth Ellen Homrighaus, 'Baby Farming: The Care of Illegitimate Children in England, 1860–1943' (unpublished PhD thesis, University of North Carolina, Chapel Hill, 2003); Ruth Ellen Homrighaus, 'Wolves in women's clothing: Baby-Farming and the *British Medical Journal*, 1860–1872', *Journal of Family*

History, 26/3 (2001), 350–72; Lionel Rose, *Massacre of the Innocents: Infanticide in Great Britain 1800–1939* (London, 1986).

4 *Western Mail,* 13 October 1893, p. 6; 15 November 1892, p. 5.

5 *Western Mail,* 11 September 1890, p. 5.

6 *Western Mail,* 14 May 1890, p. 3.

7 *Cardigan Observer and General Advertiser,* 1 August 1896, p. 3.

8 *Western Mail,* 2 January 1897, p. 8.

9 *Western Mail,* 2 August 1893, p. 7.

10 Homrighaus, 'Baby Farming', p. 10.

11 Homrighaus, 'Baby Farming', p. 3.

12 Ballinger, *Dead Woman Walking*, p. 65.

13 Arnot, 'Infant death, child care and the state', 298.

14 Anne-Marie Kilday, *A History of Infanticide in Britain: c.1600 to the Present* (Basingstoke, 2013), p. 109.

15 *Haverfordwest & Milford Haven Telegraph*, 2 August 1871, p. 3.

16 Rose, *Massacre of the Innocents*, p. 79.

17 Report from the Select Committee on Protection of Infant Life (1871) PP (HMSO, London), p. iii.

18 Quoted in Rose, *Massacre of the Innocents*, p. 88.

19 'Abortion and Child Murder', *The British Medical Journal*, 2/1825 (21 December 1895), 1583–4 (p. 1584).

20 Report from the Select Committee on Midwives' Registration (1892), PP (HMSO, London), p. 25.

21 Benjamin Waugh, 'Baby Farming', *Contemporary Review,* 57 (May 1890), 700–14.

22 Waugh, 'Baby Farming', 701.

23 Waugh, 'Baby Farming', 709.

24 Swain, 'Toward a social geography of baby farming', 155.

25 *Western Mail*, 26 December 1871, p. 3.

26 *Evening Express*, 8 May 1893, p. 3.

27 Parl. Deb. (series 3) HC vol. 351, col. 1678 (23 March 1891).

28 Homrighaus, 'Baby Farming', pp. 250−1.

29 Dr A. Wiltshire, RSCPIL, p. 27.

30 Françoise Barret-Ducrocq, *Love in the Time of Victoria* (London, 1991), p. 178.

31 Homrighaus, 'Wolves in women's clothing', 357.

32 *Western Mail*, 18 May 1888, p. 4.

33 *Western Mail*, 21 May 1888, p. 3.

34 *The Times*, 4 July 1870, p. 9, *Times* Digital Archive, https://www.gale.com, accessed 31/07/2010.

35 Sherri Broder, 'Child Care or Child Neglect? Baby Farming in Late-Nineteenth-Century Philadelphia', *Gender and Society*, 2/2 (1988), 128–48 (p. 139).

36 *Haverfordwest & Milford Haven Telegraph*, 2 August 1871, p. 3.

37 *The Welshman*, 1 March 1872, p. 4.

38 Mr A. Gernon, RSCPIL, 1871, p. 31.

39 Dr A. Wiltshire, RSCPIL, 1871, p. 28.

40 *Western Mail*, 21 June 1871, p. 4.

41 Waugh, 'Baby Farming', 713.

42 *Haverfordwest & Milford Haven Telegraph*, 2 August 1871, p. 3.
43 *South Wales Daily News*, 3 March 1894, p. 6.
44 'Professional Baby-Farming', *The Examiner*, 4 October 1879, p. 1273.
45 Waugh, 'Baby Farming', 711.
46 *Western Mail*, 5 December 1874, p. 8.
47 *The Cambrian*, 31 May 1872, p. 6.
48 Rose, *Massacre of the Infants*, pp. 93–4.
49 *Haverfordwest & Milford Haven Telegraph*, 8 March 1882, p. 3.
50 *Pembrokeshire Herald*, 31 March 1882, p. 2.
51 'Correspondence', *Pembrokeshire Herald*, 24 March 1882, p. 2.
52 *The Cambrian*, 12 May 1865, p. 5.
53 *Western Mail*, 21 February 1881, p. 3.
54 *Western Mail*, 8 February 1877, p. 8.
55 Waugh, 'Baby Farming', 711.
56 *Western Mail*, 3 March 1894, p. 7.
57 'Editorial Comments', *Western Mail*, 5 March 1894, p. 4.
58 *Haverfordwest & Milford Haven Telegraph*, 2 August 1871, p. 3.
59 Arnot, 'Infant death', 273.
60 Arnot, 'Infant death', 275.
61 Homrighaus, 'Wolves in women's clothing', 350.
62 A Bill for the better Protection of Infant Life (1871).
63 Committee for Amending the Law in Points wherein it is Injurious to Women, *Infant Mortality: Its Causes and Remedies* (Manchester, 1871), pp. 1–41.
64 Daniel J. R. Grey, 'What woman is safe...?' coerced medical examinations, suspected infanticide, and the response of the women's movement in Britain, 1871–1881', *Women's History Review*, 22/3 (2013), 403–21 (p. 404).
65 CALPIW, *Infant Mortality*, p. 4.
66 CALPIW, *Infant Mortality*, pp. 7–8.
67 CALPIW, *Infant Mortality*, p. 9.
68 CALPIW, *Infant Mortality*, p. 32.
69 Dr Wiltshire, RSCPIL, 1871, p. 28.
70 Ernest Hart, RSCPIL, 1871, p. 13.
71 'Licensed Infanticide', *John Bull*, 11 January 1868, p. 25.
72 *Bristol Mercury & Daily Post*, 26 June 1880, p. 8.
73 *Western Mail*, 15 January 1873, p. 3.
74 Census Return, 1871, Llanddausant, Carmarthenshire, RG10/5473, https://www.findmypast.co.uk, accessed 23/04/2012.
75 *The Cambrian*, 24 January 1873, p. 8.
76 *Western Mail*, 13 March 1873, p. 4.
77 *The Cambrian*, 31 May 1872, p. 6.
78 *Western Mail*, 5 December 1874, p. 8.
79 *Haverfordwest & Milford Haven Telegraph*, 2 August 1871, p. 3.
80 *Western Mail*, 18 May 1888, p. 2.
81 *Western Mail*, 5 December 1874, p. 8.
82 CALPIW, '*Infant Mortality*', p. 21.

83 Guy Lushington, *The Law of Affiliation and Bastardy: Comprising the Bastardy Laws Amendment Act, 1872* (London, 1904, reproduced Whitefish, Montana, 2010), p. 11.
84 *The Welshman*, 2 November 1883, p. 4.
85 *Western Mail*, 22 July 1870, p. 4.
86 *Western Mail*, 20 June 1871, p. 4.
87 *Western Mail*, 19 June 1871, p. 3.
88 *Western Mail*, 20 June 1871, p. 4.
89 Anna Davin, *Growing up Poor: Home, School and Street in London 1870–1914* (London, 1996), p. 97.
90 *Western Mail*, 18 January 1873, p. 4.
91 *Western Mail*, 8 December 1874, p. 6.
92 *The Times*, 8 May 1896, p. 13, *Times* Digital Archive, https://www.gale.com, accessed 31/07/2010.
93 *Haverfordwest & Milford Haven Telegraph*, 2 August 1871, p. 3.
94 *The Cambrian*, 31 May 1872, p. 6.
95 Waugh, 'Baby Farming', 701.
96 *Evening Express*, 1 December 1905, p. 3.
97 *Evening Express*, 2 December 1905, p. 2.
98 *South Wales Daily News*, 12 September 1905, p. 5.
99 *The Cambrian*, 15 September 1905, p. 2.
100 *South Wales Daily News*, 2 December 1905, p. 6.
101 *Evening Express*, 3 November 1904, p. 2.
102 Lucia Zedner, *Women, Crime and Custody in Victorian England* (Oxford, 1991), p. 40.
103 Kilday, *A History of Infanticide*, p. 86.
104 Kilday, *A History of Infanticide*, p. 84.
105 The National Archives (hereafter TNA), Statement from Eliza Goodchild, 13 August 1907, HO 144/861/155396.
106 *Western Mail*, 24 July 1907, p. 5.
107 *South Wales Daily News*, 24 July 1907, p. 5.
108 TNA, Statement from Mrs Emily Stroud, 16 July 1907, HO 144/861/155336.
109 TNA, Statement by Stanley Vivian Rees, Clewes Hotel, Salford, HO 144/861/155336.
110 *South Wales Daily News*, 24 July 1907, p. 5.
111 *Western Mail*, 8 June 1907, p. 5.
112 *Western Mail*, 6 June 1907, p. 5.
113 TNA, Letter to Under Secretary of State from Head Constable W. McKenzie, Cardiff City Police, 8 August 1907, HO 144/861/155336.
114 TNA, Statement from Stewart H. MacPherson, Cardiff City Police, 8 August 1907, HO 144/861/155336.
115 Ginger Frost, *Living in Sin: Cohabiting as Husband and Wife in Nineteenth-Century England* (Manchester, 2008), p. 35.
116 Ivy Pinchbeck and Margaret Hewitt, *Children in English Society: From the Eighteenth Century to the Children Act 1948*, Vol II (London, 1973), p. 384.
117 *South Wales Echo*, 13 August 1907.
118 TNA, Letter to Mr Shee from Secretary of State Herbert Gladstone, 2 August 1907, HO 144/861/155336.

119 Jill Pellow, *The Home Office, 1848–1914: From Clerks to Bureaucrats* (London, 1982), p. 70.
120 TNA, Home Office Minutes, 8 August 1907, HO 144/861/155336.
121 Ellen Ross, *Love and Toil: Motherhood in Outcast London, 1870–1918* (Oxford, 1993), p. 184.
122 Colin Heywood, *A History of Childhood: Children and Childhood in the West from Medieval to Modern Times* (Cambridge, 2001), p. 59.
123 Census Return, 1911, Mynyddislwyn, Newport, RG14/PN32031, https://www.findmypast.co.uk, accessed 19/11/2012.
124 Census Return, 1911, Dunvant, Swansea, RG14/PN32735, https://www.findmypast.co.uk, accessed 19/11/2012.
125 *South Wales Daily News*, 30 July 1907, p. 6.
126 TNA, Letter written by Herbert Gladstone, 9 August 1907, HO 144/861/155336.
127 Anne Logan, *Feminism and Criminal Justice: A Historical Perspective* (Basingstoke, 2008), p. 130.
128 TNA, Home Office Minutes, 14 August 1907, HO 144/861/155336.
129 TNA, Declaration of Sheriff and Others, 14 August 1907, HO 144/861/155336.
130 Glamorgan Archives (hereafter GA), Finger Print & Photographic Register 1904–1908, No. 877, D/DCONC/C-3/2/1, p. 98.
131 *South Wales Daily News*, 2 December 1905, p. 6.
132 TNA, Letter to Under Secretary of State from Head Constable of Cardiff City Police, 31 July 1907, HO 144/861/155396.
133 TNA, Letter written by Herbert Gladstone, 9 August 1907, HO 144/861/155336.
134 Harry Hendrick, *Child Welfare: England 1872–1989* (London, 1994), p. 46.
135 Ballinger, *Dead Woman Walking*, p. 70.
136 Hendrick, *Child Welfare*, p. 47.
137 Rose, *Massacre of the Innocents*, pp. 110–11.
138 *Pembrokeshire Herald & General Advertiser*, 26 September 1873, p. 4.
139 Waugh, 'Baby Farming', 710.
140 *Haverfordwest & Milford Haven Telegraph*, 2 August 1871, p. 3.
141 Mr Ernest Hart, RSCPIL, p. 14.
142 Report from the Select Committee on Midwives' Registration, p. 26.
143 *Evening Express*, 11 October 1895, p. 4.
144 *South Wales Daily News*, 1 November 1895, p. 6.
145 Report from the Select Committee on Midwives' Registration, p. 10.
146 Graham Mooney, 'Still-Births and the Measurement of Urban Infant Mortality Rates, c. 1890–1930', *Local Population Studies*, 53 (1994), 42–52 (p. 44).
147 *Western Mail*, 20 January 1877, p. 6.
148 Report from the Select Committee on Midwives' Registration, p. 10.
149 Infant Life Protection Act, 1897, 60 & 61 Vict. c. 57.
150 Rose, *Massacre of the Infants*, p. 161.
151 Infant Life Protection Act, 1897.
152 Ross, *Love & Toil*, p. 195.
153 Pinchbeck and Hewitt, *Children in English Society*, p. 634.
154 *The Pembroke County Guardian and Cardigan Reporter*, 2 November 1906, p. 4.

155 W. Clarke Hall, "The Children Act, 1908," being the Third Edition of the Law Relating to Children. "The Children Act, 1908," and other statutes relating to the protection of children: *With notes and forms* (London, 1909, reproduced Milton Keynes, 2010), p. 3.
156 *Evening Express*, 5 September 1908, p. 3.
157 Broder, 'Child Care or Child Neglect', 138.
158 *Haverfordwest & Milford Haven Telegraph*, 9 February 1910, p. 3.
159 *Carmarthen Journal*, 8 June 1917, p. 4.
160 Registration of Births and Deaths Act 1874, 37 & 38 Vict., Ch 88, 1.
161 *Carmarthen Journal*, 8 June 1917, p. 4.
162 *Cambria Daily Leader*, 20 June 1917, p. 1.
163 *Carmarthen Journal*, 8 June 1917, p. 4.
164 Pinchbeck and Hewitt, *Children in English Society*, p. 604.
165 Rose, *Massacre of the Innocents*, pp. 184–5.
166 Rose, *Massacre of the Innocents*, p. 186.
167 TNA, Statement by Stanley Vivian Rees, Clewes Hotel, Salford, HO 144/861/155336.

Chapter Three

'Did you not come to me, my dear?'[1]: Abortion and the abortionist

In 1899 Mrs Elizabeth Thomas was convicted of causing the death of a young barmaid from Cardiff, Miss Agnes Lewis, on whom she had allegedly performed an illegal abortion with the use of instruments.[2] Mrs Thomas was portrayed by the press as a typical working-class unqualified abortionist positioned at the centre of a female network. Community networks provided support to desperate women at a time when abortion seemed to be the only personal or economic solution to unwanted pregnancies. In fact, many abortionists faced economic hardship themselves; hence, performing illegal operations in return for a financial reward was a calculated risk. Abortion was a felony, so there is little evidence to be found of this activity except from criminal cases, or if a woman became seriously ill following the abortion, resulting in a death with a subsequent inquest. Given the nature of the crime, and the public appetite for sensational cases, the press immediately seized upon any opportunity to uncover and publish personal details regarding the victims and the offenders. Therefore, when the subject of abortion is viewed in a wider context, criminal cases are incredibly revealing from a social perspective, as well as expanding on the medical and legal issues relating to the crime. Despite this, abortion has not received a great deal of attention because, as Angus McLaren points out, it might not be viewed as a suitable subject for historians.[3] McLaren also highlights the problems of research due to 'the difficulty, if not impossibility, of establishing the incidence of the acts which were illegal and therefore hidden from public scrutiny'.[4] By the end of the nineteenth century, many women practised abortion as a form of birth control, including single women desperate to extricate themselves from the hardship associated with maintaining illegitimate offspring. Both abortion and concealment of birth were criminal offences, yet the element of risk associated with concealing an infant's body was far greater than the danger of dying as a result of an illegal operation. Even so, there were still considerably more cases of infanticide brought before the courts than cases involving criminal abortion.

The extensive press reporting of criminal cases exposes the complexities of relationships between the women who resorted to abortion and those who formed part of the female networks within Welsh communities. Clearly, women were not isolated, because they were well aware of how, and where, to acquire the services of abortionists. The names of well-known suppliers of abortifacients were also common knowledge. Owing to the secretive nature of a concealed pregnancy and birth, women were alone and without reassurance or support. However, abortion appeared to be a shared experience, as women were usually cared for by female companions during and after the operations. Companions also provided accommodation for a few days for recovery of the patient, if necessary.

Given the legal and ethical nature of abortion, the majority of medical practitioners refused to perform illegal operations.[5] Not surprisingly, this reluctance encouraged women to seek the services of unqualified abortionists, or certain medical practitioners who were not averse to carrying out illegal operations. The *British Medical Journal* (*BMJ*) criticised those medical men 'who prostitute their medical knowledge by using it to relieve – for excessive fees – foolish girls from the consequences of their folly'.[6] Needless to say, women were blamed for incidences of abortion.

Men were seldom mentioned in criminal trials, except for the occasional censure from a judge during the summing-up of a case. In fact, there were few cases where men were indicted, even though it was well known that they often pressured women to undergo illegal operations. Even though evidence is lacking, important insights into the practice can be obtained from various sources such as newspapers, medical journals, parliamentary reports and contemporary journals. The press coverage of many abortion trials was considerable, because the number of persons usually involved generated a great deal of local interest. To add further public interest, newspapers published intimate details about the individuals concerned, especially as the news broke and when the offenders appeared at the coroners' inquests. Some newspapers published detailed sketches of the offenders and victims, which added yet another dimension to abortion cases.

Scrutiny of abortion cases exposes the victims' identities, why they turned to abortionists in the first instance and to what extent both single and married men were complicit in the decision. Men often paid for illegal operations or purchased abortifacients on behalf of women. The victims of abortion are the focal point in this chapter; but it is equally important to assess the role of the abortionists, their social class, whether they were male or female, doctors or unqualified operators. Similarly, an assessment of the manner in which these individuals were dealt with by the judiciary, and the community's response to their activities, is just as relevant. Criminal cases provide evidence of doctors who performed abortions for a fee and those who refused on legal and ethical grounds. The medical profession roundly condemned doctors who carried out illegal abortions. As Michael Thomson explains, 'In demonising abortion and abortionists it was, of course, critical to promote the fiction that abortion was not provided by physicians and that regular and irregular practitioners were readily distinguishable.'[7] The cases referred to in this chapter provide examples of 'regular' and 'irregular' doctors, and of practitioners who existed somewhere in-between. Abortionists were subjected to the full force of the law if convicted and were handed down lengthy prison sentences for their part in the destruction of infant life.

Angus McLaren's study of abortion in nineteenth-century England found that women seeking illegal operations were mostly working- and lower-middle class. Middle-class women 'could afford more skilled methods', which meant that abortions remained private and were unlikely to come to public notice. This explains why the majority of criminal cases were amongst the working classes rather than the well-to-do.[8] Not surprisingly, the issues of gender and class were prominent features in cases of abortion. Therefore, this chapter explores how the issues of gender and class shaped women's lives and influenced their decisions concerning unwanted infants. Apart from endangering their own lives, women were confronted with the option to either break the law and risk detection, or to raise children whom they could not afford to support.

The aim of this chapter is to explore abortion as another option available to desperate single women. The very idea that illegal abortionists practised in darkened rooms for the benefit of promiscuous single women is rather misleading, as the following cases will prove. The chapter is based on twenty-one cases brought before the courts, including three publicised inquests, reported in the press in the period 1884–1919. As it was a criminal offence, abortion appeared to be a practice carried out in private with little known about the circumstances surrounding the act. Even though evidence is lacking, newspapers are extremely enlightening and are drawn upon as a key source in this chapter because the press clearly exposes the interaction of a number of individuals on both a personal level and within the wider community. The first section of this chapter addresses the sale and illegal use of abortifacients as a means of birth control for married women and as a last resort for single women who had 'a mishap'. The second and third sections of the chapter discuss criminal abortion cases reported in the press in the periods 1884–1900 and 1901–19. The reason for the division of cases is because there was a noticeable difference between rates of conviction prior to 1900, compared to those reported in the early decades of the twentieth century. Each indictment referred to within the chapter reflects an individual's set of circumstances and also uncovers common themes between all cases. The cases are examined from different perspectives to explore why verdicts differed over the decades and to what extent gender and class affected the outcome of criminal trials.

'The first two doses put me right'[9]: Abortifacients and birth control

Throughout the centuries, women have resorted to abortion, relying on instruments of various kinds and remedies ranging from potions concocted by herbalists to lead pills supplied by post. Mr Walcott reported to the commissioners of inquiry in 1834 that women induced abortion 'from the interest they give the man in preventing a birth, which presents the alternative of a prison, or (to him) a heavy weekly expense'. He was also aware that men approached medical practitioners for drugs for the purpose of bringing on an abortion.[10] Mr Walcott argued that the severity of the new Bastardy Clause would reduce cases of abortion. Yet, women still resorted to the practice throughout this period while putting their health at risk and proving injurious to the unborn baby if the procedure failed. Abortifacients contained harmful substances such as cantharides (Spanish fly), mercury, powdered savin, juniper essence, colocynth, quinine and gin, gunpowder and lead pills.[11] Many women relied on abortifacients and, in the case of married women, often with their husbands' knowledge.

If noxious pills and potions failed to produce the desired result, a woman was more likely to turn to an abortionist to 'put her right'.[12] The *BMJ* argued that it was difficult 'to make women see any moral difference between early getting rid of the product of conception and using measures to prevent pregnancy altogether. The latter practice is far too common, especially among married women.'[13] Katie Fisher's research 'revealed a common distinction drawn between abortions and bringing on a period' in those determined to limit family size.[14] This was particularly apparent for married women who found it necessary to practise birth control, either through choice or for economic reasons.

The first law to make abortion a criminal offence was included in Lord Ellenborough's Act in 1803. The law decreed that if a miscarriage was procured before quickening (around the fifth month) the crime was punishable by transportation or corporal punishment. Abortion later than that point was a capital offence, although it became a non-capital offence in 1837.[15] The introduction of the Offences Against the Person Act in 1861 made it a criminal offence for a woman to procure her own miscarriage. It was also an offence for any person to administer drugs or use instruments to bring about miscarriage. Section 58 pertaining to the Act stated that:

> Every Woman, being with Child, who, with Intent to procure her own Miscarriage, shall unlawfully administer to herself any Poison or other noxious Thing, or shall unlawfully use any instrument or other Means whatsoever with the like Intent, and whosoever, with Intent to procure Miscarriage of any Woman, whether she be or not be with Child, shall unlawfully administer to her or cause to be taken by her any Poison or other noxious Thing, or shall unlawfully use any Instrument or other Means whatsoever with the like Intent shall be guilty of a Felony, and being convicted

> thereof shall be liable, at the Discretion of the Court to be kept in Penal Servitude *for Life* or for any Term not less than *Three* Years, – or to be imprisoned for any Term not exceeding *Two* Years, with or without Hard Labour, and with or without Solitary confinement.[16]

Section 59 of the same Act related to any person who supplied 'Poison or other noxious Thing', or any instruments knowing that they were intended to procure a miscarriage. A person could be found guilty of a misdemeanour and, at the discretion of the court, could be imprisoned for three years or any term not exceeding two years, with or without hard labour.[17] The law on abortion remained as such until the Abortion Act in 1967. More than a century had elapsed before the law was amended, but as Barbara Brookes explains, 'It was not until fertility control was regarded as a widely accepted social goal, and a necessary part of health care for women, that abortion moved out of the criminal context and into the mainstream of the health services.'[18] Equally, Michael Thomson points out that 'The shift from prohibition to a greater reliance on medical discretion within this period provided the conditions that made the Abortion Act in 1967 possible.'[19]

Criminal abortion cases were few in number, and the evidence indicates that most prosecutions related to offences committed in the urban districts of south Wales. In 1908, the Seventy-first Annual Report of the Registrar General reported that there were seven deaths caused by abortion or miscarriage in south Wales, comprising six cases in Glamorgan and one case in Pembrokeshire.[20] These particular figures were not associated with criminal cases since procuring abortion was accounted for under the Offences Against the Person Act 1861. In both England and Wales during 1908 there were seventeen criminal cases of procuring abortion. The judicial statistics reported that in the period 1893–1910 there were 278 criminal cases of procuring abortion in England and Wales. The number of cases fluctuated considerably from year to year. For instance, the statistics reveal that in 1893 there were twenty-two criminal cases of abortion, yet in 1894 there was a significant decrease to a total of nine cases. The lowest number of criminal cases was six, recorded in 1901, and the highest number of thirty was recorded in 1909.[21]

As there were few prosecutions, the evidence proves that the law was difficult to police, particularly as self-administration of drugs, or self-induced abortion, normally occurred during the early stages of pregnancy and took place in the privacy of the home. The police in Swansea were criticised regarding the lack of interest in abortion cases, but in their defence the superintendent reported that:

> the victims were ashamed to confess their own criminality, and whilst the facts were generally well known to their circle of friends, none of them would take the responsibility of a prosecution. The traffic has been carried on all over Wales with impunity and the utter inability of the law to cope with it has been severely condemned.[22]

Then again, given the nature of the act, it was difficult for police to detect and prove abortions had been performed unless a woman died or was critically ill after the procedure.

Obviously, it was impossible to establish the number of women who resorted to abortion. However, Amand Routh, an obstetric physician, calculated the estimated loss of population by adopting the moderate estimate of four abortions to each stillbirth to achieve a total of 98,680 abortions, premature labours and stillbirths in 1910, and 96,925 in 1911 in England and Wales.[23] Based on the estimated figures, and in comparison to the low rate of fatalities, abortion appeared to have been a relatively safe practice. In fact, the greatest risk to women was infection derived from illegal operations; although the majority of abortionists had acquired the necessary skills to perform operations on a regular basis with relative safety.

The number of abortifacients widely accessible on the market was considerable, yet their effectiveness was often questionable, as well as dangerous to health. One brand was Towle's Pennyroyal and Steel Pills for Females. In a veiled message the product claimed that it would 'quickly correct all irregularities, remove all obstructions and relieve the distressing symptoms so prevalent with the sex'.[24] This popular brand was advertised extensively throughout Wales in both rural and urban newspapers, including Welsh-language newspapers such as *Y Celt*.[25] Dr Mackay's 'Marvellous' Female Remedy claimed that it was 'the only trustworthy and reliable preparation in the world for all irregularities, never failing in bringing about all that is desired speedily and safely'. Mrs W. commented in one testimonial that 'The first two doses put me right', with only one such endorsement purporting to be from a single woman.[26] Regardless of the testimonial's authenticity, this advertisement implied the promotion of a product for the benefit of married women rather than a product to encourage immoral behaviour amongst single women. Another remedy was Blanchard's Apiol & Steel Pills. Blanchard also offered for sale an 'Illustrated book containing valuable information on how all Irregularities and Suppressions may be entirely avoided or removed by simple means.'[27] These products were affordable and readily available by mail order, even though the 'drugs or quasi mixtures of various kinds' were reported to be 'useless for the purpose'.[28]

In 1895 the *BMJ* argued that abortions would continue for as long as the press printed advertisements providing men with the opportunity to avoid paternity and girls were scared of the shameful prospect of unmarried motherhood. Criticism was levelled at newspapers because 'the mere fact of their extensive publication was an incentive both to immorality and crime'.[29] The ineffectiveness of remedies and the financial incentives for the publication of advertisements prompted J. Rutherford Hill of the Pharmaceutical Society of Great Britain to complain that 'some strong measures are urgently called for to stop the use of public newspapers and magazines for such nefarious purposes'.[30] As medical professionals were anxious about the seemingly increased use of abortifacients, it could be argued that women were habitually self-administering drugs to 'keep them regular'. Women frequently administered drugs soon after a missed period, and it was possible that these delays in menstruation were not due to pregnancy, but underlying physical causes such as anaemia or anxiety.[31] The *BMJ* argued that 'medical men for good reasons, and after consultation, think it necessary to induce abortion; but whoever heard of their trusting to drugs to do it?'[32] Doctors continued to criticise the effectiveness of abortifacients, despite their popularity and widespread use.

Men repeatedly coerced women to take pills and potions to procure a miscarriage, and they were likely to be present at the time of ingestion to ensure that administration of the drugs actually occurred. Françoise Barret-Ducrocq found that 'quite a number of men seem to have regarded it as an obvious, almost a normal expedient'.[33] The following cases exemplify prevailing attitudes. Newspaper reports reveal that William Davies, a Swansea town councillor, attempted to preserve his reputation when he instructed his servant, Elizabeth Pugh, to obtain drugs to induce a miscarriage. When that attempt failed, Davies suggested that she should go to America 'so as not to get him into disgrace'. Elizabeth Pugh later gave birth and subsequently sued him for maintenance.[34] Another case caused a sensation at Carmarthenshire Assizes in 1892 when William Alexander Miller was charged with supplying drugs to Catherine Bassett in order to bring about an abortion. Forty-one-year-old Miller was a shop assistant and described as well educated.[35] He was also understood to be a married man.[36] Obviously, a married man usually had much to lose if his extramarital affairs came to light. According to press reports, Catherine Bassett stated that Miller 'had seduced her under the promise of marriage, and when she became pregnant he brought her a bottle of mixture, which he told her, would, if she took it three times a day rid her of her child. She took a small amount while he was there but spat it out.'[37] Miller claimed that, 'I did it at her own desire and request.'[38] He was convicted of the charge and sentenced to six months in prison with hard labour.[39] There appeared to be no mention that Catherine Bassett would be charged with any offence, even though ingestion of the drugs meant that she was an accomplice to the crime.

During this period the law decreed that no person should administer to herself any noxious poison to induce her own miscarriage, although prosecutions remained few in number. It is significant to find that the only woman in the sample charged with inducing her own miscarriage was Mrs Alice Jones. She was reported to be of respectable appearance and married to 'a lazy husband, who had done but one day's work since 1915'. The commissioner was sympathetic to the 'terrible story of her life' and bound her over to the sum of £10 'to come up for judgement if called upon in 12 months'.[40] That demand for abortifacients caused considerable concern amongst the medical profession was firm evidence that many women relied on drugs to 'put them right'. Given the extensive advertising in the Welsh press, it is plausible that the number of women who resorted to abortion by the use of abortifacients could certainly be underestimated. Furthermore, it is highly unlikely that suppliers of abortifacients, such as Towle's Pennyroyal or Blanchard's Apiol and Steel Pills, would have funded extensive advertising if it was not financially viable. As expected, when the drugs failed to produce the desired result, the only option for many women was to terminate the pregnancy by the illegal use of instruments.

'A shady kind of skill'[41]: Abortion and the abortionist 1884–1900

Motivated by financial rewards, abortionists repeatedly ignored the legal penalties associated with illegal operations, and they were as accessible to women as abortifacients. A typical case revealed that a number of individuals were involved, including single and married men and women, 'regular' and 'irregular' doctors, unqualified operators and, of course, the reliable networks that permitted abortionists to thrive in the first place. One particular network consisted of three members of the same family, namely Dr John Hopkins, his daughter Mary Hopkins and her future husband, John Rees. Dr Hopkins practised in Carmarthen and was well known for his 'shady kind of skill', a skill also attributed to his daughter.[42] In 1884, Emily Cope died after Andrew Bayntun, the father of her unborn child, had made arrangements for her to travel from Bath, in an advanced stage of pregnancy, to give birth while under the care of the doctor. This case exposes the father's role in the woman's death, seldom seen in other cases referred to in this chapter. At the inquest held in Carmarthen town, Mary Hopkins was noticeably evasive. She claimed that Emily Cope arrived on the doorstep unannounced and unknown to her and Dr Hopkins. Even more implausible was Dr Hopkins's statement that he was not sure if the woman was pregnant or not, even though all witnesses testified that Emily Cope was in an advanced stage of pregnancy. Dr Hopkins denied that the young woman had been confined at his house and argued that the cause of death was inflammation of the lungs. Yet, the post-mortem indicated that twenty-two-year-old Emily Cope had recently given birth, and the cause of death was due to blood poisoning as a result of emptying the womb.[43]

Forty-five-year-old Andrew Bayntun, from Cardigan, was a surgeon-dentist and known to be acquainted with the doctor. Although married, he claimed to be living apart from his wife at the time. Andrew Bayntun admitted that he and Emily Cope had

had an intimate relationship and never denied paternity.[44] Emily Cope wrote three days after the birth to tell him that the baby had died. Again, Andrew Bayntun admitted that he did not ask what had become of the infant and Dr Hopkins never mentioned it. Baby clothes were found amongst Emily Cope's belongings, which implied that preparations had been made for the birth. Both men were charged with murder at the coroner's inquiry and were 'protected from the violence of the shouting and tumultuous throng by a large body of police' on leaving the court.[45]

The evidence suggests that, under normal circumstances, abortionists were widely accepted within local communities until charged with an offence. Public attitudes shifted between outright condemnation and a curious desire to discover personal details regarding the individuals concerned. Press reports reveal that when Dr Hopkins and Andrew Bayntun appeared at the Glamorgan Assizes, the court was crowded and there were 'the most strained feelings of excited interest apparent'. It was reported that, nevertheless, the judge ordered all females out of the court, which was a common practice. The evidence put forward in abortion cases was not considered a suitable subject for respectable women, even though they were naturally interested in the outcome. The prosecution admitted that they had no evidence against Andrew Bayntun for either murder or manslaughter. Therefore, he was acquitted by the jury, although he was ordered to remain as a witness to be cross-examined. The post-mortem confirmed that the child was near full maturity; however, there was no conclusive evidence to prove that an instrument had been used to induce an abortion. The prosecution argued that if Dr Hopkins was not guilty of murder, then there was a case for manslaughter based on his culpable neglect, yet the judge disagreed. He pointed out that the case was suspicious, but there was no evidence of murder because the doctors could not say if an abortion had been performed. According to medical testimony, Emily Cope died from blood poisoning as a result of parturition. No doctor confirmed whether Dr Hopkins could have done anything to cure her; therefore the judge directed the jury to find the man not guilty of murder.[46]

Andrew Bayntun never denied his involvement in the case. As Angus McLaren found, single men 'were prosecuted as much for their sexual activities as for their involvement in abortion that made such "immorality" public knowledge', and that the prosecution of unscrupulous men provided an opportunity for the public to see that the abortion law was not aimed at women alone. McLaren maintains that when single women died as a result of illegal operations, men were likely to be prosecuted because they were usurping the girl's parents and their right to control their daughters.[47] This was relevant in Andrew Bayntun's case, even though McLaren was referring to single men in particular. Both Andrew Bayntun and Dr Hopkins plotted Emily Cope's visit while she was in an advanced stage of pregnancy; therefore a stillbirth was probably the intended outcome. The fact that Bayntun never enquired about the dead infant was perhaps proof enough. Just like many other men in similar circumstances, he seized control of the situation, but precisely what happened to Emily Cope while in the care of Dr Hopkins was not established.

Dr Hopkins was depicted as a disreputable doctor in the press reports; however, unqualified abortionists were also active in local communities, and this chapter considers one such notable example. Mrs Mary Kew, a well-known character in Cardiff, was an unqualified abortionist and recognised locally as 'Mother Kew'. Like many abortionists, she also practised as a midwife. In 1888 Mrs Kew was arrested for attempting to perform an abortion with the use of instruments upon Mrs Emma Stone. The woman was critically ill after the operation, and unlikely to survive; therefore, it was agreed that she should provide a statement to the police.[48] The *BMJ* advised doctors that it was desirable when appropriate to record dying depositions in criminal abortion cases. The statement proved to be crucial evidence against the person who carried out the operation if the woman died; they were sought provided that the patients' chances of recovery were not prejudiced by making a deposition.[49] Dying depositions were submitted as evidence in a number of cases referred to in this chapter, although the legality of some statements was challenged in court. Hence, successful legal challenges led to the acquittal of prisoners. Mrs Kew was given the opportunity to cross-examine Mrs Stone at her bedside and asked, 'Did you not come to me, my dear, and say that you had a bad husband, and that as there were already five children you did not want another. Didn't you beg me to do the thing for you?'[50] Mrs Stone died later from blood poisoning.[51] Naturally, Mrs Kew's involvement in her death caused considerable local gossip. The *Western Mail* reported that Mrs Kew's arrest has had the 'usual effect of loosening tongues, and statements of a startling nature are being freely made'.[52] A local woman alleged that Mrs Stone had used an instrument on herself. Apparently, she admitted to using the wooden instrument herself in the first week following a visit to Mrs Kew.[53] An examination revealed marks on the head of the foetus where it had come into contact with a sharp instrument puncturing the walls of the womb.[54] Mrs Kew was charged at the Glamorgan Assizes with feloniously killing and murdering Mrs Emma Stone. In her defence, Mrs Kew's counsel argued that Mrs Stone's dying depositions were inadmissible as evidence because the conditions to render them admissible had not been complied with. Firstly, Mrs Kew was not legally represented when the depositions were taken, and secondly, no notice had been provided for the woman to acquire a solicitor in sufficient time. The defence counsel put forward that Mrs Kew had 'pretended to perform the operation for the sake of gain, but she never did anything to cause those wounds'. It was put to the jury that when Mrs Stone found that there was no miscarriage, she used the wooden instrument herself during the time period suggested by the doctor.[55] Mrs Kew's acquittal was secured because Mrs Stone had incriminated herself and the depositions were inadmissible in court.

The following year, in 1889, Mrs Kew appeared at Glamorgan Assizes, yet again charged with feloniously using certain instruments upon a nineteen-year-old single woman, Bessie Embery, with intent to procure a miscarriage. Mrs Kew was also charged with attempting to procure an abortion by administering a dose of castor oil, and with concealing the birth of the child. She pleaded guilty to the charge of concealment. Again, Mrs Kew had no legal representation at the police court, although the judge ordered her defence at the assizes. Women, and indeed children, were removed from the court before opening the case. Bessie Embery had visited Mrs Kew's home accompanied by two friends, Elizabeth Chaplin and Amelia Jenkins. Elizabeth Chaplin operated as part of a network, and she was responsible for introducing the young woman to Mrs Kew. She also helped Bessie Embery to pay for the abortion at a cost of two guineas. Initially, Mrs Kew refused to perform the operation on the grounds that she had not long been discharged for her part in Mrs Stone's death. Despite pressure from desperate women, abortionists were reluctant to operate in some cases, but they were usually won over by the prospect of financial reward.

Bessie Embery pleaded with Mrs Kew and promised that she would tell no one. After more than six operations, Bessie Embery finally gave birth prematurely at six months.[56] The baby was taken away by another woman and handed to Mrs Kew to dispose of. Mrs Kew informed the court that she put the baby in the closet and threw eight buckets of water over it.[57]

In summing-up, the judge pointed out that Elizabeth Chaplin was almost equally as culpable as Mrs Kew, and she could have been charged as an accomplice. Mrs Kew was convicted and sentenced to seven years' imprisonment. The sentence was sensationally received in court, while a clapping of hands was heard in the balcony, which was promptly suppressed. Mrs Kew appeared to take calculated risks on a regular basis, yet the circumstances surrounding this particular indictment made it difficult to evade the law in this case. In fact the police were optimistic in securing a conviction, especially as they had learned from past experience not to arrest Mrs Kew without firm evidence beforehand. The press conveniently used criminal abortion cases as a means to police women's sexuality, although Bessie Embery was not portrayed as immoral to the same extent as other single women in similar cases. According to the *South Wales Echo*, she was a servant who had 'the misfortune to become pregnant'.[58] The press presented an image that was representative of a desperate young servant girl abandoned by some man, so common in the public imagination, rather than a promiscuous young woman, which was often the case.

The community's acceptance of women like Mrs Kew, that is until charged with an offence, revealed public attitudes on the subjects of abortion and infant life protection. Patricia Knight maintains that in England, 'Women performing abortions or selling pills do not seem to have been regarded locally with any antagonism. If there had been any great hostility towards them it is difficult to see how they could have continued to flourish.'[59] Mrs Kew was under surveillance as she pursued her nefarious activities, yet there was only one instance prior to 1889 when the police successfully charged the woman of an offence. Oddly enough, this was in May 1879 when she was charged with fortune-telling and imprisoned for one month as a rogue and a vagabond.[60] Interestingly, the prison sentence did not deter Mrs Kew, because she was still telling fortunes in 1888. It was reported that Mrs

Kew's 'patrons in soothsaying included lady members of the most fashionable circles in Cardiff'.[61]

Abortionists were readily accessible between Carmarthen and Cardiff, even to the extent of keeping the business in the family. Despite the criminal trial of Dr Hopkins in 1884, his daughter, by now Mrs Mary Rees, seemed to have little fear of the law. Unperturbed, Mrs Rees continued to practise until arrested in Swansea in July 1888. Meanwhile, her assistant Louisa Wilson, a midwife, also known as Mrs Earle, was arrested in Cardiff. The two women were arrested due to the critical state of twenty-four-year-old Mrs Maud Williams after Mrs Rees allegedly performed an illegal operation. As Mrs Williams's health deteriorated, an application was made to her husband to consent to his wife providing a statement. At first he refused because he feared it would disturb her too much, and he also believed that his wife would survive. Mrs Williams gave her statement to the police, in the presence of a magistrate and a solicitor. Both women were also afforded the opportunity to cross-examine Mrs Williams at her bedside.[62]

In December 1888, Mary Rees and Louisa Wilson were charged at Glamorgan Assizes with the wilful murder of Mrs Maud Williams. The press reported that both women were respectably dressed and followed the case with the 'most intense interest'. Even though a number of witnesses were called, the case broke down for the prosecution. Yet again, the defence counsel questioned the legality of Mrs Williams's statement. The defence argued that the depositions were defective because the evidence was recorded in the presence of a justice who played no part in the committal of the two women. The depositions were also flawed because the caption with the charge against the accused was only included afterwards. Hence, it was considered that, in the absence of the depositions, it was unreasonable to ask the jury to convict the accused. There was a second indictment against the two women for attempting to perform an illegal operation, but as the evidence was virtually the same, the prosecution was unable to proceed with that case either.

Irrespective of the acquittal in Mrs Williams's case, the two women faced a third indictment of feloniously procuring a miscarriage upon Mrs Mary Jane Collier.[63] Details of the case revealed that Louisa Wilson's role was to acquire patients for Mary Rees, and this was achieved via a newspaper advertisement. In a veiled message it read, 'Ladies, Married or Going to be – valuable information – Two stamps, addressed envelope, Madame Cerise Hahn, Hamilton Street, Canton, Cardiff.'[64] Mrs Collier responded to the advertisement and informed the court that the purpose of the visit was to obtain information regarding contraception, although it is apparent that Louisa Wilson knew she was required to perform an abortion. It was revealed in court that when Mrs Collier returned for the operation, Mary Rees did not follow the usual procedure to induce a miscarriage, and instead used her finger to start this process, rather than an instrument, therefore limiting any damage to the womb.[65] Mrs Collier was critically ill following the miscarriage. Given that Mary Rees had not used an instrument, the doctor did not suspect an illegal operation had taken place because there was no evidence of wounds or lacerations. Then again, she was a well-practised abortionist and was, no doubt, aware of the most appropriate procedure that would cause the least damage to the womb, if any. Apparently, Mrs Collier's husband had known nothing about the abortion until the police came to the house. Mrs Collier had five children, and this was reported to have been her second miscarriage in twelve months.[66]

Mary Rees was under surveillance; therefore, the police were keen to prosecute given the opportunity, especially as the force was criticised for its alleged indifference to practising abortionists. In court, the defence argued that 'the case rested on the uncorroborated testimony of Mrs Collier, as an alleged accomplice'. The defence was unsuccessful in this case and both women were convicted of the charge.[67] The judge told thirty-two-year-old Mary Rees that you 'have forced on me the certainty that you carry on a trade of procuring abortion of young women', and sentenced her to ten years' imprisonment.[68] She was transferred to Woking Prison and described in the prison register as having an 'imperfect education'.[69] The judge sentenced thirty-one-year-old Louisa Wilson to five years for procuring patients and participating in Mary Rees's practices.[70] She too was removed to the same prison and also reported to have an 'imperfect education'.[71]

It is interesting to discover that both Mary Rees and her husband John Rees were on trial at Glamorgan Assizes at the same time. In an entirely separate case, John Rees, a commercial traveller, was indicted for performing an illegal operation upon Alice White, a single woman who was employed at Swansea Laundry. Alice White was thought to be about six weeks pregnant, yet despite two visits to the doctor was unable to gain a conclusive medical opinion about possible pregnancy.[72] It was reported that, accompanied by a friend, Alice White asked John Rees to perform an operation. He agreed but insisted that it must be kept quiet 'on account of his poor missus'. This was because Mary Rees, his wife, was still on remand awaiting trial. Press coverage indicated that Alice White only had one guinea after pawning her watch, and at first the man had refused to operate, saying he 'would not touch her under five guineas'. After some deliberation John Rees reduced his fee and performed the operation, but Alice White was not convinced that it had been carried out correctly. When nothing happened she asked for the payment to be returned, which he agreed to do after some protest. Press reports revealed that instruments normally used by an accoucheur were found at John Rees's house, although these had been fabricated by a blacksmith and not by an instrument maker.[73] It could have been, as suggested by doctors, that Alice White was not pregnant and that other physical causes might have led the young woman to believe otherwise.

The cross-examination of single women in court was a humiliating experience. However, the majority of cases under review concerning married women reveal that they were not subjected to the same degrading experience in court, even though all were accomplices to an unlawful act. For single women, their alleged sexual activities were disclosed to the court and sensationalised later by the press. In Alice White's case, her defence was undermined when she was forced to admit to having received money for 'immoral purposes'. Obviously, her testimony was discredited when John Rees's defence counsel claimed that 'the girl's story was partly invented and was very improbable'.[74] He admitted that John Rees's conduct 'might have been disgusting, indecent and fraudulent'. The defence argued that the Crown should put forward witnesses 'who would speak not of suspicious circumstances, or of disgusting circumstances, of immoral thoughts and acts, but who would state that the man did really attempt to procure a miscarriage'. The defence insisted that John Rees had only pretended to perform the operation, and that the jury needed to consider the intent rather than the act itself. Despite the fact that he was the husband of the infamous abortionist Mary Rees, Alice White's testimony was discredited because the girl was known to have received immoral earnings and was accused of lying in court. The judge also contended that, 'The principal witness was a woman of undoubted bad character, and it had been urged that she was, therefore, not to be relied on.' John Rees was acquitted and discharged from court.[75]

Considering this case from a gendered and class perspective, Alice White was employed as a low-paid worker in a laundry, and it was usually poorly paid female employment that forced some women to accept immoral earnings in the first instance. According to the judge and the defence counsel, Alice White did not comply with the norms of female respectability and morality. Naturally, abortionists denied all knowledge of the charges brought against them. Therefore, apart from vengeance on the victims' part, the evidence provides no obvious reason why women would make false accusations. After all, the victims were also accomplices to the crime and, given the prevailing sexual double standards, little could be achieved when the legal procedure was such a humiliating experience.

When a woman contravened the norms of respectability, regardless of the man's conduct, the press were inclined to report the case in a negative manner. The death of Mrs Elizabeth Christiansen in 1896, following an illegal operation, resulted in the broadcast of her personal life in both the local and national press. The *South Wales Daily Post* ran with the headlines, 'The Swansea Sensation' and 'Past Life of the Deceased'. Elizabeth Christiansen was estranged from her husband and reported to be an 'unfortunate'. Yet she maintained an outward appearance of respectability, while her late parents had enjoyed 'general respect and esteem'. As a young woman, the press described her as being of a '"wild" disposition, a trait which in after life developed and exhibited itself more strongly', and that 'the subsequent career of the unfortunate woman can only be described as "shady"'. Elizabeth Christiansen, also known as Evans, was not referred to as a prostitute by the press, but it was reported that 'Among the sisterhood of the fallen in the town Elizabeth Evans was much liked.'[76] While Elizabeth Christiansen lay dying, her close friend, Mrs Margaret Williams from Llanelli, was dragged from the South Dock at Swansea, having been found drowned. She had been beaten about her face, but the post-mortem revealed that the injuries had not caused her death. She was reported to have received a summons for keeping a brothel at Llansamlet.[77] Her friendship with Margaret Williams might explain how Elizabeth Christiansen was associated with the 'fallen' in Llanelli, and why the press connected this incident with her case. Apparently Elizabeth Christiansen had a number of gentlemen friends, although she was associated with one man in particular. David Griffiths, a married man from Llanelli, was understood to be the father of the unborn child, and he was known to have been supportive under the circumstances. The press suggested that 'her morality was confined exclusively to one man', although it was soon pointed out that 'The facts already known completely disposes of it.' David Griffiths was mentioned at the inquest, but there appears to be no account of him being called as a witness.[78]

Elizabeth Christiansen was portrayed as a 'fallen woman', which was a middle-class term used to describe a woman who was once respectable. J. A. Banks argues that 'this was because there were no "fallen ladies". There were, it is true, no fallen gentlemen either, but this was because there were no fallen men.'[79] Similarly, as Carol Smart points out, 'In the (hetero) sexual sphere we have two categories of women, the respectable and the "fallen"; with men however the law appears to recognize only one category, the respectable.'[80] The contemporary view on this was expressed by Dr Kerr, who maintained that 'women fell from a higher level than men, and therefore sank lower. On this account it was more difficult for the former to reform.'[81] Using the powers of the press to openly control women's sexual behaviour, numerous stories circulated in the newspapers regarding Elizabeth Christiansen's past long before the inquest began. This prompted the coroner to censure the press before proceedings began, and the police also complained that 'mouths were now shut' because of what the papers had reported on the case.[82] In fact, other cases of criminal abortion had the opposite effect of 'loosening tongues' within the community. Elizabeth Christiansen's determination to keep quiet about the operation meant that no statement was taken from the dying woman. Consequently, any statement uttered prior to her death could not be used as evidence. The verdict of the coroner's jury was that Elizabeth Christiansen died from blood poisoning following lacerations to the uterus, but there was no direct evidence as to who had performed the operation.[83]

Evidently, Elizabeth Christiansen had an unenviable past. Therefore, the press did not miss the opportunity to publish salacious details even though the woman had died. However, when twenty-five-year-old Agnes Lewis died following an illegal operation, the press adopted an unusual approach not visible in other cases concerning single women. The young woman was described as 'a very good-looking girl, with a nice fresh-coloured complexion, and a head of luxuriant hair'. It was said that 'Her vivacity and sunny disposition gained for her many friends.'[84] Agnes Lewis had undergone an illegal operation, yet the press still considered her to be a respectable young woman. Elizabeth Christiansen and Alice White, however, were recognised as immoral; therefore, it was apparent that the two women were not deserving of the same level of respect as popular young barmaid Agnes Lewis.

The majority of cases of criminal abortion involved working-class women but Lily Maud Challenger's experience reflects the situation from a middle-class perspective. Twenty-three-year-old Lily Challenger was the very respectable and well-liked daughter of the manager of Messrs Vivian and Sons Fuel Works, Swansea. Seemingly, as far as the press were concerned, the need to resort to abortion did not necessarily preclude a woman from being referred to as respectable in some cases. So it is not surprising to find that the press drew a distinction between abortions performed amongst allegedly immoral, working-class single women and the experiences of middle-class women undergoing the same illegal operations. This chapter considers one such instance. In this case Lily Challenger's fiancé, Elliot Muller, controlled the situation from the outset, aided by Dr Timothy Jones and assisted by medical student Henry Richards. Initially Jones provided Muller with medicine, which he insisted would do Lily Challenger 'no harm whatever', although, as in many cases, it did not have the desired effect. Jones then suggested an operation, but Muller was unable to pay the fee, so it was agreed that payment would be made at a later date. It was reported that Lily Challenger objected at first but, after some pressure on Muller's part, she finally consented to have the abortion. Jones operated on the young woman on five separate occasions, and all were in Muller's presence. On the fifth and fatal occasion Jones operated while Richards administered chloroform, again in Muller's presence. Only this time there were complications, and Muller was forced by Jones and Richards to assist in the operation. Lily Challenger died at home shortly after the miscarriage. When arrested, Jones realised the gravity of the situation and assumed that a long-term prison sentence was inevitable, which, he said, 'would keep me away from drinking a considerable time'. Similar to women in the same position, Jones revealed his own vulnerability when he said, 'It is that ------ Muller that has brought me into this trouble.'[85] Muller eventually paid Jones just 15s. 6d to perform the illegal operation. Lily Challenger's experience differed to every other case considered in this chapter because there appeared to be no female support network to rely upon, clearly visible in working-class cases. Normally, middle-class women could afford to pay for skilled doctors, so any operations remained private. Therefore, evidence suggests that support networks existed mostly for the benefit of working-class women, rather than for those women from the middle classes.

Both Timothy Jones and Henry Richards appeared at Glamorgan Assizes in November 1896 charged with wilful murder. Not surprisingly, there were calls for Elliot Muller to be prosecuted for his participation in the operation. However, Muller was the key prosecution witness even though he was regarded as an accomplice; without his evidence it was impossible for the prosecution to proceed with the case.[86] The judge directed the jury to find Jones guilty of murder, but the lesser verdict of manslaughter was returned instead because there was no malice aforethought to justify the charge of murder. The judge was somewhat dissatisfied by the verdict and told Jones that 'the jury have sought to secure you the clemency that probably would have been extended to you by the Crown if you had been convicted of murder and recommended to mercy'. The judge said that Jones had once been a 'man of creditable position' in the medical profession but he had turned to drink, which had degraded him and brought him to participate in such nefarious practices. Jones was sentenced to life imprisonment, which caused a sensation in court.[87] The doctor did not conform to the middle-class expectations of a man in his position, and he had disgraced himself both professionally and morally.

It is interesting to discover that Dr Timothy Jones had appeared in court nine years earlier to testify in a case of concealment of birth at Pontardulais (discussed in Chapter Five). As the man was drunk at the time, the examination could not proceed, so the case was dismissed for want of evidence.[88] Jones admitted to dependency on alcohol, therefore affecting his ability to retain patients, or to attend to new patients in a professional manner. Hence, when he was presented with an opportunity to benefit financially, he was unable to resist. In fact, Jones's desperation mirrored that of female abortionists who were also in straitened circumstances. Jones was sentenced to life imprisonment for committing an illegal operation in return for the paltry sum of 15s. 6d, while Muller escaped unscathed regardless of inadvertently causing his fiancée's death. It was reported that, enraged, Lily Challenger's father took the law into his own hands and attacked Muller with a whip at the railway station as he fled to Liverpool and from there to foreign parts.

Henry Richards was sentenced to five years' penal servitude for his part in the operation.[89] However, following an appeal against the judge's sentence, Richards was released from prison a few months later. The *Western Mail* commented that 'A jury, it seems, are able to reduce this charge of murder to that of manslaughter – and Jones, therefore, suffers a "lifer" but they cannot reduce a charge of murder to being an accessory after the fact of manslaughter – therefore, Richards is free.' It was also pointed out that the judge had made another error when he sentenced Richards 'illegally to five years'. The sentence was reduced to two years and later withdrawn following a review.[90] Jones had been handed down the maximum sentence of penal servitude allowed by the law, but this was later challenged because other abortionists had received lesser sentences in similar cases. Over time, there were frequent attempts to obtain an amendment to Jones's sentence. Finally, in May 1905, a petition for his release, extensively signed by many people in Swansea, was presented to the Home Office. It was reported that the intervention of some influential people, and the promise of relatives to take care of Jones, might secure his release after he had served the tenth year. Jones had been in prison for nine years at this point in time.[91] In November 1905, Jones was released from Parkhurst Prison, Isle of Wight.[92] It was reported that 'he had benefited greatly' since experiencing, what Jones termed, 'the sweet enjoyments of freedom'.[93]

Numerous press reports exposed both the dominance and the importance of support networks to women within local communities.

The police in Swansea had been strongly criticised for the lack of intervention in what was clearly a well-established network, although the authorities had secured a conviction against the infamous abortionist, Mrs Mary Rees, but not for long. Yet again, and seemingly unmoved by a lengthy prison term for her part in Mrs Collier's case in 1888, Mary Rees was linked to the death of Mrs Fanny Dorcas Parsons in 1898. Mrs Parsons was a friend who had visited Mary Rees regularly while in prison. It was reported that Mrs Parsons, accompanied by her friend Mrs Sarah Davies, went to Mary Rees's home, which was where the operation allegedly took place. Sarah Davies's performance at the inquest revealed how witnesses closed ranks and repeated their well-rehearsed lines of evidence. For instance, in the inquest Sarah Davies continually denied knowing Mary Rees. In response to questioning she replied, 'I had never seen the woman before with my eyes, if I was never to move from this chair, never before in my life.' Finally, under pressure, the woman admitted that she was acquainted with Mary Rees. This case resulted in an open verdict because the authorities were unable to prove that Mary Rees had carried out an illegal operation, although it was indicated that future proceedings would not be ruled out if further evidence came to light.[94] More to the point, if Mary Rees had adopted the same procedure as used in Mrs Collier's case, the doctor would have found little evidence to prove that an illegal operation with instruments had taken place.[95] Mary Rees, then Mary Hopkins, may well have operated on Emily Cope, from Bath, when she gave birth at the home of Dr Hopkins mentioned previously. If so, this might explain why there appeared to be no medical evidence to prove that an instrument had been used in that case. Despite a long-term prison sentence in Mrs Collier's case, Mary Rees was able to step back into her role as an abortionist, which also proved the woman's acceptance within the community. Moreover, the reported frequent visits of many women to her home confirmed that there was a demand for the abortionist's services at that time. However, in September 1901, the *Carmarthen Weekly Reporter* told of Mary Rees's death from consumption, describing her as 'The Female Doctor', daughter of the late Dr Hopkins of Carmarthen.[96]

Existing networks, such as those highlighted in the Parsons case, help to explain why the authorities found it difficult to enforce the law, especially when abortionists were as resilient to punishment as Mary Rees. It is obvious in most cases that individuals declined to inform on each other as soon as victims fell ill or died. What is significant about these local networks is that certain individuals were often connected to other abortion cases in some form or other. For instance, at Mrs Parsons' inquest it was put to Sarah Davies that she was associated with Dr Timothy Jones, the doctor imprisoned in Lily Challenger's case. It is interesting to note that Sarah Davies was also a witness at Elizabeth Christiansen's inquest for her involvement in the case. She lived next door to the Bird-in-Hand Hotel in Swansea, where Elizabeth Christiansen died. Sarah Davies was also responsible for calling in Dr Timothy Jones to attend the dying woman. The doctor was not implicated in Elizabeth Christiansen's death, but Jones had operated on her after the miscarriage. Evidence indicates that abortionists, and those who formed the support networks, knew the appropriate doctors to summon when victims fell ill in the hope that such cases would not be reported to the authorities. Of course, it was a different matter when the victims died and the doctors had to complete the death certificates.

There is only one case referred to in this chapter whereby an abortionist was convicted of murder and sentenced to death. This case related to twenty-five-year-old Agnes Lewis, the popular barmaid at the Victoria Hotel in Cardiff, mentioned previously, who died after undergoing an illegal operation alleged to have been performed by Mrs Elizabeth Thomas. The woman was a lodging-house keeper in very straitened circumstances at the time.[97] Her situation was exacerbated because her husband was in Australia, having deserted the family fourteen years earlier.[98] Elizabeth Thomas was from a respectable background, because her parents were known as 'quiet, steady, respectable people' from Roath.[99] At Glamorgan Assizes, Elizabeth Thomas was charged with the wilful murder of Agnes Lewis.[100] The post-mortem found that the young woman had given birth prematurely, which had been brought on by 'unnatural means'.[101] A month beforehand, a doctor had confirmed that Agnes Lewis was about four and a half months pregnant. The same doctor was called when she lay critically ill at the Tavistock Hotel under the care of a close friend, Louisa Cooper. The doctor found that Agnes Lewis had miscarried, and was suffering from pelvic cellulitis, peritonitis and septic poisoning. As the case concerned a well-liked barmaid, the seated public at the coroner's inquest consisted of medical men and a host of licensed victuallers and bar frequenters.[102] At the assizes, large crowds had gathered outside the court long before the doors opened, while the ladies' gallery 'was crammed with unusual rapidity'. Indeed, women were fighting on the steps in an attempt to gain admission, and many who secured seats were of the 'respectable class'.[103]

Elizabeth Thomas denied the charge and reportedly told a witness that 'I did not touch her' and 'I am blamed for her death, but there are others in it besides me.'[104] The defence counsel put it to the jury that Agnes Lewis had approached Elizabeth Thomas to perform the operation, but she refused. It was alleged that Agnes Lewis then went somewhere else for the operation and returned to stay with Elizabeth Thomas before being taken to the Tavistock Hotel by Louisa Cooper. Apparently Agnes Lewis informed one doctor that the operation had taken place at a nurse's house in Chepstow.[105] This might well have been the truth, because it was reported that she came from the village of Woolaston, situated six miles from Chepstow.[106] The reputed father of the unborn child was seldom mentioned in court cases, yet in this case the defence counsel contended that the real culprit was not in the dock. He did not know who this man was; he might be present in the court, or 'he might be hiding his head, as he ought to do, somewhere for the shame and ultimately the tragic death that was the result of his conduct'. Unfortunately, 'The man gratified his desires; the woman had to bear the burden and shame.' The judge also expressed 'his feelings of horror and disgust of a man who seduced a woman and thus indirectly brought about all this appalling calamity'. The jury could not concur on a verdict, and it seemed that Elizabeth Thomas would be acquitted at one point. However, the jury finally returned a guilty verdict with a strong recommendation to mercy. It was reported that when the judge asked Elizabeth Thomas if she had anything to say, she replied, 'I never did wrong. I never touched Agnes Lewis – I never touched her on my honour.'[107]

It was alleged in court that Louisa Cooper knew far more about the operation than she was prepared to divulge. In fact, she had previously stayed with Elizabeth Thomas for four or five months when her first baby was born. Louisa Cooper was known to have had four or five miscarriages. This case provides clear evidence of how the female network functioned to assist women in need but, more importantly, women in Elizabeth Thomas's position were often financially desperate, which exposed their own vulnerability as well. Women in similar circumstances to Agnes Lewis relied on someone like Elizabeth Thomas who, despite being convicted of a criminal act, maintained an essential role within the community. She claimed that others were involved, yet the individuals concerned appeared as witnesses for the prosecution. Therefore, Elizabeth Thomas had to accept sole responsibility for the young woman's death despite the fact that key witnesses withheld vital evidence. The stance taken by the press in reporting this case was notable, particularly the way that the defence counsel and the judge roundly condemned the father, whoever he may have been. Agnes Lewis's popularity within the community obviously held sway over the press reporters, which was in stark contrast to the reporting of Alice White's case. Elizabeth Thomas was known to participate in this kind of practice; therefore, she was not accorded any degree of sympathy for her alleged role in the death of Agnes Lewis.

Surprisingly, Dr Timothy Jones's name emerged in the press yet again. The press pointed out that the public found it difficult to understand the difference between the crime committed by Elizabeth Thomas and that of Dr Timothy Jones. The doctor, a 'professional and educated man was found guilty simply of manslaughter, whereas this ignorant woman has been convicted on the capital charge'.[108] Elizabeth Thomas was sentenced to death, but this was later commuted to penal servitude for life. The trial judge, Mr Justice Bucknill, visited her in prison afterwards. He 'expressed his sorrow for her and her children, and promised to do all he could for her'.[109] In August 1904, the Home Secretary had reportedly received information that supported the evidence put forward on Elizabeth Thomas's behalf.[110] As a consequence, the sentence was reduced to twelve years, while her good conduct secured a further remission of four years. Elizabeth Thomas was later released from Aylesbury Prison in December 1907.[111]

During the 1880s, Dr Hopkins, Mary Rees, Louisa Wilson and Mary Kew were charged with murder, but all were acquitted. This proves the jury's reluctance to convict the accused of wilful murder in cases of criminal abortion. Renowned for their nefarious practices, it is not surprising to find that Mary Kew, Mary Rees and Louisa Wilson were convicted upon indictment of the lesser charge of procuring an abortion, in much the same way as the lesser charge of concealment of birth affected the outcome in infanticide trials. The need to practise birth control amongst the working classes was met with opposition from the medical profession because it was considered it would promote immoral behaviour, particularly as illegal operations and the increasing use of abortifacients were both a social and health issue. Dr Timothy Jones and Elizabeth Thomas were the only abortionists to be convicted for causing the deaths of two women during the 1890s. Yet, there was no proof that Elizabeth Thomas had actually performed the operation. Bearing in mind that Agnes Lewis was clearly a well-liked young woman, and had also been employed at one of the best restaurants in Cardiff, it could be argued that Elizabeth Thomas was made a scapegoat because the other individuals who were party to the operation were summoned as prosecution witnesses.[112] The issues of gender, class and respectability were apparent in all ten cases, and definitely affected the outcome of criminal trials during these two decades.

'I never done such a thing'[113]: Abortion and the abortionist 1901–19

Abortion was an option for single women who had 'a mishap', while married women were more determined to control their own fertility and limit family size. Katie Fisher points out that at the beginning of the twentieth century, increasing numbers of married couples practised birth control, corresponding at the same time with the sustained decline in the average family size.[114] The middle classes had access to information on methods of birth control during this period, although doctors were reluctant to promote contraception amongst the working classes because it was considered that such freedom would lead to immorality.[115] It was also the case that contraceptives were affordable to the middle classes, yet the cost was often prohibitive for many working-class couples. Dr Richard Prichard, the medical officer for the Llandaff and Dinas Powis rural districts, argued in 1906 that, 'With the advancement of education and the greater demand for luxuries, there is a strong temptation to limit the family by voluntary control unless strong religious sentiments over-rule the iniquity of the practice.'[116] Religious sentiment did not seem to deter Reverend

Evan Jenkins from Garnant, Carmarthenshire. When Reverend Jenkins was told that his wife was expecting their third child, he obtained drugs to bring on an abortion. As the man was known to beat his wife, the court granted her an order of separation.[117]

The feminist movement campaigned extensively on a number of issues during this period, including birth control. This was apparent in 1914 when an article on pregnancy and feminism appeared in the *BMJ*. It stated:

> On the surface of the Woman's Movement floats the great vessel known as the *Vote*, and there are lots of little ships around it with sails trimmed to carry them into Franchise Harbour and Equal Representation Bay; but these things are only on the surface. There is underneath them a deep ground swell of discontent – in many cases well founded – of dissatisfaction with the life of womankind under certain circumstances, and of actual rebellion against the imposed self-sacrifice of the mother's lot.[118]

Repeated pregnancies and childbirth took their toll on women, both physically and mentally, not to mention the stress of another child to feed and clothe. As a physician obstetrician, Amand Routh disagreed with the use of birth control because he claimed that 'every method of artificial conception is harmful both in its physical and its moral effect'.[119] Routh's attitude was nothing out of the ordinary, as many medical practitioners were more concerned with curbing immoral behaviour amongst the working classes than encouraging birth control.

Half the criminal cases referred to in this chapter during the years 1884–1900 resulted in a conviction. However, that was not the case with eight criminal abortion trials recorded during 1901–19. The third part of this chapter addresses the reason why only one person was convicted of performing an illegal operation during this time period, even though four women died from complications associated with abortions.

Press coverage of the case against Mrs Henrietta Veall, from Cardiff, proves illuminating. In November 1908, it was alleged that Mrs Henrietta Veall had performed an illegal operation upon thirty-year-old Mrs Clara Lamprey, described as a 'quiet, respectable woman' with three children. Mrs Lamprey was encouraged to make a statement as her condition deteriorated following the alleged abortion. Mrs Veall was taken by the police to Mrs Lamprey's bedside, where the depositions were recorded in the presence of the relevant authorities. In response to the accusations, Mrs Veall claimed, 'I never done such a thing.' Naturally, the case caused a great deal of attention locally, and crowds gathered outside Mrs Lamprey's house, hoping to catch a glimpse of Mrs Veall in police custody. Mrs Lamprey eventually recovered from the operation.[120] Meanwhile, Mrs Veall was held in prison on remand from week to week until Mrs Lamprey had recovered sufficiently to attend court.[121] The *Cardiff Times* reported that, although still weak, Mrs Lamprey appeared in court for the first time stylishly dressed in a grey outfit wearing a brown fur boa and brown hat.[122] While such descriptions appear to be completely irrelevant to any case, the press usually reported on the attire worn by both men and women charged with the offence, and some witnesses did not go unnoticed either. A person's attire was thought to reflect the wearer's respectability, or lack of it in some cases. As an accomplice to the criminal act, perhaps Mrs Lamprey wished to impress upon the court that she was a respectable married woman and dressed accordingly. At Glamorgan Assizes it was pointed out that Mrs Lamprey, a 'comparatively poor woman', had paid Mrs Veall eighteen shillings for the operation. The defence counsel contended that Mrs Lamprey had sent for Mrs Veall in order to make a 'shameless confession'. Referring to Mrs Lamprey's statement, the defence argued that 'One who could make such a confession might not be believed unless there was sufficient corroboration, and he submitted that in this case there was no conclusive corroboration.' Despite efforts by the defence, Mrs Veall was convicted and sentenced to three years' imprisonment. In summing-up, the judge stated that 'it was a very serious case, because a poor woman was nearly killed'. However, a number of abortionists had been acquitted even in cases that resulted in the victims' deaths.

Respectability played a substantial role in determining the outcome of criminal trials. An offender's perceived respectability increased the probability of an acquittal, although female abortionists known to have once been respectable were dealt with less favourably. Mrs Veall was known to the police as 'a respectable woman, but she had given way to drink, and for some time had been suspected of this kind of thing'.[123] Therefore, based on police evidence, the woman did not conform to the prevailing ideology of respectability and morality. Indeed, Mrs Veall represented the typical working-class abortionist, whose motive to perform illegal operations was as a means to earn a living. Likewise, Mrs Lamprey's decision to have an abortion was due to financial constraints. Hence, economic pressures forced both women to be complicit in a criminal act, but the responsibility for performing the operation lay with Mrs Veall and not with the accomplice, Mrs Lamprey. Indeed, Mrs Veall risked imprisonment for what appeared to be just eighteen shillings, while Mrs Lamprey no doubt went on to suffer further miscarriages because financial circumstances dictated it.

Given the support of female networks, abortionists were predominantly married women. Then again, there were fewer male abortionists because doctors were less likely to perform illegal operations. In March 1910, Dr Arthur Preece Walters was indicted at Glamorgan Assizes for the wilful murder of Mary Florence Lewis in December 1909. It was reported that the young woman, accompanied by her friend Mrs Lewis, visited Walters in a room that he occupied at Pontypridd. Female friends often provided single women with somewhere to stay after illegal abortions rather than patients returning home and risking detection. Mrs Rees, a sister to Mrs Lewis, provided her with a bed following the medical procedure, and soon after the visit to Dr Walters, Florence Lewis gave birth prematurely. It was reported that Mrs Lewis's husband buried the fully-formed baby in the garden, although it was exhumed later by police.[124] Three weeks later Florence Lewis died from peritonitis and blood poisoning, although the superficial post-mortem could not prove that an illegal operation had taken place. In his evidence, Dr Wilcox from the Home Office explained about 'the danger of blood-poisoning setting in if a woman travelled on a cold day so soon as the deceased did, after the birth'. Aided by the doctor's testimony, Walters was acquitted of wilful murder because there was no conclusive medical evidence to prove that an illegal operation had taken place.[125] Therefore, Walters was acquitted again on a second charge of illegally using instruments.

Dr Arthur Preece Walters faced a third indictment for performing another illegal operation. Mrs Hannah Polsford had also visited Walters in November 1909 to purchase medicine to induce a miscarriage, but it proved ineffective. The first step taken by a number of women in response to unwanted pregnancies was to self-administer drugs. However, the ineffectiveness of certain drugs meant that women returned to undergo illegal operations, which proved to be far more lucrative for abortionists. Mrs Polsford consulted Walters once more and agreed to an operation, but she was taken ill soon after the miscarriage. The woman repeatedly denied to her doctor that her condition was the result of an operation, although Mrs Polsford was prompted to confess her involvement with Walters after reading about the death of Florence Lewis in the local newspaper. Upholding his professional duty, the doctor reported Walters to the police, and he was subsequently arrested.

At Merthyr Police Court, Mrs Polsford was described as 'a very respectable married woman, she had had children before, and it would be a matter of pain to her and her relatives if her name was published'. The press were requested to refrain from publishing her name, and this was agreed.[126] Even though Mrs Polsford was an accomplice, she still retained her anonymity. At Glamorgan Assizes, Mrs Polsford said, 'I do not approve of giving evidence.' She continued, 'I went for medicine, and I do not want to incriminate myself.' Evidently, Mrs Polsford was advised by her lawyer how to respond to questioning. The witness, Mrs Davies, was equally reticent and said that 'She saw nothing more than a bottle of medicine given to Mrs Polsford.' The prosecution asked if Mrs Polsford could be treated as a hostile witness, but the judge pointed out to her that, 'You are not bound to give evidence if you think it will incriminate yourself.' As a result, the prosecution was unable to proceed with the case, and Walters was acquitted yet again.[127]

For seven weeks, prior to his arrest, a friend allowed Walters to lodge with him because he was 'in very poor circumstances' and also permitted him to use a back room to see callers and receive letters.[128] When arrested, Walters was found with an instrument in his pocket, while two others were discovered at his lodgings. If Walters was in the habit of carrying medical instruments in his pocket, then it is of no surprise that women were suffering from life-threatening infections following his illegal operations. Moreover, claims were made that Dr Walters 'was not a specified practitioner'.[129] The rumour proved correct, because three years later it came to light that his real name was Richard Harrison. In

1913, he was charged with falsely issuing death certificates under the assumed identity of A. P. Walters. The real Dr Arthur P. Walters was present at Harrison's trial at Glamorgan Assizes.[130] The judge sentenced Harrison to twelve months' hard labour. In fact, Harrison had previously served a twelve-month sentence, with hard labour, for a similar offence at Maidstone.[131] It was ironic that Harrison was acquitted of wilful murder and performing illegal operations, yet he served twelve months' hard labour for issuing false death certificates.

The illegal activities of doctors like Richard Harrison, alias Arthur Preece Walters, and Dr Timothy Jones, prompted the Select Committee on Midwives' Registration to comment that in cases of criminal abortion, 'it is only a very inferior class of medical man who would yield to a temptation of that kind'. Dr Farquharsen remarked, 'It is a matter of hunger more than morality.'[132] Evidence proved that doctors also fell upon hard times. Doctors often made their living based on reputation as well as medical skill. Therefore, once a doctor's character was called into question, he gained a reputation of another kind, rendering it difficult to secure both patients and an income.

Mrs Polsford's initial response was not to incriminate herself. Did the desire for anonymity at the police court, and her refusal to provide evidence at the assizes, mean that the doctor who laid evidence had betrayed the woman's confidence? Or was it the case that the doctor had been obliged, as part of his professional duty, to report Walters to the police, being confident that Mrs Polsford would not be charged with an offence? Doctors faced the dilemma of whether to maintain 'professional secrecy' for their patients' sake, or to report the crime to the police. John Campbell, a medical man, explained that the doctor is 'both a citizen and a trusted advisor to the patient'. Campbell argued that as citizens, doctors were bound to prevent criminal offences such as abortion, but at the same time they must not break a patient's confidentiality. He maintained that when a doctor attended a woman who was dying as a result of an illegal operation, he was bound to secrecy, but upon the woman's death the bond no longer existed. The coroner could be informed, and the abortionist brought to justice. Campbell also pointed out that by maintaining secrecy the doctor was actually shielding the criminal who committed the offence – the woman who was a 'willing victim' – as were those who supported her throughout the illegal procedure. As a doctor, his duty was 'to save life regardless of the moral character of the patient'.[133]

Gender and class issues were inherent in all abortion cases, but the case against Mrs Anna Lloyd in 1913 illustrates the inequalities. When Mrs Lloyd appeared before the magistrates, the press reported that 'the statements made were of so unpleasant a description that we have been compelled to refrain from giving them in detail'.[134] Therefore, it is not surprising to find that the magistrates requested that all women should leave the court. There was some applause at this announcement.[135] Four locally well-known persons from Swansea were indicted, but it was thirty-four-year-old Mrs Anna Lloyd who was charged with 'feloniously and unlawfully using a certain instrument upon Annie May Lewis of Morriston with intent to procure a miscarriage'. This case was unusual because there were three other individuals charged with aiding and abetting in the alleged offence, namely Mrs Harriet Stephens, Mrs Hannah Ankers and Glyn Morris. The three were also charged with unlawfully, wickedly and maliciously conspiring together to bring about the offence.[136] Eighteen-year-old Annie May Lewis was a single woman who worked in the sorting room and cleaned the office at Morriston Tinplate Works. Glyn Morris, a married man, was an accountant and employed at the same tinplate works. It was alleged that, in March 1913, while Annie May Lewis was cleaning the office, Morris took advantage of his position and had 'improper relations' with the girl that resulted in pregnancy.[137]

Annie May Lewis had previously consulted two doctors; one prescribed medicine, but the other doctor refused to have anything to do with her. In similar circumstances to those witnessed in the Lily Challenger case, Morris accompanied the girl to consult herbalist John Thompson on four separate occasions. He instructed the herbalist 'to do the best he could for her', and that 'he did not care how much it cost'. Later, when the medicine failed, Morris was reported to say that he knew a woman in Swansea who would 'put her right'. Annie May Lewis alleged that Mrs Lloyd had performed the illegal operation on her at the White Hart Hotel, where she was to remain for a few days to allow time for the miscarriage to occur. She began to feel unwell after the operation; meanwhile, her worried father was trying to locate her whereabouts. Glyn Morris and Mrs Lloyd panicked. As part of the cover-up, Mrs Lloyd took Annie May Lewis home to fetch clothes with the excuse that she had offered the girl employment; the intention was for both to return to the White Hart Hotel. It was alleged that beforehand, Mrs Lloyd had told Annie May Lewis, 'If you die with pain don't say I did anything to you to-day because I would get 14 years, and Mrs Ankers and Mrs Stephens would get seven years each.' Annie May Lewis's mother refused to let her return with Mrs Lloyd as planned, and that night she was seriously ill as a result of the operation.

It was common for support networks to close ranks when individuals were arrested or called to testify in court, particularly in cases where victims had died. Even as victims lay dying, some were very cautious not to implicate themselves, or anyone else, including the abortionists. Annie May Lewis survived the operation, and press reports show that as each person was arrested they incriminated each other. Mrs Stephens denied any knowledge of an operation and said, 'Aren't you going to bring Mrs Ankers into it?' Mrs Ankers was later arrested and she asked, 'Is Glyn Morris caught?'[138] When arrested Mrs Lloyd said, 'I think it is a shame that Mr Glyn Morris should tamper with a little girl like that, and bring other people into trouble.' The woman also asked, 'Is Glyn Morris locked up?'[139] The women were adamant that Morris must accept responsibility for his actions.

Women assisted each other in times of crisis, but not without taking risks. Having said that, compared to the estimated number of women who resorted to abortion, perhaps the danger was not as great as one might expect. As an accomplice to the crime, the judge cautioned Annie May Lewis in court: 'It is my duty to tell you that if your evidence is what I understand it is going to be, you are equally guilty of the crime which is alleged against all these four people. That being so, you are not bound to give any evidence unless you are so pleased.'[140] The fact that four offenders were charged, instead of one individual, meant that each person was represented in court. As a consequence, the defence lawyers intimidated Annie May Lewis in the witness box and characterised the girl as a liar. The defence counsel pointed out that Mrs Lloyd was not a poor woman, and asked why would she perform the operation and 'run the risk of prosecution for the paltry sum of three guineas'.[141] The defence also added that Mrs Lloyd's husband was 'a man of utmost respectability, employed in an important public office in the town'.[142] A position which no doubt carried with it some influence. After a three-day trial, extensively covered by the press, Mrs Anna Lloyd was acquitted and the charge of conspiracy against the others was not proceeded with. All four were discharged, and 'heartily congratulated by their friends'. As the acquitted left the court amidst a large crowd, there was 'a good deal of booing, chiefly on the part of the women'.[143] The magistrates maintained that prosecution of the case was justifiable, and it does beg the question why each person incriminated the others as they were arrested in turn if no crime had been committed. The defence counsel summed up that Annie May Lewis had lied about the operation, although it seems from the evidence available to us that Mrs Lloyd was probably culpable, and she and Glyn Morris had conspired to perform the operation. The girl had been dangerously ill, and the doctor confirmed that an illegal operation had taken place. Yet as a working-class girl defending herself in court against eminent lawyers who represented well-known middle-class individuals, Annie May Lewis had little chance of retaining her moral character. Morris had abused his position to take advantage of her sexually and acted with impunity.

Most abortionists were unqualified, though certain doctors were not averse to performing illegal operations. However, chemists also played a considerable role. One case heard at the Glamorgan Assizes, at the same time as that of Mrs Anna Lloyd's, involved a fully-qualified Cardiff chemist, Ernest George Watts. The man was charged with performing illegal operations upon Elizabeth Lloyd in January 1913. Before the woman gave evidence, the judge told her that as an accomplice there was no need to answer questions that would incriminate her. The chemist denied the charge. Watts denied that 'he had done anything more than examine the girl twice'. Watts was acquitted and discharged from court.[144] In his evidence to the Select Committee on Midwives' Registration, Dr Farquharson claimed that some abortionists were failed medical students, who had trained for a year or so and then became chemists' assistants, and from there turned into 'depraved persons'. He also pointed out that even though chemists were registered, it did not prevent them from 'selling oceans and tons of medicine each year for the purpose of causing abortion'.[145] Many unprincipled chemists and herbalists were charlatans, because they fraudulently sold medicines for the purpose of inducing miscarriages. John Thompson, the herbalist in Mrs Anna Lloyd's case, testified against Glyn Morris. As a result, Thompson exposed himself as a charlatan, which subsequently ruined his business. Under cross-examination, Thompson admitted that Morris purchased medicine to procure a miscarriage; therefore, he was implicated for knowingly selling it for that purpose. He denied keeping medicines for illegal purposes.[146] These two chemists were neither doctors nor typical abortionists. It was evident that some chemists were positioned comfortably alongside abortionists, and they were often renowned locally to 'put a woman right'.

The questions of morality and respectability were usually confined to cases concerning single women who had survived illegal operations. However, these particular issues were evident in a court case concerning a married mother-of-four, because her alleged lack of morality had a negative impact on her case. In 1919 Mrs Esther Davies died as a result of an illegal operation while her husband was serving in HM Forces abroad. The operation was reportedly performed by a certified midwife, Mrs Mary Lavinia Beynon, the wife of a police inspector with the Borough Police Force. Mrs Davies owned a motor car, and worked as a voluntary driver for the Ministry of Munitions at Swansea. The main witness in the case was her close friend, Nurse Winifred Poulson. The two women frequently went away on trips in the motor car, and they sometimes met with gentlemen friends on their excursions. Of course, this behaviour was immediately seized upon by the defence when Nurse Poulson was asked whether going away with Mrs Davies on weekend trips with gentlemen was a respectable way to behave.[147] The woman's respectability was questioned even further when a police detective alleged that Mrs Davies 'had led a very gay life and her reputation was very unenviable'. Her alleged immorality was brought into question and, in doing so, placed an element of doubt on whether Nurse Poulson's testimony could be relied upon.

Three doctors provided medical evidence in this case, and all agreed that Mrs Davies's condition was 'consistent with an ordinary miscarriage, followed by neglect'. When Dr David Davies visited Mrs Davies, he was informed by her that she had suffered a miscarriage at Swansea the previous Friday. The doctor assumed that it had been procured, owing to septicaemia and the severity of her condition.[148] The pathologist at Swansea Hospital confirmed that death was caused by general peritonitis and septicaemia, and that there was no direct evidence of a miscarriage brought on by the use of any instruments.[149] Doctors were expected to maintain 'professional secrecy'; however, Mrs Davies's doctor told the court that he had 'treated her for a certain disease', which the defence pointed out was when her husband was away serving in the army. Once this ambiguous statement was published in the local press, it might have been deduced that the woman had been treated for a sexually transmitted disease, therefore damaging her reputation even further. At Swansea Police Court, the defence counsel pointed out that 'there was no such jury in this country convicting the accused upon such evidence given by the prosecution'.[150] The defence argued that Mrs Beynon was a highly respectable midwife and if she was put on trial at Glamorgan Assizes she would be acquitted, so he asked the magistrates not to proceed. The bench found that there was a *prima facie* case; therefore, Mrs Beynon was committed for trial.

When Mary Lavinia Beynon was acquitted of wilful murder at Glamorgan Assizes, the verdict was received with applause, which was immediately suppressed. The press reports indicated that Mrs Beynon was 'heartily congratulated by many of her friends upon the result'. The judge stated that, 'I have much pleasure in saying that I entirely agree with the verdict.' He said, 'I don't believe that you had anything to do with it.' From the outset, it was unlikely that Mrs Beynon would be convicted of wilful murder, even if she did perform the operation. Nurse Poulson was a single woman summoned to court to testify against the person alleged to have committed the offence, yet she left court with a slur on her own character. Referring to the defence counsel, Nurse Poulson said, 'after taking my character away I have lost everything, my practice and my home'.[151] The fact that Mrs Davies's husband was away defending the country during the war, while she enjoyed weekend trips with gentlemen friends, obviously had a negative impact on the case. Given that her husband was in Russia, and he had not been home for three years, Mrs Davies probably had no option but to terminate the pregnancy for fear of the consequences.

During the years 1901–19 there were seven cases of illegal operations, one case of self-induced miscarriage and another concerning self-administration of drugs to procure a miscarriage.

However, Mrs Henrietta Veall was the only abortionist to be convicted of the charges made against her. Indeed, had she maintained her respectability and not turned to drink, then an acquittal would have been likely, especially as Mrs Lamprey survived the operation. After the devastating loss of life during the First World War, infant life preservation was even more important, but that was not reflected in the verdicts as a deterrent. It was evident that most juries had no desire to convict abortionists of wilful murder, particularly as women were both 'willing victims' and accomplices.

Conclusion

This chapter has scrutinised newspaper accounts of criminal trials as a means to investigate and understand the practice of abortion within Welsh communities. Indeed, the powers of the press should not be underestimated as a valuable source for social historians for this subject area. The reporting of criminal trials was extensive, uncovering a wealth of detailed information: far more than has been addressed in this chapter. It is evident that doctors were reluctant to promote birth control amongst the working classes, although the medical profession acknowledged that married women sought the right to control their own fertility to limit family size. The press reports revealed that abortionists, supported by female networks, operated in Welsh communities quite openly. Amand Routh maintained that criminal abortion was 'more probable where the women are unmarried';[152] however, the particular cases considered in this chapter indicate that there was no difference between the numbers of married and single women who resorted to abortion. Based on twenty-one cases in total, the deaths of twelve women occurred as a result of abortion, of whom six were married, one woman was reported to be a widow, and five women were single. A total of nine women survived the illegal operations, of whom four were married, and five women were known to be single.

Men had long coerced women to induce miscarriages, particularly in the case of single women. The common perception was that only promiscuous single women sought abortions, where the operation took place in a dimly lit room or in a doctor's surgery in some back street. Yet, half of those who resorted to abortion were reported in the press to be respectable married women who induced miscarriages, often with their husbands' knowledge, and some routinely used abortifacients to 'keep them regular'. Therefore, the gradual shift in attitudes regarding birth control resulted in married couples making joint decisions to limit family size, which eased the family's economic burden. Given the nature of illegal operations and the risk to women's health, abortion was later perceived less as a criminal offence than as one that should be dealt with as a medical issue. The early decades of the twentieth century witnessed a change in middle-class attitudes regarding criminal abortion, and this might explain the lack of convictions during 1901–19 compared to the last two decades of the nineteenth century.

The issues of gender, class and respectability feature considerably in abortion cases, and it is no surprise to discover that the alleged sexual improprieties of most single women were evident for all to see. In complete contrast, men's sexual deviances remained invisible, as did their identities and presence in court in the majority of cases. The evidence indicates that more women were convicted for performing illegal operations than men. In fact, Dr Timothy Jones was the only man convicted of the offence, although nine men were charged altogether, including four doctors in the period under investigation. It is also the case that poorer female abortionists, such as Mrs Mary Kew and Mrs Elizabeth Thomas, were more likely to be convicted, when compared to the acquittals of Mrs Anna Lloyd and Mrs Lavinia Beynon. It was also the case that female abortionists were married women, therefore seemingly strengthening the network via experience and knowledge in such matters. No abortionists, apart from Mrs Henrietta Veall, were convicted in the period 1901–19. Dr Timothy Jones and Mrs Veall were known to drink and both had made a habit of performing illegal operations. Persistent offenders, such as Mary Kew and Mary Rees, were often under police surveillance; hence, when the evidence was stacked against them, the women were finally convicted of the offences.

It is noteworthy that considerable numbers of respectable women crammed into the public galleries when abortionists stood trial, even though such proceedings would have been considered inappropriate. This was reflected in some cases when all women, and children in Mary Kew's case, were ordered out of court; a frustrating experience given the local interest and the difficulty of gaining court access in the first instance. Women were vociferous, both inside and outside of the courtroom, and many eagerly voiced their opinions at the verdicts. In fact, the public response in court was also a measure of feeling for the accused or, indeed, some witnesses, and such behaviour could possibly have influenced the juries in certain cases.

There is no evidence to indicate that abortionists had any intention to murder the victims, since the motivation to perform the operations arose from the desire to gain financial rewards only. Death occurred as a result of ignorance and negligence, not malicious intent. However, procuring a miscarriage was a felony. If a woman died the law decreed that it amounted to murder, yet the jury was reluctant to convict on a capital offence. Elizabeth Thomas was sentenced to death, although it could be argued that the sentence was disproportionate in comparison to the verdicts reached in other abortion trials, particularly as establishing proof was crucial in her case. Based on the evidence in the majority of cases, manslaughter would have been a more appropriate indictment rather than the capital offence of wilful murder. Juries might have been more inclined to secure a conviction for manslaughter in such cases. This tendency is obvious in cases of concealment of birth and infanticide, because juries were reluctant to convict women of murder, or even the lesser charge of concealment of birth.

In most cases of criminal abortion there were a number of accomplices, including the woman herself. Therefore, some abortionists were punished as a visible deterrent, while other participants escaped unscathed. Obviously, due to its incredibly personal nature, and illegal procedure, the extent of the practice during this period will remain hidden. However, despite the risks, abortion remained an option for single women and a means to avoid the unenviable situation of unmarried motherhood.

Notes

1 *Western Mail*, 25 May 1888, p. 3.

2 *South Wales Echo*, 21 November 1899, p. 2.

3 Angus McLaren, *Birth Control in Nineteenth-Century England* (London, 1978), p. 231.

4 McLaren, *Birth Control*, p. 231.

5 Barbara Brookes, *Abortion in England, 1900–1967* (Kent, 1988), p. 54.

6 'The Traffic in Abortifacients', *The British Medical Journal*, 1/1987 (14 January 1899), 110–11 (p. 111).
7 Michael Thomson, 'Abortion Law and Professional Boundaries', *Social & Legal Studies*, 22/2 (2013), 191–210 (p. 196).
8 McLaren, *Birth Control*, p. 243.
9 *Baner ac Amserau Cymru*, 12 August 1896, p. 2.
10 Report from His Majesty's Commissioners of Inquiry into the Administration and Practical Operation of the Poor Laws (1834), PP (HMSO, London), p. 180a.
11 Françoise Barret-Ducrocq, *Love in the Time of Victoria* (London, 1991), p. 129.
12 *The Cambrian*, 13 March 1896, p. 3.
13 'The Traffic in Abortifacients', 110.
14 Kate Fisher, *Birth Control, Sex, and Marriage in Britain 1918–1960* (Oxford, 2006), p. 118.
15 Shani D'Cruze and Louise A. Jackson, *Women, Crime and Justice in England since 1600* (Basingstoke, 2009), pp. 82–3.
16 An Act to consolidate and amend the Statute law of England and Ireland relating to Offences Against the Person 1861, Vic. 24 & 25, c. 100, Section 58.
17 Offences Against the Person Act 1861, Section 59.
18 Brookes, *Abortion in England.*
19 Thomson, 'Abortion Law and Professional Boundaries', 192.
20 Causes of Death in Registration Counties, Seventy-first Annual report of the registrar-general (1908) BPP 1909 XI [Cd.4961] 397, www.histpop.org, accessed 26/05/2018.
21 Table A: Assizes and Quarter Sessions 1893–1910: Number of Persons for Trial and Nature of Offences in Each Year From 1893–1910, Judicial Statistics, England and Wales, Part 1 Criminal Statistics (1910).
22 *Western Mail*, 26 July 1888, p. 3.
23 Amand Routh, 'A Lecture on Ante-Natal Hygiene: Its Influence Upon Infantile Mortality', *The British Medical Journal*, 1/2772 (14 February 1914), 355–63 (p. 357).
24 *The Cambrian*, 8 July 1898, p. 2.
25 *Y Celt*, 21 October 1892, p. 2.
26 *Baner ac Amserau Cymru*, 12 August 1896, p. 2.
27 *The Carmarthen Weekly Reporter*, 11 August 1910, p. 1.
28 Report from the Select Committee on Patent Medicines (1914) PP (HMSO, London), p. 239.
29 'Abortion and Child Murder', *The British Medical Journal*, 2/1825 (21 December 1895), 1583.
30 J. Rutherford Hill, 'Criminal Abortion', *The British Medical Journal*, 2/1978 (26 November 1898), 1655.
31 'The Traffic in Abortifacients', 110.
32 'The Traffic in Abortifacients', 110.
33 Barret-Ducrocq, *Love in the Time of Victoria*, p. 129.
34 *Western Mail*, 23 June 1894, p. 5.
35 *Carmarthen Journal*, 25 March 1892, p. 8.
36 *Western Mail*, 25 January 1892, p. 5.
37 *Carmarthen Journal*, 25 March 1892, p. 8.
38 *Western Mail*, 26 January 1892, p. 7.

39 *Carmarthen Journal*, 25 March 1892, p. 8.
40 *Rhondda Leader*, 26 July 1919, p. 1.
41 *Western Mail*, 26 July 1888, p. 3.
42 *Western Mail*, 26 July 1888, p. 3.
43 *Western Mail*, 16 July 1884, p. 3.
44 *Western Mail*, 6 November 1884, p. 4.
45 *Western Mail*, 30 July 1884, p. 4.
46 *Western Mail*, 6 November 1884, p. 4.
47 Angus McLaren, 'Illegal Operations: Women, Doctors, and Abortion, 1886–1939', *Journal of Social History*, 26/4 (1993), 797–816 (p. 805).
48 *Western Mail*, 25 May 1888, p. 3.
49 'The Duties of Medical Practitioners in Cases of Criminal Abortion', *The British Medical Journal*, 1/2875 (5 February 1916), 206–7 (p. 207).
50 *Western Mail*, 25 May 1888, p. 3.
51 *South Wales Echo*, 6 June 1888, p. 4.
52 *Western Mail*, 25 May 1888, p. 3.
53 *South Wales Echo*, 6 June 1888, p. 4.
54 *South Wales Echo*, 7 August 1888, p. 4.
55 *Cardiff Times*, 11 August 1888, p. 7.
56 *South Wales Echo*, 14 March 1889, p. 3.
57 *South Wales Echo*, 1 February 1889, p. 2.
58 *South Wales Echo*, 14 March 1889, p. 3.
59 Patricia Knight, 'Women and Abortion in Victorian and Edwardian England', *History Workshop*, 4 (1977), 57–69 (p. 62).
60 *Cardiff Times*, 17 May 1879, p. 2.
61 *Western Mail*, 25 May 1888, p. 3.
62 *Western Mail*, 27 July 1888, p. 1.
63 *Western Mail*, 19 December 1888, p. 2.
64 *Western Mail*, 11 June 1888, p. 1.
65 *Western Mail*, 19 December 1888, p. 2.
66 *Western Mail*, 18 August 1888, p. 3.
67 *Western Mail*, 19 December 1888, p. 2.
68 *South Wales Daily News*, 20 December 1888, p. 2.
69 West Glamorgan Archive Services (hereafter WGAS), Swansea Prison Nominal Register, 2/1a, April 1887–August 1889, p. 474.
70 *South Wales Daily News*, 20 December 1888, p. 2.
71 WGAS, Swansea Prison Nominal Register, 2/1a, p. 308.
72 *South Wales Daily News*, 20 December 1888, p. 2.
73 *Western Mail*, 5 December 1888, p. 4.
74 *Western Mail*, 20 December 1888, p. 2.
75 *South Wales Daily News*, 20 December 1888, p. 2.
76 *South Wales Daily Post*, 9 March 1896, p. 3.
77 *South Wales Daily Post,* 6 March 1896, p. 3.
78 *South Wales Daily Post*, 9 March 1896, p. 3.
79 J. A. Banks, *Victorian Values* (London, 1981), pp. 85–6.
80 Carol Smart, *Women, Crime and Criminology* (London, 1977), p. 117.

81 Norman S. Kerr, *Female Intemperance* (London, 1880), p. 8.
82 *The Cambrian*, 13 March 1896, p. 3.
83 *South Wales Daily Post*, 9 March 1896, p. 3.
84 *Western Mail*, 13 October 1899, p. 5.
85 *South Wales Echo*, 20 November 1896, p. 2.
86 *Reynolds's Newspaper*, 13 September 1896, p. 1.
87 *South Wales Echo*, 21 November 1896, p. 2.
88 *South Wales Daily News*, 3 November 1887, p. 2.
89 *South Wales Echo*, 21 November 1896, p. 2.
90 *Western Mail*, 5 March 1897, p. 4.
91 *Cardiff Times*, 20 May 1905, p. 7.
92 *The Cambrian*, 17 November 1905, p. 4.
93 *Weekly Mail*, 25 November 1905, p. 10.
94 *Evening Express*, 18 February 1898, p. 3.
95 *Western Mail*, 19 December 1888, p. 2.
96 *Carmarthen Weekly Reporter*, 20 September 1901, p. 1.
97 *Western Mail*, 17 October 1899, p. 3.
98 *South Wales Echo*, 21 November 1899, p. 2.
99 *Western Mail*, 17 October 1899, p. 3.
100 *Western Mail*, 21 November 1899, p. 6.
101 *Western Mail*, 13 October 1899, p. 5.
102 *Western Mail*, 17 October 1899, p. 3.
103 *Western Mail*, 21 November 1899, p. 6.
104 *South Wales Echo*, 20 November 1899, p. 3.
105 *South Wales Echo*, 21 November 1899, p. 2.
106 *South Wales Daily News*, 27 October 1899, p. 4.
107 *South Wales Echo*, 21 November 1899, p. 2.
108 *South Wales Echo*, 21 November 1899, p. 2.
109 *The Cambrian*, 13 December 1907, p. 2.
110 *Cardiff Times*, 6 August 1904, p. 3.
111 *The Cambrian*, 13 December 1907, p. 2.
112 *Western Mail*, 13 October 1899, p. 5.
113 *The Cardiff Times*, 14 November 1908, p. 6.
114 Fisher, *Birth Control*, p. 1.
115 For a general overview on birth control see Brookes, *Abortion in England*; Fisher, *Birth Control*; Knight, 'Women and Abortion'; McLaren, *Birth Control*; McLaren, 'Illegal Operations'; Angus McLaren, 'Women's Work and Regulation of Family Size: the question of abortion in the nineteenth century', *History Workshop*, 4 (1977), 70–81; Angus McLaren, 'Abortion in England, 1890–1914', *Victorian Studies*, 20/4 (1977), 379–400; Angus McLaren, 'Contraception and the Working Classes: The Social Ideology of the English Birth Control Movement in Its Early Years', *Comparative Studies in Society and History*, 18/2 (1976), 236–51; R. Sauer, 'Infanticide and abortion in nineteenth-century Britain', *Population Studies*, 32/1 (March, 1978), 81–93.
116 *Weekly Mail*, 14 April 1906, p. 4.
117 *Western Mail*, 13 February 1899, p. 6.

118 'Pregnancy and Feminism', *The British Medical Journal*, 2/2772 (14 February 1914), 355.
119 Routh, 'A Lecture on Ante-Natal Hygiene', 356.
120 *The Cardiff Times*, 14 November 1908, p. 6.
121 *Weekly Mail*, 12 December 1908, p. 1.
122 *The Cardiff Times*, 16 January 1909, p. 6.
123 *Weekly Mail*, 3 April 1909, p. 3.
124 *Merthyr Express*, 26 February 1910, p. 9.
125 *Weekly Mail*, 19 March 1910, p. 7.
126 *Merthyr Express*, 5 March 1910, p. 9.
127 *Weekly Mail*, 19 March 1910, p. 7.
128 *Merthyr Express*, 26 February 1910, p. 9.
129 *Evening Express*, 18 February 1910, p. 3.
130 *Rhondda Leader*, 19 July 1913, p. 7.
131 *Cambria Daily Leader*, 17 July 1913, p. 6.
132 Report from the Select Committee on Midwives' Registration (1892), PP (HMSO, London), p. 31.
133 John Campbell, 'The Position of the Medical Practitioner Called in to Attend a Case of Procured Abortion', *The British Medical Journal*, 2/3180 (10 December 1921), 985.
134 *Cambria Daily Leader*, 9 June 1913, p. 3.
135 *Cambria Daily Leader*, 18 June 1913, p. 6.
136 *Cambria Daily Leader*, 25 July 1913, p. 5.
137 *Cambria Daily Leader*, 9 June 1913, p. 3.
138 *Cambria Daily Leader*, 25 July 1913, p. 5.
139 *Cambria Daily Leader*, 18 June 1913, p. 6.
140 *Cambria Daily Leader*, 25 July 1913, p. 5.
141 *Cambria Daily Leader*, 28 July 1913, p. 5.
142 *Cambria Daily Leader*, 26 May 1913, p. 13.
143 *Cambria Daily Leader*, 29 July 1913, p. 3.
144 *Cambria Daily Leader*, 24 July 1913, p. 5.
145 Report from the Select Committee on Midwives' Registration, p. 31.
146 *Cambria Daily Leader*, 25 July 1913, p. 5.
147 *South Wales Weekly Post*, 13 September 1919, p. 2.
148 *South Wales Weekly Post*, 20 September 1919, p. 2.
149 *South Wales Weekly Post*, 8 November 1919, p. 1.
150 *South Wales Weekly Post*, 20 September 1919, p. 2.
151 *South Wales Weekly Post*, 8 November 1919, p. 1.
152 Routh, 'A Lecture on Ante-Natal Hygiene', 356.

Chapter Four

'The insanity of reproduction'[1]: Insane motherhood and parental child murder

In February 1879, thirty-year-old Annie was charged with the wilful murder of her eight-week-old infant. Annie's motive, however, was not desperation, shame or poverty, because she was the middle-class wife of a ship's captain from Llanelli. In this case, Annie was suffering from an attack of insanity associated with childbirth, which was recognised at the time as 'puerperal insanity' or 'puerperal mania'. The condition was acute, and the symptoms normally developed during the early days or weeks after childbirth. The commonly recognised symptoms exhibited by the mother included incessant talking, incoherent speech, an excited temperament and a wild-looking expression. It was also possible for mothers to suffer from insanity at a later stage following childbirth, which was generally linked to prolonged spells of lactation and diagnosed at the time as 'lactational insanity'. This form of attack was melancholic in nature, whereas the symptoms of 'puerperal insanity' could be both manic and melancholic.[2] The mothers who suffered from the melancholic form were depressed and emotional, and often complained of 'feeling lost'. They were restless and lacked sleep; they refused food, had little to say and were affected by memory loss. The more disturbing symptoms included suicidal and homicidal impulses, delusions, hallucinations and the hearing of voices. Cases of child murder as a result of 'puerperal insanity' or 'lactational insanity' were rare in comparison to the number of asylum admissions for the same disorders. Yet, the consequences were devastating for the few mothers who succumbed to homicidal impulses and killed their children while insane.

The provision and expansion of public asylums during the nineteenth century provided a suitable setting for the growth of the predominantly all-male psychiatric profession. Indeed, Joan Busfield points out that 'Institutions became the linchpin of nineteenth-century mental health provision and the places where psychiatry clearly emerged as a separate speciality within medicine and where madness was transformed into mental illness.'[3] Mentally affected women were admitted to the newly constructed asylums, where they provided alienists, later known as psychiatrists, and medical men with the opportunity to trial various treatments, some of which could only be described as a violation of women's bodies; although such treatments were considered to be beneficial to the patient at the time. Interestingly, Hilary Marland's study of the Royal Edinburgh Asylum casebooks revealed that 'the asylum seems to have functioned as a refuge', where women could rest, have proper meals and be free of the daily hardship of their lives. Marland points out that many women preferred to be in the asylum than at home and were keen to leave their domestic roles behind.[4] Nancy Theriot argues that 'the symptoms of puerperal insanity involved a denial of motherhood and a reversal of "feminine" traits'. Theriot maintains that women 'acted out their rebellion; male physicians who for ideological and professional reasons were disposed to define women's behaviour as "insanity" legitimized women's rebellion as illness'.[5] Whether women rebelled against domestic male dominance or found the asylum a place of respite, the asylum casebooks reveal the women's struggle against puerperal insanity.

A commonly held view of alienists was that many family doctors were not adequately trained to treat mental illness; their expertise lay with anatomical and physiological knowledge and not with mental physiology and psychology.[6] As contemporary medical journals have shown, the debates between both professions as to who was most qualified to treat patients with puerperal-related mental illness continued for decades. Consequently, professional tensions developed into three-sided debates between doctors, alienists and lawyers as the courts established a link between insanity and infanticide.[7] As Roger Smith points out, 'Insanity was a label used by juries to describe women who were passive by nature and circumstance, even in the face of active violence.'[8] Hence, such criminal cases were both a medical and a legal issue. This led medical specialists to argue that, with limited medical knowledge, lawyers were not in a position of authority to frame laws to manage the criminally insane.

This chapter draws upon county asylum records, Broadmoor Criminal Lunatic Asylum case files, medical journals and newspaper reports to examine the issues of female insanity and the impact that mental illness had on the lives of affected women and their families. The inclusion of Glamorgan County Asylum casebooks for the years 1874–76, 1886–87, 1895–96 and 1905–06 provides the medical background to the criminal case studies of Catherine, Annie, Mary and Margaret, who murdered their own children while in a state of insanity.[9] The women's cases are discussed from the point at which the crime was perpetrated, their detention at Broadmoor and potential discharge back into the community. From a medical, legal and social perspective, the criminal cases present crucial evidence of the women's states of mind at the time of the crime and how the medical profession, asylum superintendents, the judiciary and the Home Office dealt with each case. These particular cases also provide evidence that concealment of birth and the killing of newborn infants by their mothers while in a fit of transient insanity was not the same as puerperal insanity.

A review of the patient casebooks from Glamorgan County Asylum identified women with puerperal-related mental illness. The most informative sections of the casebooks were those at the time of admission, because it was at this point that the mothers exposed their feelings and the circumstances surrounding their breakdown. In fact, the records revealed the number of mothers who came perilously close to committing child murder had it not been for their timely admission to the asylum.

This chapter is based on the experiences of female insanity, motherhood and child murder. However, a case review of one father, who killed his seven-year-old daughter, is also included here. He was found to be insane by a jury and, therefore, detained at Broadmoor indefinitely. Even though this particular case relates to the killing of an older child, it is explored because it provides an opportunity to consider how a paternal child murderer, who was understood to be insane, was treated in relation to maternal child murderers. To ignore this case of paternal child murder would present a one-sided view of parental child murder. From a gendered perspective, Natalie Zemon Davies suggests that 'we should be interested in both women and men, that we should not be working only on the subjected sex any more than a historian on class can focus entirely on peasants. Our goal is to understand the significance of the sexes, of gender groups in the historical past.'[10] Inclusion of the father's case emphasises how the courts, the press and the local communities considered the man's insane behaviour in comparison to their attitude to the offending mothers, when all the parents involved had killed their own children. In a study of patients detained at Broadmoor and Perth asylums, Jonathan Andrews found that older children were much more likely to be victims of insane men, rather than insane women, and that violent attacks on newborn babies and infants were most likely to be committed by women.[11] Therefore, the criminal cases provide the opportunity to consider gender in relation to both insanity and child murder.

'She seemed unsettled in her mind'[12]: Recognition of 'puerperal insanity'

Women who committed child murder as a consequence of 'puerperal insanity' were considered to be insane. They were treated differently from women who concealed their pregnancy, gave birth in secret and committed the crime of child murder while in a frenzied state, either during or directly after childbirth. Some women who gave birth under these circumstances were judged to be distraught and mentally disturbed at the time, but they were not considered to be insane. In most cases, single mothers committed infanticide to be free of the burden and the shame of giving birth to an illegitimate child. In comparison, mothers recognised as suffering from 'puerperal insanity', or 'lactational insanity', often committed child murder in a delusional state to protect their children from harm and suffering in the future, so the motives for sane and insane mothers to kill their infants were in opposition to each other.

Throughout the latter part of the nineteenth and early twentieth century, doctors and alienists debated whether or not 'puerperal insanity' existed as a condition directly caused by parturition. For example, medical superintendent J. Thompson Dickson stated that 'there is a potentiality of insanity either by hereditary transmission or specially and accidentally induced, but not associated with the parturient condition'.[13] In his opinion, M. D. McCleod maintained that:

> Insanity of a parent or ancestor tends to produce in an individual a strong susceptibility to insanity, or allied nervous

> disorder – a pathological sensitiveness – a proneness to break down under exciting causes, which would not affect a person with a healthier pedigree.[14]

One aetiological factor that medical men agreed upon was that of 'hereditary taint', which was regarded as a cause of insanity in general. For that reason, many within the medical profession were of the opinion that a latent predisposition to mental illness could be triggered by other factors. Alienist John Conolly, a prominent figure in the earlier Victorian period and an advocate of non-restraint of patients, maintained that in a greater number of cases of 'puerperal insanity' patients were already of a peculiar mental character before becoming pregnant, and were even likely to have inherited a peculiar mental constitution.[15] 'Puerperal insanity' was, as Alan Rigden explained, an acute mania which could render the patient liable to attack by any one of the 'so-called causes of insanity such as fright, shock, undue worry, or a neurotic inheritance'.[16] Medical man Robert Boyd noted that hereditary predisposition rendered females more prone to insanity in pregnancy and after childbirth, but it did not delay their recovery.[17] This suggests that when a mother was mentally weaker than normal, childbirth disturbed her already precarious mental balance. Hence, when the balance was restored, she was capable of returning to normal, albeit in a rather fragile state.

Puerperal patients were treated by alienists or psychiatrists, yet the illness was associated with the parturient condition. Aleck Bourne explained that obstetrics and psychiatry lay on the 'border line of two specialities of medicine'. Therefore, both groups of medical men were 'in danger of neglect because each repudiates the responsibility of special study'.[18] Dr Cuthbert Lockyer maintained that the best solution would be to employ a fully trained obstetrician in asylums and mental hospitals in order that patients could be treated equally by an alienist and an obstetrician.[19] 'Puerperal insanity' usually affected mothers during the early days or weeks following childbirth, although another issue frequently debated at the time was at what point the puerperal state ended and the lactational state began. John Baker, deputy superintendent at Broadmoor, reported that not all medical men were in agreement on this point. Baker 'regarded, as puerperal, those in which the crime of infanticide took place within two months of parturition, and as lactational, those in which the child-murder occurred later'. Baker pointed out that Thomas Clouston set a limit of six weeks from the birth for puerperal insanity, whereas J. Batty Tuke fixed at one month, but allowed two months for debatable cases.[20]

The expansion of the field of psychiatry during the latter half of the nineteenth century led to the classification of mental illnesses into four categories: mania, melancholia, dementia and idiocy. Whether insanity affected mothers during pregnancy, childbirth or lactation, the symptoms presented the same as for mania and melancholia, and patients were classified accordingly on admission to the asylum. Dr T. B. Hyslop, who was assigned to Bethlem Asylum, found that an attack of puerperal insanity was likely to begin at night and seemed to be the result of 'the dream-state, the continuation of the dream taking the form of terrifying hallucinations or illusions'.[21] Patients suffering from delusions could be dangerous and possessed of violent, homicidal and suicidal tendencies. Suicide was associated with the melancholic state and, as Asa Janson points out, 'A shift occurred within dominant medical opinion in Britain from a belief that suicide was a possible outcome of melancholia in the early nineteenth century to one which held that a majority of melancholics were "suicidal" at the dawn of the twentieth century.'[22] As melancholia was often insidious and chronic, the depression was likely to be well established by the time its effect on the mother was obvious to the family. Baker pointed out that:

> the patient is, as a rule, sanely conscious of many things and usually coherent, but it begins to dawn on the friends that the mind is gradually giving way, yet, owing to some perverse reasoning, they defer placing her under asylum care and treatment, even if the woman herself begs to be safeguarded.[23]

The fact that the symptoms of mania were distressing for the patient and her family probably explains why more puerperal cases were admitted to asylums when compared to cases of melancholia.

Early treatment was crucial, not only for the sake of the mother but also to protect her infant, and other children in some cases. This was evident in the case of twenty-four-year-old J. B., who was struck down by the illness three days after her second confinement; records indicate that she tried to strangle her baby while suffering from both suicidal and homicidal tendencies.[24] Under similar circumstances, thirty-two-year-old E. T. developed symptoms four days after the birth. She too was suicidal and had threatened to kill her baby.[25] Two weeks after the birth, twenty-five-year-old M. C. suffered suicidal and violent tendencies when she stopped feeding the baby.[26] Likewise, it was noted that twenty-one-year-old H. J. attempted to kill her five-week-old baby after her milk supply failed.[27] All four patients suffered from puerperal insanity, either within a few days or within five weeks following the births. The patients experienced the same symptoms; they behaved in a similar manner and all were discharged from the asylum following diagnosis and treatment as being recovered, largely because treatment was administered soon after birth. It was also apparent that the women's ill health could have resulted in four potential cases of infanticide, proving that early admission was crucial in order to protect infants from their mothers. The medical records highlight another common symptom: all four patients suffered from failed lactation. Dr Hyslop found that the effects of suppressed lactation or a difficult labour were well known to bring on a puerperal attack.[28] This was the case when twenty-four-year-old J. M. was mentally disturbed after a long and difficult labour that resulted in the use of instruments during the birth.[29]

Not all mothers were discharged from an asylum in good mental health, despite treatment. Clearly, admission was not soon enough for thirty-five-year-old E. R., a collier's wife who was reported to be bewildered and confused three to four weeks after the birth of her child. Records show that E. R. was not admitted to an asylum until nine months later, by which time the medical superintendent noted that 'she has lost her senses and wants to come here to get better'. By June 1878, E. R. had become 'incoherent, demented and idle'. She died seven years later in January 1881 after being transferred to the Joint Counties Asylum Carmarthen.[30] Failure to treat mothers during the early weeks after childbirth meant that it was difficult to render a cure in some cases, especially if melancholia was well established. One patient, S. B., was admitted in 1874 due to an attack of insanity following a miscarriage. A year later she displayed symptoms of restlessness, memory loss, idleness and was very unsteady on her legs. By the time S. B. died in 1877 of 'general paralysis', records show that she was 'mindless, feeble in her bodily health and helpless'.[31]

During the Victorian period the intrusive treatments for 'puerperal insanity' ranged from restraint, blood-letting, solitary confinement, cold baths and the application of leeches to the head, to blistering the back and neck as a way to control the patient's mind and body. Practitioners claimed that such treatments were advantageous to patients. Patients were kept quiet with the administration of sedatives, namely morphia, chloral and potassium bromide; sedatives were likely to have been administered in lieu of restraints as the use of such devices diminished. Refusal of food and medication was a common symptom of insanity, particularly in melancholic patients, who often had a wish to die. As a consequence, a substantial number of asylum patients were subjected to the brutal treatment of forcible feeding. During the period 1874–76 it was recorded that three of the nine patients at Glamorgan Asylum were force-fed, yet during the years 1895–96 just one patient in fourteen was forcibly fed. Henry Sutherland, a physician, held that forcible feeding was necessary after all other attempts had failed. For instance, 'persuasion, arguments, threats, influences causing shame to the patient, and occasionally yielding to some delusion or peculiar manner of taking food'. Sutherland recognised the moral causes for the refusal of food including 'all emotional influences connected with a dislike to food, such as real grief, which the insane are sometimes quite capable of feeling when first separated from their friends; suicidal intention; and also delusions'.[32] Forceful methods were used to open the patient's mouth to enable the gag to be put in place, which often caused cuts and broken teeth. Once the throat and oesophagus had become overly sore and irritated from repeated feeding, patients were fed through the nose or the bowel instead. This practice applied to both insane men and women and was administered on moral and medical grounds.[33] Records show that one patient, J. M., was force-fed, after which it was noted that 'she has taken nourishment much more readily'.[34] In another case it was recorded that, after being force-fed, H. F. was 'quieter and takes food willingly'.[35] However, the practice of forcible feeding went far beyond administering food in the interest of the patient's health.

Assistant medical officer L. Harris-Liston was in the practice of force-feeding if patients had refused food for just twenty-four hours in a well-nourished person or if a weaker person missed two meals.[36] Sutherland found that, in his experience, 'the display of the feeding apparatus on a table is sometimes sufficient to induce the patient' to take food. He also discovered that he could force compliance by having patients witness another being force-fed, and informing them that they would be fed in the same manner. Sutherland was also in the habit of instructing force-fed melancholic patients to hold each other down to be forcibly fed in turn, or administering a beef tea enema to a strong man in front of other patients as a remedy to ensure compliance.[37] In a study of the Bethlem Asylum records, Sarah Chaney found that when it came to force-feeding, distinctions were made between voluntary and involuntary patients. While it was not a written rule or a legal requirement, at Bethlem 'voluntary boarders were never force-fed'.[38] Forcible feeding was a medical question, but it was also one of physical and mental control. As a very enthusiastic advocate of force-feeding, W. Herbert of the North Wales Counties Asylum pointed out that where force-feeding is administered, 'The patient seems to realise sooner that he is mastered.'[39] It was argued at the time that force-feeding was necessary, but it could be regarded today as a cruel violation of the bodies and minds of both men and women. The treatments employed by asylum staff to save time, such as those adopted by Sutherland, pointed to the fact that insane persons were thought to be insensitive and mindless to such abuse.

Delusions were a disturbing symptom frequently recorded in the patients' notes. David Wright's findings concerning patients at the Buckingham Asylum are comparable to those patients recorded at the Glamorgan Asylum. Patients commonly feared poisoning and believed that family members and friends were plotting to kill them. Wright found that delusions of guilt and persecution were common and often made reference to the Devil acting in a 'persecutory' role.[40] G. L. said that 'the Devil told her to kill her husband and children'.[41] Delusions were at the root of suicidal and homicidal thoughts or acts, and it was difficult to establish a patient's recovery until they were brought under control with treatment.

Not all mentally ill mothers were admitted to an asylum. Middle-class mothers were more likely to receive medical care at home. They might also be afforded a change of scenery and only referred to the asylum, probably a private one, if treatment failed at home. Poorer women were admitted to county asylums and cared for by alienists experienced in dealing with mothers worn down by frequent births, poverty and hardship. John Conolly found that poor patients acclimatised to asylums much better than middle-class patients did to private asylums since the latter were used to being indulged and felt difficulty in adjusting to the confinement.[42] A mother's domestic role was generally central to the running of the family household; therefore, concerted efforts were made to create some form of normality at the asylum to aid the mother's recovery. Patients were encouraged to carry out light domestic duties to prepare them to take up their role again as wife and mother. Yet, some mothers were so mentally disturbed that a cure was rendered impossible and they never returned home, depriving children and husbands of their presence.

It is interesting to note that there were few single mothers diagnosed with 'puerperal insanity' at both Glamorgan Asylum and Dundee Asylum, compared to the number of cases concerning married mothers who were suffering from the same illness.[43] Geoffrey Clarke believed that the actual number of single mothers admitted with 'puerperal insanity' could be higher, because some women claimed to be married for social reasons.[44] This prompts the question as to why few single mothers were diagnosed with puerperal insanity. Morag Campbell points out that 'Women not conforming to socially accepted standards were hence perhaps seen as unsuitable for the puerperal insanity diagnosis.'[45] At Glamorgan Asylum, in the years 1874–76, there were only two puerperal-related cases of single mothers who had recently given birth. Twenty-two-year-old domestic servant E. H. was diagnosed as puerperal after giving birth three months previously. It was recorded that she had been seduced by her master.[46] A single mother, twenty-two-year-old E. T., was diagnosed with melancholia after giving birth to an illegitimate child three weeks previously. There was no mention of 'puerperal insanity' because she was recorded as a congenital imbecile.[47]

There were only three recorded cases concerning single mothers during 1877–80 in Glamorgan Asylum, although the medical superintendent did not diagnose the patients as suffering from 'puerperal insanity'. Single mother S. L., a twenty-year-old servant, had given birth six or seven months previously. Even though her symptoms were the same as those experienced by married mothers, E. R. was not diagnosed with puerperal insanity.[48] For sixteen-year-old servant M. F., her case notes revealed that the supposed cause of her mental illness was due to her giving birth in a toilet at a brothel.[49] A. W. was diagnosed with chronic mania, although the supposed cause was the birth of an illegitimate child.[50] It was possible that some patients were single and only claimed to be married, therefore distorting the actual number of admissions concerning single women. It was also the case that single mothers did not suffer from the physical strain and hardship of successive pregnancies and childrearing when compared to married mothers. This might explain why, with regard to single women, there were so few asylum cases assigned to 'puerperal insanity'. Then again, the casebooks might well replicate the findings of Campbell's research at the Dundee Asylum. Campbell maintains that single mothers did not conform to the prevailing ideological standards set for married women and were therefore not worthy of the diagnosis of 'puerperal insanity'.[51]

'Puerperal insanity' and 'lactational insanity' were very much disorders of the nineteenth century, so by the early twentieth century the illnesses were no longer diagnosed as such. The conditions were more likely to be termed 'puerperal psychosis', 'exhaustive psychosis' and 'confusional psychosis'. This was because the symptoms of 'puerperal insanity' and 'lactational insanity' presented the same as those of mania and melancholia found in patients not linked to the parturient condition. Insanity associated with childbirth is diagnosed today as postpartum psychosis and is treated as a psychiatric emergency.[52] Dorothy Sit *et al* describe the illness as 'an overt presentation of bipolar disorder that is timed to coincide with tremendous hormonal shift after delivery'. It is also vital that an accurate diagnosis of postpartum psychosis is made without delay in order that patients can receive the correct treatment to allow for a full recovery, to prevent further attacks and to reduce the risk to mothers and their children.[53] Just as it is now, nineteenth-century medical specialists found that recognition of mental illness, and early intervention, proved crucial. Otherwise, many more infants would have been murder victims; hence, there would also have been far more cases of insane mothers entering the asylum via the criminal courts.

'I have all along advised that she should be watched'[54]: Insanity and child murder

The Glamorgan Asylum records revealed that infants born to mothers with suicidal and homicidal tendencies were potential victims of child murder. Katherine Watson points out that 'puerperal psychotic illness is a relatively rare cause of the crime'.[55] This raises the question: how prevalent was puerperal-related mental illness in relation to the number of infants killed by their mothers in Wales? During this period, women from Wales who committed child murder on the grounds of insanity were detained at Broadmoor. In the period 1870–1914 the Admissions Register for Broadmoor Criminal Lunatic Asylum recorded that eleven women were admitted from Wales. Ten of the eleven women had killed their own children, while one woman had killed her nephew.[56] Therefore, bearing in mind that sixty-five cases of puerperal-related insanity were recorded at Glamorgan Asylum during the years 1874–76, 1886–87, 1895–96 and 1905–06, it can be seen that infanticide as a result of insanity was rare.[57]

John Baker carried out a comprehensive study of female admissions in the years 1864–1902. Baker found that infanticidal mothers formed the bulk of the female population at Broadmoor; 253 had killed their children, while another thirty-three infants had suffered violence at the hands of their mothers. Twenty newborn infants were killed as a result of puerperal insanity, and twelve of the twenty mothers were discharged after a short detention. Only sixteen women in total had killed illegitimate infants, and they were found to be insane on the grounds of 'transient frenzy'. However, Baker was doubtful of a correct diagnosis in such cases because the women were usually able to recollect the details of the crime afterwards.[58] This signifies that there was very little inclination to find single women insane when they were charged with murder. Only two of the eleven women admitted to Broadmoor from Wales had murdered their illegitimate infants.

Baker recorded that infanticide occurred more frequently as a result of 'lactational insanity' than it did in association with 'puerperal insanity'. He noted that infanticides occurred in the following proportions: insanity of pregnancy 5 per cent, puerperal insanity 35 per cent, and insanity of lactation 60 per cent. Baker claimed that fewer cases occurred in the early days after parturition. In fact, most infanticides happened during the later stages of the puerperal period and were due to the disorder of the melancholic type. The acts of drowning and poisoning were most likely to be committed during the later stages following parturition and as a result of melancholia.[59] Baker found that:

> Rarely did the mother deny the act, but excuse herself on the plea that the child is happy in Heaven. They soon realise

> the gravity of the act, melancholic despair seizes them, their only wish is to die, and they cry out to be led to instant execution. This is followed by a confession in a mechanical manner where they shed no tears; express no remorse, but stare vacantly in front of them.[60]

The following four case studies relate to the experiences of Catherine, Annie, Mary and Margaret, who were admitted to Broadmoor in 1873, 1879, 1883 and 1895 respectively. In line with Baker's assessment, it appeared that there was little difference between the homicidal and suicidal acts exhibited by the four mothers in comparison to the behaviour of other infanticidal women who were also detained at Broadmoor for the same offences.

Baker explained that the motive of mothers who killed their children, or attempted suicide, was often due to an 'irresistible impulse' that overpowered them while mentally weak. He pointed out that:

> At first an obsession, it becomes a delusion; the thought of suicide projects itself into her mind, she cannot leave the child behind, it must be sacrificed first; the dreadful thought is banished again and again only to recur with renewed intensity, until it really seems to fascinate, and finally overwhelm her – the deed is done, and a ruined home is the result.[61]

The following case studies corresponded with Baker's explanation for mothers who succumbed to 'an irresistible impulse'.

In December 1872, thirty-eight-year-old Catherine was charged with wilful murder after she drowned her daughter, aged one year and eight months, in a pool of water in the garden.[62] It was reported that her husband was a coker at the Pyle works and was known to be 'a steady and industrious man' in 'comfortable circumstances'. Catherine was known to be a 'kind and affectionate mother' and very fond of the child. One neighbour reported that Catherine had laid out the dead infant carefully on a heap of clothes and had covered her with a barley sack, which had been turned in a fashion similar to that used with bedclothes.[63] When asked why she had killed the child, Catherine replied that, 'I don't know. I was tired of life', and that the Devil told her to do it.

Catherine's doctor stated at the coroner's inquest that he had treated her for the past twelve months, but between April and June he found her to be 'in an unsound state of mind and could not be held responsible for her acts'. In the doctor's opinion, Catherine had been suffering from melancholia and dementia, and that 'on the day that the offence was committed she was deranged'. One witness reported that Catherine was in the habit of 'putting her hair into her mouth, and pulling her clothes to pieces'. Yet, her husband stated that, 'he did not notice that she was low-spirited of late'.[64] The coroner informed the jury 'that they had nothing to do but return a verdict of wilful murder'. It was apparent that juries were ill at ease in delivering verdicts of wilful murder in cases where mothers had killed their children while insane. In Catherine's case the jury foreman said, 'We find that the prisoner did it wilfully.' The coroner replied, 'And that is equivalent to wilful murder.'[65] In March 1873, at the Spring Assizes held at Swansea, Catherine was acquitted of wilful murder on the grounds of insanity. Therefore, Catherine was 'to be kept in strict custody until Her Majesty's pleasure be known'.[66] While Catherine was detained at Cardiff and Swansea gaols, both governors confirmed that 'she was of weak intellect since she had been in prison'.[67] The Home Secretary issued Catherine's warrant and she was admitted into Broadmoor on 23 May 1873 where she was to be kept until lawfully removed or discharged.[68]

Catherine was a working-class mother, but the subject of the second case study, Annie, was the middle-class wife of a ship's captain. In 1879 Annie killed her eight-week-old daughter after an attack of 'puerperal insanity' that began two weeks after the birth of her first child.[69] There was no indication from those within her social circle that Annie was mentally unstable in any way prior to the birth. Her servant stated that Annie was doing very well until she stopped breastfeeding after just two weeks. Annie showed symptoms of depression; she passed sleepless nights and lost interest in the baby, her friends and the household. She complained of feeling lost and later attempted suicide by taking an overdose of the sedative chloral.[70] George Robertson, physician-superintendent at Edinburgh Asylum, maintained that 'The desire to die and to find oblivion is not a rare symptom of melancholia', and that the early stage is the most dangerous.[71] Annie displayed symptoms of 'puerperal insanity' and was treated accordingly by her doctor at home.

Annie's doctor advised that a change of scenery would be beneficial. Medical superintendent J. Thompson Dickson claimed that 'A prompt and complete change of surroundings, absolute rest, nutritious diet and stimulants judiciously administered, will in most cases ensure recovery.'[72] The change in setting had no positive effect because Annie remained mentally unstable and required constant attention. Meanwhile, the baby was left in the servant's care, and when it was returned to her she took no notice at first but then began to accept it. As Annie settled, she was frequently left alone with the baby when at her parents' house, and also when she returned to her own home four days prior to the tragic event. At this time Annie was seen by her neighbour, who pointed out that she 'looked very wild', but said 'the baby was getting on nicely'.[73] Annie continued to be indifferent, but not enough to warrant her family to keep constant watch over.

Annie killed the baby while she was in a delusional state, and immediately admitted to her servant that she had tied a ribbon tightly around its neck.[74] Alan Rigden, a medical officer, pointed out that:

> There is no condition known to alienists that shows more violent manifestations; the whole mental life of the woman is reduced to a state of turmoil; ideas and images present themselves to consciousness with such bewildering rapidity that nothing is fully cognized; before an idea can be more than partially conceived another arises, displacing the first.[75]

Annie's symptoms were very similar to a typical case described by Rigden. In his experience, a patient was 'quiet and self-absorbed' and would take no interest in the baby. While in a disturbed mental state, a patient might attempt suicide. If so, the attempt was usually made at the beginning of the illness. Depression was predominant, but the patient soon became aggravated while talking rapidly to herself, shouting or singing.[76] Once Annie had lapsed into a melancholic state, she attempted suicide and then committed infanticide. J. Stanley Hopwood maintained that 'deliberate homicidal acts are not possible in the maniacal state' soon after the birth. Acts of homicide and suicide become more common at a later stage, during the puerperal period, once the patient is in a melancholic state with delusions of unworthiness.[77] Annie's doctor stated that 'persons who suffer from this complaint frequently commit suicide or destroy their children'. It was reported that the doctor was not surprised when he heard that she had taken the life of her child.[78]

Despite Annie's care and treatment, Broadmoor's superintendent noted that 'The measures which were taken for watching her appear to be have been of an inadequate character.'[79] However, monitoring the insane patient at home did have its difficulties. One point raised by Thomas Clouston, superintendent at Cumberland and Westmorland Asylum, was 'the impossibility of making friends understand and guard against the cunning and method that are so often found in madness'.[80] The decision whether to admit a patient placed doctors in a difficult position. In Clouston's opinion, safety of the patient and family was paramount. He maintained that a suicidal person should be admitted to an asylum, and most definitely so if both suicidal and homicidal impulses were present.[81] As a middle-class mother, Annie was more likely to be treated at home to avoid the indignity of being admitted to an asylum.

Annie was not immediately arrested, because she was too ill to be removed from her home. Therefore, a police constable kept watch over her. Annie did not attend the inquest either, which was conducted in her absence. As an amateur singer Annie was very popular in Llanelli, yet there appeared to be some kind of morbid fascination by the public to witness her in the magistrates' court in a deranged state. A large crowd had gathered; but, owing to Annie's mental state her solicitor requested that the court be cleared of onlookers. The hearing continued in private. Her solicitor hoped that the jury's verdict would be one of 'murder whilst in an unsound state of mind'.[82] Irrespective of his plea, the coroner pointed out that the jury was not in the position to say what state of mind she was in at the time of the crime. Annie's doctor felt that this was a case in which the magistrates should not commit:

> Firstly, because sound mind and discretion were essential to wilful murder, and these the accused did not possess; and, secondly, because the accusation rested mainly upon the assertions which the accused herself had made. The statements of an insane person could not, he held, be used as evidence against that person, especially, as she had, at the same time, made other statements which were manifestly untrue.[83]

The jury returned a verdict of wilful murder. An application for bail was rejected because the coroner had issued a warrant charging Annie with wilful murder. She was committed for trial at the assizes and taken to Carmarthen gaol on 5 February 1879. The Bench was in no doubt that Annie was suffering from 'puerperal insanity' and instructed the Clerk to write to the Home Secretary enclosing detailed evidence to prove that she had committed the crime while insane. Annie did not face a criminal trial because she was declared insane beforehand and, therefore, not fit to plead. This meant that she was not considered to have sufficient intellect to understand the trial proceedings and the details of evidence. Baron Alderson explained the legal definition of unfitness to plead, referring to the case *R v. Pritchard* (1836): 'Is the accused of sufficient intellect to comprehend the course of proceedings of the trial, so as to make a proper defence – to know that he might challenge any of you to whom he may object – and to comprehend the details of evidence?'[84] Annie's warrant was signed by the Home Secretary on 14 February 1879, and she was admitted to Broadmoor ten days later.[85]

On admission, Annie was described as 'weak, also both suicidal and dangerous with a chief delusion that she was very sinful'.[86] Her records revealed that within four months she had 'improved in bodily and mental health, was cheerful and was taking an interest in ordinary events'.[87] The prognosis for mothers struck down with 'puerperal insanity' having just given birth to their first child was good, and this was the case for Annie. In fact, Hopwood found that for some women 'the attack of insanity was of such a transitory nature that by the time their trial was over and they reached the asylum the attack had subsided, and they were sane on reception and remained sane'.[88]

Annie recovered, although that was not the case for middle-class mother Mary, whose husband held a prominent position as borough analyst with Swansea Corporation. In November 1883, thirty-five-year-old Mary drowned her two-year-old daughter after she suffered a period of depression. In much the same way as Annie, Mary would sit down and take no interest in life. Harbouring the same morbid thoughts as Catherine, the subject of the first case study, Mary said that she was tired of her life. It appears that Mary was worried about her child, as she said she did not know what would become of the little girl after she had gone.[89]

In his experience, George Robertson found that patients did not conceal their feelings regarding suicide, although they did not point it out in so many words, often saying such things as their life was not worth living.[90] Even though Mary had suicidal thoughts, the family did not believe it was necessary to keep watch over her. Mary immediately admitted to her servant that she had drowned her daughter, although she stated she did not know why; however, she was convinced that the child was in heaven. While the doctor tried to revive the child, Mary sat in the same room without any signs of tears or distress. The doctor described Mary as 'insane as she wore a stolid, dazed look, and was quite indifferent to everything that was going on around her'.[91] Afterwards, like Annie, Mary remained closely guarded in her home rather than taken into custody.[92]

Mary's husband held a prominent role in the public sphere and had considerable social standing within the community. This may have had some bearing on the jury's attitude at the coroner's inquest, which was held at their home. The foreman stated, 'We are most anxious to avoid the ugly word "murder", and preferred to say that she took the infant's life while of unsound mind.' The foreman requested Mary's immediate admission to the asylum to avoid the degradation of prison, but that was beyond the remit of the coroner without communication with the Home Office, although he assured the jury that while in prison 'she would be kept better there than in her own house'.[93] Via the press, the jury wished to 'express their utter disgust at the vile and contemptible anonymous letters' sent to the couple regarding her husband's alleged affair, 'believing that they had a tendency to add materially to the unfortunate woman's mental depression'.[94] The press reported that the 'unfortunate lady' was removed to prison where her friends would be allowed to attend to her.[95]

In view of her husband's social position, members of the jury might well have been acquainted with him. In fact, it seems that four months earlier, he had seconded the nominations for the foreman and another member of the jury to the council of the Swansea Liberal Association.[96] Therefore, this might explain why the jury found that they were ill at ease in passing a verdict of wilful murder. There was also the stigma attached to the confinement and certification of an insane family member to consider. As the coroner's inquest was held at the couple's home, the jury encroached into their private sphere, which possibly made the men feel uncomfortable due to the enormity of the case set out before them. According to Akihito Suzuki, 'the existence of a lunatic in a family itself destabilised the boundary between the public and private spheres and invited forceful intervention from the outside world'.[97] Even taking into account possible bias by the press in this case, the newspapers consistently highlighted the attitude of the ruling middle classes when someone from their own ranks fell within the jurisdiction of the law and all its social implications.

The magistrates' court was nearly empty when Mary arrived, which was in contrast to Annie's court appearance. Mary was committed for trial and admitted to Swansea gaol. Again, like Annie, Mary was certified insane because she was unfit to plead in court. Mary's incarceration in gaol was short, and she was removed to Broadmoor just ten days later. In February 1884, three months after the tragedy, two prominent MPs presented a petition to the Home Secretary to assist in Mary's case. It was also in that same month that Mary was scheduled to appear at the Glamorgan Assizes, but she was unable to attend; therefore, the witnesses were dismissed and the trial was postponed.[98] Yet again, Mary did not attend the next scheduled assizes in May 1884. At this point the judge instructed the governor of the gaol to strike her case from the calendar until further orders.[99] It was also reported that she had contemplated suicide years earlier when a rope was found in her room.[100] There was a history of insanity in the family; therefore, hereditary predisposition was considered to be a contributory factor to Mary's periods of depression, and it also complicated her recovery.

Annie and Mary were middle-class mothers with servants in attendance, while working-class mother Catherine was reported to be in 'comfortable circumstances', but thirty-two-year-old Margaret from Nevern, Pembrokeshire, was from a poorer background. In June 1895 Margaret was charged with the wilful murder of her infant daughter. Her husband was a small farmer, although his illness had caused poverty and deprivation. Margaret had been depressed for nearly two years following the birth of her youngest child. Ten months after the birth, Margaret's doctor confirmed that she was suffering from suppressed lactation, depression, insomnia and dyspepsia, probably brought on by the stress of her husband's illness. Three months later he treated her for incipient insanity and advised a change of scene, but under surveillance. Margaret's health improved and that was the last time the doctor attended her. On the doctor's advice, the family had exercised a certain amount of supervision over her movements.

Similar to Mary, in a disordered state and believing her youngest child would be better in heaven, Margaret suffocated her daughter, aged two years and seven months, early one morning. She had attempted to kill the infant fourteen months before but had been prevented from doing so just in time. Margaret made yet another attempt on the child's life two months later. On this occasion Margaret refused to hand over the infant and was reported to have said that 'she could do what she liked with her own child'. The doctor had advised all along that Margaret should be watched because she was a possible danger both to herself and her children.[101] Margaret admitted killing the child to her ten-year-old daughter very soon afterwards. In his evidence, her brother-in-law reported that Margaret had said, 'if she had had the opportunity she felt that she could have killed the other two and then herself, lest they might suffer after she had gone'. He understood that to mean that Margaret's intention was to commit suicide. She then asked him to get his shotgun and shoot her in the farmyard.[102] Hopwood explained that when some mothers killed their children, the original idea was one of suicide, and not murder: 'In these cases the prevailing idea is a wish to die, but for some reason she shrinks from committing suicide and resorts to murder as a means to an end.'[103] This might well have been the case for Margaret, because she asked to be shot immediately, therefore putting an end to her life as well. She was also mentally affected in the same way as Mary, because Margaret also expressed no emotions of grief and remained in that state until arrested. Margaret was taken into police custody that day and detained at Fishguard, in contrast to middle-class mothers Annie and Mary, who remained in their homes under police surveillance.

At the coroner's inquest there was no attempt to evade the use of the ugly word 'murder', or a repeat of the difficulties expressed by the jury in Mary's case. The evidence was heard in Welsh because of Margaret's inability to speak English. While it was the intention of the press to report the case accurately in English, it was possible to lose some meaning in translation. The coroner's jury returned a verdict of wilful murder, but wished to add the rider that Margaret did it when in a state of insanity. The coroner said that, 'It would be out of order to add to the verdict, but the press would, no doubt, take notice of it as being the desire of the jury.'[104] Margaret was brought before the magistrates two days later. In common with both Annie and Mary, she was completely oblivious to what was going on around her. Margaret was committed for trial at the assizes and transferred to Carmarthen gaol.

On admission, Margaret was reported to be suffering from delusions, and that she felt a terrible urge to kill herself rather than be hanged. She saw strangers in her cell, who would run after her but say nothing. She reported that 'Voices tell her to do certain things, and these she must do.'[105] Margaret later admitted in gaol that 'she had been feeling bad, low and miserable for nearly 2 years before getting into trouble'.[106] Margaret was scheduled to appear at the Winter Assizes in November 1895, although, like Annie and Mary, she was not subjected to a criminal trial. The *South Wales Daily News* reported that even if Margaret were to appear at the tribunal 'she would not be able to put in a plea of any description, because being a certified lunatic, there would be no reason in the formality', and that it was 'relatively rare for a monomaniac to be spared the ordeal of a trial before one of Her Majesty's judges'. The Home Secretary issued Margaret's warrant and she was received into Broadmoor on 29 July 1895.[107]

Margaret was described as a dark, heavy, melancholic woman. Apparently, there was no insanity or consumption in her family, and both her parents were sober.[108] She remained very depressed and suicidal. The medical superintendent noted that 'Speaking Welsh only, it is difficult to know what passes in her mind.'[109] Therefore, detention in an asylum in England far away from her family probably hindered her recovery; she was possibly confined in a world of her own and unable to communicate effectively. Margaret believed that her poor health was part of her punishment. She was very agitated, biting her handkerchief and saying that, 'she must bite herself to pieces as she had killed her little child'.[110] Baker believed that 'Even at their mental best many of these mothers are haunted by the ever-present shadow of their crime, which spreads around an almost universal tendency to sadness.'[111] It was less likely that Margaret would make a full recovery because the depression had taken hold during the previous two years. Baker claimed that poorer women always seemed to be pregnant or nursing, which made them susceptible to a mental breakdown. He also found this to be the case with over-lactation, which he described as 'ruinous for mother and child'.[112] Margaret was detained at Broadmoor for eight years and constantly hindered by guilt. Following a period of illness, Margaret died in November 1903, aged forty, 'exhausted' from blood poisoning.[113]

It was evident at the coroner's inquest that Margaret was not safe to be at large. It was reported that her husband 'had observed something wrong with her mind for eighteen months past, and by reason of her mental state he had exercised a certain amount of supervision over her movements, and he had also consulted medical men as to her condition'.[114] Thomas Clouston was of the opinion that nearly every case of puerperal and lactational insanity, amongst the poor, would recover sooner in an asylum. He believed that homicidal cases should be placed in an asylum, and if both impulses were present, then the patient must be removed to safety. Clouston also pointed out that relations may be opposed to this course of action, but if the patient should kill someone or commit suicide then the medical man would be blamed.[115] As David Wright points out, 'many families chose not to send an insane family member to the asylum; others waited months or even years before deciding'.[116] In his experience Hopwood found that 'Although the relatives recognise a change in the patient, they often fail to realise that it is the start of a serious mental condition until a tragedy takes place which could have been avoided had medical advice been sought earlier.'[117] Dr Eliza Walker Dunbar, one of the first women doctors to qualify in the UK, in 1872, noticed that patients 'do not rightly appreciate the causes of their depression, and fail sometimes to mention them'.[118] In Margaret's case, the family chose to watch her movements rather than admit her to an asylum; besides, her removal might well have placed the family under additional strain as women formed an integral part of the household economy.

According to Baker's assessment, Catherine, Annie, Mary and Margaret probably acted on an 'irresistible impulse' when they killed their infants, which was exacerbated by delusions.

Apparently, Margaret admitted that 'all she knew was that an inexplicable impulse impelled her to do so'.[119] Nevertheless, from a legal perspective, the claim 'irresistible impulse' was not that well received by those who framed the laws on insanity. 'Irresistible impulse' was a medical term, but when applied in a court of law, it was more complex. Roger Smith points out that 'Jurists could not see how to maintain a distinction between an irresistible and an unresisted impulse,' and that 'It was feared that irresistible would become a euphemism for "unresisted".'[120] Medical experts were not convinced that lawyers had enough understanding of the complexities to manage the mentally insane, and that it was not possible to apply the same forms of punishment to an insane person as one would to a sane person who committed the same crime.

Contemporary medical journals exposed both the rivalry and the struggle for recognition between scientific medical experts and lawyers and judges. In fact, medical specialist C. A. Mercier complained that 'The controversy between the medical and the legal professions that has raged for so long round this subject is now rapidly extending.'[121] Medical men argued 'whether those who framed the law did or did not make themselves fully acquainted with the pathological states of the body comprised under the terms of insanity', and 'whether it is reasonable, or indeed possible, for those persons to frame just laws who only have a partial knowledge of the subject matter about which the laws that they were framing are concerned'.[122] Mercier questioned whether insane criminals should be immune from prosecution. He explained that medical men, as expert witnesses in court, are asked to show why the offender, 'who up to the time of the crime has been sufficiently sane to be allowed, rightly or wrongly, to be at large, should, now that he has committed a crime, receive the benefit of the plea of insanity'.[123] Medical experts recognised that some form of punishment should be administered to criminally insane persons, while at the same time arguing that the criminally insane should be protected from the full force of criminal law. Dr L. Weatherly claimed that, in his opinion, punishment should be proportionate to the crime. Criminal persons should be placed in an environment where he or she could go through a process of rehabilitation, the aim of which was to restore mental stability.[124]

Annie, Mary and Margaret were transferred to Broadmoor while under committal, although other women from Wales recorded in the Broadmoor Admissions Register were all tried at the assizes beforehand, including Catherine.[125] The jury at the coroner's inquest were most concerned about Mary's detention in Swansea gaol, yet she was only held for ten days before admission to Broadmoor. Annie was removed to Broadmoor within eighteen days, while Margaret was detained in Carmarthen gaol for seven weeks before being transferred to Broadmoor, which meant that her detention was far longer than that experienced by middle-class mothers Mary and Annie. Catherine was held on remand from December 1872 until her trial in March 1873, and then she was finally removed to Broadmoor in May of that same year.

The evidence indicates that Catherine, Mary and Margaret killed their youngest infants while suffering from the melancholic form of insanity. Each mother had also suffered the loss of children before the tragedies took place. At what point their other children had died in relation to the deaths of the victims has not been established, but grief may well have contributed to the mothers' depressed states. Medical superintendent A. C. Clark maintained that 'when a mother has lost a child the subject was sure to engross her thoughts, to prey upon her mind with the intensity of disease, and to colour her delusions afterwards'.[126] Catherine had given birth to five children, but one child had died before she took the life of her youngest. This was also the case for Mary, as it appeared that she had previously lost one of her six children. In Margaret's case, two of her six children had died prior to the tragedy. It seemed that Catherine and Margaret's symptoms emerged when their infants were about eight months old or so, and were possibly brought on due to the strain of lactation. Over a period of months the depression took hold and the tragedies ensued. As a middle-class mother, Mary might not have experienced the strain of motherhood in the same way as Catherine and Margaret had done. However, Mary had suffered periods of depression for a number of years, and there was also a history of insanity in her family. In Annie's case she had only given birth to one child and had suffered mental disturbance during the first two weeks. Under these circumstances her prognosis for a full recovery was good.

In all four cases the symptoms were the same as those experienced by mothers admitted to the Glamorgan Asylum. It was also the case that the patients treated in the early stages of 'puerperal insanity' usually recovered, while the mothers admitted some months, or even one or two years, later following the onset of melancholic symptoms were less likely to make a full recovery and may well have died in the asylum. Together, the medical journals and the Glamorgan Asylum casebooks provide a means with which to explain the symptoms of puerperal-related mental illness, and the four criminal cases serve to explain the tragedy of infanticide as a consequence of insanity.

'I have never noticed anything about his state of mind'[127]: Paternal child murder

Mothers were more likely to murder newborn babies and infants, while fathers tended to murder older children. Jade Shepherd analysed sixty cases of paternal child murderers detained at Broadmoor in the years 1869–1900. Shepherd found that 'a careful study of representations of murderous fathers suggests that attitudes towards paternal child-murder were more similar to those expressed in cases of female infanticide than has been supposed'.[128] The case concerning a father from Carmarthen supports Shepherd's findings. In December 1887, Henry was accused of the wilful murder of his seven-year-old daughter after she suffered a fatal injury to her throat. Henry's behaviour was similar to that of the four mothers in that he immediately admitted what he had done. He said, 'I did it with a razor', and, 'I would have done the same with the other child had she been here.'[129] Margaret also admitted an urge to kill her other children had they been present at the time. Henry was prone to occasional epileptic attacks since falling from a horse, while his excessive alcohol consumption only aggravated the condition.[130] The inclusion of Henry's case in this chapter highlights the parallels between insane paternal and maternal child murderers.

When Henry appeared before the coroner and the magistrates' court, there were no sensationalist headlines in the press, unlike with other such murder cases. The *Western Mail* reported on the 'Carmarthen Tragedy', while the local newspaper, the *Carmarthen Journal*, was just as low-key with the headline 'The Murder at Carmarthen'.[131] These restrained headlines provided a striking contrast to the *Llanelly and County Guardian*'s reporting of Annie's case with the sensationalist headlines of 'The Strangling of a child by its Mother' and 'Deplorable case of Mania'.[132] In Catherine's case, the *County Observer and Monmouth General Advertiser* reported on the 'Shocking Murder of a Child by its Mother at Pyle'.[133] The *Western Mail* ran with the headline 'Shocking Murder in Pembrokeshire' and 'Child Suffocated by its Mother' in Margaret's case. Again, *The Cambrian* reported Mary's case as that of 'A Mother Drowning Her Daughter in a Bucket'.[134] The eye-catching headlines revealed the manner in which the mothers had killed their infants, yet there was no mention of how Henry had murdered his daughter or that her father was the perpetrator. The press emphasised that each mother had defied the ideological role of motherhood and natural protector, which made the crimes even more shocking.

Public opinion was very much swayed by the influential press reporting in murder trials, providing considerable coverage in cases of concealment of birth and infanticide. Martin Weiner points out that the Home Secretary, William Harcourt, was particularly interested in acquiring press clippings of capital cases during the 1880s. By the end of the nineteenth century, 'newspaper clippings were expected to be sent, along with judge's reports and other official documentation, to Whitehall'.[135] However, this practice also occurred in cases concerning the criminally insane on their admission to Broadmoor. Amongst Henry's admission records was a handwritten report from *The Standard* regarding his trial, with a note attached referring to the newspaper report books for other press clippings relating to his case. In fact, by the time Margaret was admitted to Broadmoor in 1895, the request for press reports was included on the pre-printed form accompanying her warrant.[136] Even accounting for possible bias and occasional inaccuracies in reporting, the authorities clearly recognised the value and influence of press reports. The reports provided details of what was known locally of the offender's behaviour, possibly omitted in court, and it was also a way of gauging public opinion, particularly in capital cases.

In Henry's case, the *Carmarthen Journal* reported that 'The crime is admitted in all its terrible and determined brutality, and the only defence possible is either that the prisoner was insane when he committed it, or was suffering from the effects of drink, aggravated by domestic difference.' '"Drink again" is the verdict, which many of the townspeople pass as to the causes of the crime, drink intensifying other things which might be expected to lead to rash deeds.' According to local inhabitants, Henry 'was not insane, except in so far as drink may have temporarily affected his mind'. As far as the local people of Carmarthen were concerned, they knew Henry's temperament far better than the medical experts. Interestingly, when Henry appeared before the magistrates, there was no hostile demonstration from the crowds that had gathered outside, but that did not stop the people from nearly stepping on each other as they rushed to obtain the best seats in court.[137]

During the latter decades of the nineteenth century, the temperance movement was well established in Wales and, combined with Nonconformity, many people viewed drink as an unnecessary evil. The historian W. R. Lambert maintains that 'The connection of the temperance movement with the kill-joy prejudices of Welsh nonconformity meant that excessive drinking was treated as a sin, not as a psychosomatic disorder and still less as a disease.'[138] According to one witness, Henry 'had a quick temper. I never heard of his being unable to take care of himself, nor that he was insane.' Henry's doctor knew him as 'a man who drank heavily from time to time'.[139] Another witness commented that, 'I have never noticed anything about his state of mind, unless when he had taken liquor.'[140] The Joint Counties Asylum was situated in Carmarthen; therefore, the townspeople knew what constituted an insane person in the community, and Henry did not fit that profile.

Considering Henry's case from a medical perspective, John Charles Bucknill was of the opinion that 'Men who have suffered from blows or wounds on the head or from sun-stroke are, we know, peculiarly liable to this frantic kind of drunkenness, and often from small amounts of stimulants.' Bucknill argued that 'As they know their weakness and the dangers of indulgence, they ought to be held liable to heavy punishment when they commit crime in their self-made fury, but certainly not to suffer the extreme penalty of the law.'[141] G. F. Blandford believed that an insane offender should be held responsible to a certain extent, 'but instead of hanging a man who committed a murder through drink, he would send him, not to Broadmoor to smoke his pipe for the rest of his life, but to penal servitude, where he could do some useful work'.[142]

Henry was deemed fit to plead in court, and unlike the four mothers who were clearly insane, he displayed no obvious signs of insanity. It had long been argued that women were constantly at the mercy of their biological makeup. The prevailing view of the time was, as Joan Busfield explains, 'Women rather than being in control of themselves (having agency) were under the control of their biology. Men had the power (the will) to control their bodies – agency was assumed; women did not.'[143] Catherine's insanity was recognised by the authorities; however, she was still committed for trial at the assizes, so it was unlikely that Henry would be spared the ordeal. He was indicted at the Carmarthenshire Assizes with 'having feloniously, wilfully, and of malice aforethought killed and murdered' his daughter. The judge urged Henry to plead not guilty after he admitted, 'I did not know what I was doing at the time, but I did it.'[144] The *Carmarthen Journal* reported it was a foregone conclusion that the verdict would be one of insanity.[145] Shepherd found that many working-class men were kind and affectionate towards their children prior to violent crime, and that defence counsels put forward the argument that a loving and kind father had no reason to kill his child, so he should be regarded as insane.[146] The witnesses all confirmed in court that Henry was a kind, affectionate father.

The superintendent of the Joint Counties Asylum examined Henry and found 'no manifest delusion or failure of intellect', although he was 'morbid, emotional, his will feeble, and powers of self-control almost entirely destroyed'. Maternal child murder was usually explained as 'puerperal insanity' if the breakdown was shortly after childbirth, or chronic mental illness that had developed as a result of insanity during the lactational period. Therefore, apart from an occasional epileptic attack, it was far more difficult to explain Henry's alleged insanity. The superintendent explained that it was not uncommon for an affected person suffering an epileptic attack 'to exercise his fury upon his children or other objects of affection'.[147] Similarly, Mr F. Whitwell held that epileptics, who suffered a sudden attack of mania, 'either exhaust their fury on themselves or those to whom, in their sane moments, they are most attached; and that such impulses are at the moment quite uncontrollable, though the perpetrator may afterwards know what he has done'.[148] Providing another explanation, Edward C. Mann had witnessed cases of 'abortive or incomplete epileptiform attacks, where there were no convulsions, and where there was no complete loss of consciousness'.[149] The defence counsel put forward that Henry must have been insane when the crime was committed. The verdict was that Henry was 'Guilty of the act charged, but at the time the prisoner was insane, so as not to be responsible according to law for the act done.' Henry was 'To be kept in strict custody until Her Majesty's pleasure be known.'[150] It was reported that while Henry was held at Carmarthen gaol, he was treated in the same way as other prisoners, 'except that his diet is rather more liberal than that of the other prisoners'.[151] As far as the authorities were concerned, it seemed that Henry bordered on deserving of punishment, yet conversely they were unsure whether he was exempt from guilt because there was no clear manifestation of insanity.

The judge and jury were sympathetic in Henry's case, and so too were the press. Daniel Grey found that 'juries could also be unexpectedly sympathetic to potentially insane men who had killed their children', and 'mimicked their treatment of women who also utilised this defence'.[152] In Dr L. Weatherly's opinion, 'The sympathy of judge and jury with a woman was well known, and he was perfectly satisfied that many of the cases of females sent to Broadmoor as having been insane would not have been so dealt with had the murderer been a man instead of a woman.'[153] However, the handling of Henry's case at the coroner's inquest, the magistrates' court, the assizes and by the press was conducted in much the same manner as that of insane mothers. Indeed, the witnesses were subjected to little or no cross-examination, apart from proving that Henry had always been 'a fond and indulgent father'.[154] There was hardly any inclination by the Carmarthenshire jury to find Henry other than insane.

Henry was admitted to Broadmoor a week later. The *Western Mail* was quick to point out that when Henry boarded the train, 'His demeanour was the very opposite to what it was at the trial. Then his plea of "Guilty" was uttered amidst piteous sobs, but on Saturday he smiled in the most light-hearted manner upon those following him as if he were going on a day's pleasure trip instead of entering upon a dreary life of a lunatic convict.'[155] This comment could be viewed in two ways. Firstly, the press had played a significant role in engendering sympathy throughout his court appearances. So, perhaps the fact that he was seen smiling was not necessarily viewed as acceptable behaviour, considering that he had murdered his daughter and escaped the death penalty. Secondly, his light-hearted manner was possibly an indication of his mental instability, although the medical superintendent 'observed no chief delusions or indication of insanity, and none were communicated to him'.[156]

Henry was detained at Broadmoor as a criminal lunatic. Criminal lunatics were defined as 'Persons charged with criminal offences who are found insane by a jury, and criminal prisoners who are certified insane while waiting trial or undergoing sentence and are removed to asylums, come within the description of criminal lunatics.'[157] R. M. Jackson argued that 'criminal lunatic' was an unfortunate term. Insane persons could be classed as lunatics, but those untried or acquitted should not be called 'criminal'.[158] According to the definition, Annie, Mary and Margaret were reported to be criminal lunatics, even though they had not faced a criminal trial. The difference in terminology was evident on Henry's warrant, which was for 'removal of a Criminal Lunatic ordered to be detained during Her Majesty's pleasure from Prison to Broadmoor'.[159] In Margaret's case, her warrant was for 'Removal from Prison to Asylum (Unconvicted Prisoner).'[160]

One notable link between all five parents was that in each case the child victims were female. Was it just coincidence, or did perhaps each parent, either subconsciously or consciously, believe that the life of a female child was not perceived in quite the same way as that of a male child? Catherine, Margaret and Henry threatened to kill their other children, who also happened to be girls. It was also noteworthy that only two of the eleven victims killed by women admitted to Broadmoor from Wales were male. However, in contrast, evidence indicates that single mothers committed infanticide whether the infant was male or female.

At Broadmoor, Henry was sometimes subject to depression, but usually known to be quiet, industrious and cheerful. For four years his records indicated that there was no change in his demeanour. Ten years later Henry remained rational and tranquil, but not very strong mentally, and he continued to suffer from epileptic attacks. Henry died at Broadmoor in May 1910 from phthisis following a detention of twenty-two years.[161] Based on the evidence at Henry's trial, and the medical interpretations, epilepsy was thought to be the cause of the violent attack on his daughter, although the consumption of alcohol may well have contributed to his outburst. Expert opinions differed as to whether a person like Henry should be punished in prison or detained at Broadmoor, and whether a person should be held responsible for their alcohol consumption when it was known that they were susceptible to epileptic attacks. Such cases prompted numerous debates between doctors and lawyers on how best to manage the insane, and to what degree an offender should be held responsible for his actions.

Beyond the confines of the asylum

The authorities did not consider mothers who had killed their own children to be as threatening as other murderers; therefore, rehabilitation and eventual discharge from Broadmoor was a high possibility. Release of patients involved an element of risk, but as Broadmoor superintendent Richard Brayn pointed out, 'If the woman is young and recovers, and appears to be able to maintain her sanity, she can hardly be detained in an asylum until past the childbearing age, and the public is not yet educated up to the idea of having her sterilised.'[162] Discharge entailed a considerable bureaucratic process since it was the Home Secretary's responsibility to issue a warrant for both admission and discharge of patients. As part of the process, the patient was assessed to ascertain whether she was in a fit mental state to return home and resume domestic duties. Both Catherine and Annie recovered sufficiently to warrant discharge, whereas Margaret, Mary and Henry died while detained at Broadmoor.

Jonathan Andrews maintains that 'Asylum superintendents, Home Office officials, and prison commissioners put considerable emphasis on the social respectability of patients' relations in the assessment for suitability for discharge, or relaxation of conditions of discharge.'[163] This particular criterion was evident in the lengthy correspondence between Broadmoor, the Home Office and the patient's family. In fact, the family's persistence, and that of other members of the community, was a contributory factor in securing a patient's discharge. Catherine's husband corresponded regularly with the Broadmoor superintendent, Dr William Orange, between 1874, the year after her admission, and 1877 regarding discharge. Catherine's father also wrote concerning his 'affectionate daughter'.[164] In October 1876, the vicar of Pyle requested Catherine's removal to the county asylum if she was not yet ready to be discharged.[165] The doctor who provided medical evidence at her trial also enquired about 'the present state of poor Catherine'.[166] The family's persistent correspondence meant that by the autumn of 1877 Catherine's discharge looked imminent, because a medical examination indicated that 'she has now remained for a considerable time in a calm and tranquil frame of mind. Although she may be looked upon as being naturally somewhat feeble-minded, we consider that the normal condition of her mental faculties is now re-established.'[167] It was also noted that 'we are by no means able to speak confidently of her again suffering from insanity'.[168] Catherine's discharge was conditional, the terms of which her husband had to abide by.

Catherine was discharged on 31 October 1877 to the care of her husband and the constant supervision of their fifteen-year-old daughter as agreed. Her husband was in a position to provide a comfortable home where Catherine could supervise and take part in the daily domestic duties.[169] Just eighteen days later, Catherine's husband wrote to Dr Orange to say that his wife 'is bearing symptoms of a relapse and she wishes to be sent back to the asylum by first opportunity. She cannot sleep night or day, and I am myself and the three children in much fear of any thing [*sic*] should happen unpleasantly.'[170] On 21 November 1877, Catherine was readmitted by warrant having relapsed into insanity 'there to remain until further orders shall be given respecting her'.[171] Brayn found that while at the asylum, patients could remain mentally stable because they lived under favourable conditions and were free from responsibility. However, once patients were discharged and attempted to resume as normal a life as possible, exposure to worry and anxiety could cause them to relapse, and thus become a danger to themselves and the public.[172] One requirement of the Criminal Lunatics Act 1884 was to submit an 'Annual Report as to the condition and circumstances of a Criminal Lunatic'. The report for the year ending 31 December 1885 stated that Catherine was very melancholic and partially demented.[173] Sixty-three-year-old Catherine died at Broadmoor in January 1898.[174]

Annie's discharge from Broadmoor was favourable. She was admitted in February 1879, yet by August of that same year her husband had requested his wife's discharge. A report concerning her mental and physical condition stated that:

> Her husband appears to be in a comfortable position in life, and is anxious to have another opportunity afforded him of taking care of her himself. If it be thought fit to discharge her to his care, it would be necessary that he should be clearly informed of the risk of the occurrence of a relapse, and that being at once reported to the authorities.[175]

That particular application failed, but in January 1880 Annie was conditionally discharged to her parents under careful supervision. Annie signed the warrant, while her father gave the undertaking to report any symptoms which may look like a recurrence of her malady.[176]

Unlike Catherine, Annie did not return to her husband on discharge. In a study of criminal lunatics released from Broadmoor and Perth asylums, Andrews found that only twenty-two out of fifty-two patients were returned to their husbands.[177] It was considered that immediate discharge to husbands might have a negative effect on the patient in the short term. M. D. McCleod advised that 'a patient who has recovered from puerperal insanity should not be allowed to resume the society of her husband too soon. A pregnancy following quickly upon an attack of this insanity is fraught with considerable danger of a recurrence.'[178] Senior assistant medical officer Geoffrey Clarke maintained that 'morbid mental symptoms commonly persist for a considerable time after the physical health has been restored, relapses are frequent, and the disease often recurs either in subsequent confinements or at other times of mental stress'.[179] Yet this advice was not always accepted, because within six months of discharge, Annie was expecting another child. In 1881 she was found to be living in Llanelli with the baby, aged one month, a nurse and a servant.[180] Records indicated that the boy was at the home of his grandparents ten years later.[181] Annie's case provides evidence that an insane mother who killed her baby could be detained at Broadmoor for a brief period, be discharged as recovered and safely have another child.

There is no evidence to indicate whether Mary's discharge was considered, due to the one-hundred-year closure of her file. However, from a social perspective, it is worth considering how Mary's middle-class husband and family managed to cope in the aftermath of her committal. When Mary's husband died in 1895, the *Western Mail* was keen to report that he was 'a man of much public spirit, during his lifetime, particularly to the cause of education'. The obituary reported that 'the most exciting incident in his life was the well-remembered child murder by his wife in a fit of mental aberration'.[182] Mary's incarceration did not signify social ruin for the family, because her husband retained his social position and continued with his public appointments. Mary was aged seventy-eight when she died in 1926, having been detained for forty-three years.

Women like Catherine and Annie were perceived as less threatening; therefore, rehabilitation and reintegration back into society was considered in a positive light. In comparison to mothers, cases of paternal child murderers were subjected to closer scrutiny. In Henry's case, the *Western Mail* commented that 'experience points to the probability that not for many years, if ever, will he be permitted again to enjoy unrestricted freedom'.[183] Henry's discharge was a possibility, provided he was considered to be mentally stable once again, although there seems to be no evidence that his discharge was ever considered. Henry's notes described him in positive terms throughout as quiet, industrious, cheerful, well-behaved, rational, tranquil, and generally in good health. This assessment would have been favourable in the case of a female patient; therefore, release would probably have been a distinct possibility. Yet Henry was not considered to be in a fit mental state to be discharged to the workhouse or to the care of family without being a danger to himself or others. In March 1905, when an annual report was carried out, his mental condition was described as 'enfeebled and epileptic'.[184] Even though Catherine and Henry were described in similar terms as regards their mental health, it seemed that as a man, who was still suffering epileptic attacks, he posed a far more serious threat to others than Catherine did.

Conclusion

In the majority of cases, insane mothers suffering from puerperal-related mental illness found their way into asylums via the usual route for treatment and care. The emerging psychiatric profession during the nineteenth century, the expanding knowledge in the field of obstetrics and the continual admission of insane patients to the asylum gave medical specialists the opportunity to trial different treatments, while simultaneously struggling for medical and professional dominance. The asylum cases were not criminal cases, but they are of significant interest to researchers of female insanity in Wales. These particular cases provide a clear distinction between temporary insanity during childbirth, used as a form of defence in infanticide trials from the eighteenth century onwards, and mental illness of a more serious kind. The casebooks present the opportunity to understand the mothers' state of mind and the symptoms and diagnosis of puerperal-related illness. However, just as importantly, the mothers' voices can be heard as they disclose the disturbing circumstances surrounding their mental breakdown.

A detailed analysis of four insane mothers detained at Broadmoor offers a different and new perspective on insanity as the cause of child murder in Wales. Also, an explanation of the illness contributes to understanding the link between insanity and child murder, and how the crime was perceived and understood in Welsh communities at the time. The criminal cases expose a number of issues, while the inclusion of Henry's case reveals gender differences and similarities in relation to child murder, insanity and the law. It is also significant that Henry was treated in much the same way by the press and the courts as the mothers had been, even though he displayed no obvious signs of insanity. Although the parents discussed in this chapter killed their children, the law relating to insanity made allowances for the biological constitution of women, which, for obvious reasons, did not extend to men.

Gender was also a factor when it came to release from Broadmoor. Henry's release back into the community was much less likely, mainly due to the gendered approach of placing women back to their 'rightful' place in the home. The issues of class and respectability were also important during the legal procedure in court, and were of equal relevance to the bureaucratic process necessary for discharge from Broadmoor.

The nineteenth century witnessed important changes in the field of mental illness, and this was reflected in social attitudes concerning insanity. The evidence shows that the attitude towards insane mothers was one of understanding and tolerance, and this was also apparent in Henry's case. Despite the fact that mothers had been detained as criminal lunatics, it was still preferable to restore them to full health in order to fulfil their natural feminine role as wives and mothers, and not as child murderers.

Notes

1 Geoffrey Clarke, MD, Senior Assistant Medical Officer, London County Asylum, Banstead, 'The Forms of Mental Disorder occurring in connection with Child-bearing', *The Journal of Mental Science,* 59 (1913), 67–74.

2 Henry Rayner, MD, 'A Discussion on the Treatment of Melancholia', *The British Medical Journal*, 2/1813 (1895), 760–6.

3 Joan Busfield, *Men, Women and Madness: Understanding Gender and Mental Disorder* (Hampshire, 1996), p. 123.

4 Hilary Marland, 'Disappointment and desolation: women, doctors and interpretations of puerperal insanity in the nineteenth century', *History of Psychiatry,* 14/3 (2003), 303–20 (p. 317).

5 Nancy Theriot, 'Diagnosing Unnatural Motherhood: Nineteenth-Century Physicians and 'Puerperal Insanity'', *American Studies*, 30/2 (1989), 69–88 (p. 83).

6 *The British Medical Journal*, 'Confusional Insanity', 1/1518 (1890), 250–1 (p. 250).

7 Tony Ward, 'The Sad Subject of Infanticide: Law, Medicine and Child Murder, 1860–1938', *Social and Legal Studies*, 8 (1999), 163–80; Tony Ward, 'Law, Common Sense and the Authority of Science: Expert Witnesses and Criminal Insanity in England, c.1840–1940', *Social & Legal Studies*, 6/3 (1997), 343–62.

8 Roger Smith, *Trial by Medicine: Insanity and Responsibility in Victorian Trials* (Edinburgh, 1981), p. 149.

9 Glamorgan Archives (hereafter GA), Glamorgan County Asylum Case Book Females, 1140–1587, 1874–1876, DHGL/10/43; Case Book Females, 3160–3605, 1886–87, DHGL/10/48; Case Book, Females, 5562–5956, 1895–1896; DHGL/10/55; Case Book, Females, 10100–10495, 1905–1906, DHGL/10/67.

10 Quoted in Joan Wallach Scott, *Gender and the Politics of History* (New York, 1988), p. 29.

11 Jonathan Andrews, 'The boundaries of Her Majesty's pleasure: discharging child murderers from Broadmoor and Perth Criminal Lunatic Department, 1860–1920', in Mark Jackson (ed.), *Infanticide: Historical Perspectives on Child Murder and Concealment, 1550–2000* (Aldershot, 2002), pp. 216–48 (p. 222).

12 *Carmarthen Journal*, 7 February 1879, p. 2.

13 J. Thompson Dickson, Medical Superintendent at St Luke's Hospital, 'A Contribution to the Study of the so-called Puerperal Insanity', *Journal of Mental Science*, 16 (1871), 379–90 (p. 389).

14 M. D. McCleod, Medical Superintendent East Riding Asylum, 'An Address on Puerperal Insanity', *The British Medical Journal*, 2/1336 (1886), 236–42 (p. 240).

15 John Conolly, MD, 'Principal Forms of Insanity: Description and Treatment of Puerperal Insanity', *Lancet,* 1 (1846), 349–54 (p. 350).

16 Alan Rigden, MD, 'Presidential Address Concerning the Insanity of Childbirth', *The British Medical Journal*, 2/2393 (1906), 1253–7 (p. 1256).

17 Robert Boyd, MD, 'Observations on Puerperal Insanity', *Journal of Mental Science*, 16 (1870), 153–65 (p. 155).

18 Aleck Bourne, Sections of Medicine, Neurology, Obstetrics, Psychiatry and Surgery, 'Discussion on post-operative and puerperal mental disorder', *Proceedings of the Royal Society of Medicine*, 17 (1924), 1–14 (p. 6).
19 Dr Cuthbert Lockyer, Sections of Medicine, Neurology, Obstetrics, Psychiatry and Surgery, 'Discussion on post-operative and puerperal mental disorder', *Proceedings of the Royal Society of Medicine*, 17 (1924), 1–14 (p. 13).
20 John Baker, MD, Deputy Superintendent, State Asylum, Broadmoor, 'Female Criminal Lunatics: A Sketch', *Journal of Mental Science*, 200 (1902), 13–25 (p. 18).
21 Dr T. B. Hyslop, Sections of Medicine, Neurology, Obstetrics, Psychiatry and Surgery, 'Discussion on post-operative and puerperal mental disorder', *Proceedings of the Royal Society of Medicine*, 17 (1924), 1–14 (p. 2).
22 Asa Janson, 'From Statistics to Diagnostics: Medical Certificates, Melancholia, and "Suicidal Propensities" in Victorian Psychiatry', *Journal of Social History*, 46/3 (2013), 1–14 (pp. 2–3) doi:10.1093/jsh/shs120.
23 Baker, 'Female Criminal Lunatics', pp. 21–2.
24 GA, Case Book, Females, 5562–5956, 1895–96, DHGL/10/55, p. 445.
25 GA, Case Book, Females, DHGL/10/55, p. 465.
26 GA, Case Book, Females, DHGL/10/55, p. 569.
27 GA, Case Book, Females, DHGL/10/55, p. 317.
28 Dr T. B. Hyslop, Sections of Medicine, p. 1.
29 GA, Case Book, Females, DHGL/10/55, p. 323.
30 GA, Case Book, Females, 1140–1587, 1874–76, DHGL/10/43, p. 252.
31 GA, Case Book, Females, DHGL/10/43, p. 576.
32 Henry Sutherland, 'On the Artificial Feeding of the Insane', *Journal of Psychological Medicine and Mental Pathology*, 1 (1875), 98–115 (pp. 98–9).
33 Sutherland, 'On the Artificial Feeding of the Insane', 98–115.
34 GA, Case Book, Females, DHGL/10/55, p. 323.
35 GA, Case Book, Females, DHGL/10/43, p. 620.
36 L. Harris-Liston, 'Artificial Feeding of the Insane', *The British Medical Journal*, 1/1885 (13 February 1897), 391–2 (p. 391).
37 Sutherland, 'On the Artificial Feeding of the Insane', 100.
38 Sarah Chaney, 'No "Sane" Person Would Have Any Idea: Patients' Involvement in Late Nineteenth-Century British Asylum Psychiatry', *Medical History*, 60/1 (2016), 37–53 (p. 42).
39 W. Herbert, 'The Forcible Feeding of the Insane', *The British Medical Journal*, 1/1731 (3 March 1894), 462.
40 David Wright, 'Delusions of gender? Lay identification and clinical diagnosis of insanity in Victorian England', in Jonathan Andrews and Anne Digby (eds), *Sex and Seclusion, Class and Custody: Perspectives and Gender and Class in the History of British and Irish Psychiatry* (Amsterdam, 2004), pp. 149–76 (pp. 166–7).
41 GA, Case Book, Females, DHGL/10/43, p. 220.
42 Conolly, 'Principle Forms of Insanity', 352.
43 Morag Allen Campbell, '"Noisy, restless and incoherent': puerperal insanity at Dundee Lunatic Asylum', *History of Psychiatry*, 28/1 (2017), 44–57 (p. 53).
44 Clarke, 'The Forms of Mental Disorder occurring in connection with Child-bearing', 68.

45 Campbell, 'Noisy, restless and incoherent', 53.
46 GA, Case Book, Females, DHGL/10/43, p. 176.
47 GA, Case Book, Females, DHGL/10/43, p. 115.
48 GA, Glamorgan County Lunatic Asylum, Case Book, Females, 1588–2069, 1877–80, DHGL/10/44, p. 473.
49 GA, Case Book, Females, DHGL/10/44, p. 169.
50 GA, Case Book, Females, DHGL/10/44, p. 461.
51 Campbell, 'Noisy, restless and incoherent', 53.
52 Royal College of Psychiatrists, 'Postpartum Psychosis: Severe mental illness after childbirth, http://www.rcpsych.ac.uk/healthadvice/problemsdisorderspostpartumpsychosis.aspx., p. 1.
53 Dorothy Sit, MD, Anthony J. Rothschild, MD, Katherine L. Wisner, 'A review of postpartum psychosis', *Journal of Women's Health,* 15/4 (2006), 352–68; Royal College of Psychiatrists, 'Postpartum Psychosis', 1–10.
54 *Haverfordwest & Milford Haven Telegraph*, 12 June 1895, p. 4.
55 Katherine D. Watson, 'Religion, Community and the Infanticidal Mother: Evidence from 1840s Rural Wiltshire', *Family and Community History*, 11/2 (2008), 116–33 (p. 117).
56 Berkshire Record Office (hereafter BRO), Broadmoor Criminal Lunatic Asylum Archives, Admissions Registers, 1868–1900, D/H14/D1/1/1/2, 1900–1906, D/H14/D1/1/2/2, 1907–1914, D/H14/D1/1/3/1.
57 GA, Case Book Females, DHGL/10/43; Case Book Females, DHGL/10/48; Case Book, Females, DHGL/10/55; Case Book, Females, DHGL/10/67.
58 Baker, 'Female Criminal Lunatics', 19.
59 Baker, 'Female Criminal Lunatics', 13–25.
60 Baker, 'Female Criminal Lunatics', 16.
61 Baker, 'Female Criminal Lunatics', 21.
62 BRO, Annual Report as to the condition and circumstances of a Criminal Lunatic, Broadmoor Criminal Lunatic Asylum, D/H14/D2/2/2/269/30.
63 *Cardiff Times*, 21 December 1872, p. 6.
64 *County Observer & Monmouthshire Central Advertiser*, 21 December 1872, p. 5.
65 *Cardiff Times*, 21 December 1872, p. 6.
66 BRO, Schedule A, Register No. 220, D/H14/D2/2/2/269/1.
67 *Western Mail*, 12 March 1873, p. 4.
68 BRO, Warrant, D/H14/D2/2/2/269/2.
69 BRO, Admissions Registers, Broadmoor Criminal Lunatic Asylum, 1868–1900, D/H14/D1/1/1/2, 1900–1906, D/H14/D1/1/1/2.
70 *Carmarthen Journal*, 7 February 1879, p. 2.
71 George M. Robertson, Physician-Superintendent Royal Edinburgh Asylum, 'Some medico-legal and practical considerations relating to melancholia', *The British Medical Journal*, 1/2623 (8 April 1911), 800–4 (p. 800).
72 Dickson, 'A Contribution', 390.
73 *Carmarthen Journal*, 7 February 1879, p. 2.
74 *Western Mail*, 5 February 1879, p. 3.
75 Alan Rigden, MD, 'Presidential Address Concerning the Insanity of Childbirth', *The British Medical Journal*, 2/2393 (1906), 1253–7 (p. 1253).
76 Rigden, 'Presidential Address', 1253.

77 J. Stanley Hopwood, M.B., B.S., Lond., Junior Deputy Medical Superintendent, The State Criminal Lunatic Asylum, Broadmoor, 'Child Murder and Insanity', *Journal of Mental Science* (January 1927), 95—108 (96).

78 *Western Mail*, 5 February 1879, p. 3.

79 BRO, D/H14/D2/2/2/290.

80 T. D. Clouston, Superintendent of the Cumberland and Westmorland Asylum, 'What cases should be sent to lunatic asylums? And when?' *The British Medical Journal*, 1/578 (27 January 1872), 96–8 (p. 97).

81 Clouston, 'What cases should be sent to lunatic asylums?' 97.

82 *Llanelly and County Guardian*, 6 February 1879, p. 3.

83 *Western Mail*, 6 February 1879, p. 3.

84 R. D. Mackay and Tony Ward, 'The Long-Term Detention of Those found Unfit to Plead and Legally Insane', *British Journal of Criminology*, 34/1 (1994), 30–43 (p. 35).

85 BRO, Warrant for the reception into the Broadmoor Criminal Lunatic Asylum, D/H14/D2/2/2/290/2.

86 BRO, Case Book, D/H14/D2/1/2/1/290, Broadmoor.

87 BRO, Case Book, D/H14/D2/1/2/1/290, Broadmoor.

88 Hopwood, 'Child Murder and Insanity', 99–100.

89 *Western Mail*, 23 November 1883, p. 3.

90 Robertson, 'Some medico-legal and practical considerations relating to melancholia', 801.

91 *Western Mail*, 23 November 1883, p. 3.

92 *Western Mail*, 22 November 1883, p. 3.

93 *Western Mail*, 23 November 1883, p. 3.

94 *Cambrian & Weekly General Advertiser*, 23 November, 1883, p. 8.

95 *South Wales Daily News*, 23 November 1883, p. 2.

96 *The Cambrian*, 6 July 1883, p. 5.

97 Akihito Suzuki, 'Enclosing and disclosing lunatics within the family walls: domestic psychiatric regime in early nineteenth-century England', in Peter Bartlett and David Wright (eds), *Outside the Walls of the Asylum: The History of Care in the Community 1750–2000* (London, 1999), 115–31 (p. 117).

98 *Western Mail*, 14 February 1884, p. 4.

99 *Cardiff Times*, 10 May 1884, p. 6.

100 *Western Mail*, 23 November 1883, p. 3.

101 *Haverfordwest & Milford Haven Telegraph*, 12 June 1895, p. 4.

102 *Western Mail*, 10 June 1895, p. 5.

103 Hopwood, 'Child murder and insanity', 104.

104 *Haverfordwest & Milford Haven Telegraph*, 12 June 1895, p. 4.

105 BRO, D/H14/2/2/513/2.

106 BRO, Schedule A, D/H14/D2/1/2/2.

107 BRO, Warrant of Removal from Prison to Asylum (Unconvicted Prisoner), D/H14/2/2/513/1.

108 BRO, Schedule A, D/H14/D2/1/2/2.

109 BRO, Case Book, 513, Broadmoor.

110 BRO, Case Book, 513, Broadmoor.

111 Baker, 'Female Criminal Lunatics', p. 25.

112 Baker, 'Female Criminal Lunatics', p. 21.
113 BRO, D/H14/D2/2/2/513/6.
114 *Western Mail*, 10 June 1895, p. 5.
115 Clouston, 'What cases should be sent to lunatic asylums?' 97.
116 David Wright, 'Getting Out of the Asylum: Understanding the confinement of the insane in the nineteenth century', *Society for the Social History of Medicine*, 10/1 (1997), 137–55 (p. 153).
117 Hopwood, 'Child Murder and Insanity', 97.
118 Dr Eliza Walker Dunbar, 'A Discussion on the Treatment of Melancholia', *The British Medical Journal*, 2/1813 (1895), 760–6 (p. 766).
119 *Cardiff Times*, 19 October 1895, p. 6.
120 Smith, *Trial by Medicine*, p. 107.
121 Chas. A. Mercier, 'A Discussion on the Plea of Insanity in Criminal Cases', *The British Medical Journal*, 2/1966 (3 September 1898), 585–8 (p. 587).
122 'Law and Insanity', *The British Medical Journal,* 1/220 (1865), 275–7 (p. 275).
123 Mercier, 'A Discussion on the Plea of Insanity in Criminal Cases', 587.
124 Baker, 'Female Criminal Lunatics', 27.
125 BRO, Admissions Registers, Broadmoor.
126 A. C. Clark, 'Aetiology, Pathology, and Treatment of Puerperal Insanity', *Journal of Mental Science*, 33/142 (1887), 169–89 (p. 180).
127 *Carmarthen Journal*, 2 March 1888, p. 3.
128 Jade Shepherd, '"One of the Best Fathers until He Went Out of His Mind": Paternal Child-Murder, 1864–1900', *Journal of Victorian Culture*, 18/1 (2013), 17–35 (p. 17).
129 *Western Mail*, 27 February 1888, p. 3.
130 BRO, Schedule A, Reg. No. 1323, D/H14/D2/1/1/15.
131 *Western Mail*, 3 December 1887, p. 3; *Carmarthen Journal*, 9 December 1887, p. 2.
132 *Llanelly and County Guardian*, 6 February 1879, p. 3.
133 *County Observer and Monmouth Central Advertiser*, 14 December 1872, p. 5.
134 *The Cambrian and Weekly Advertiser*, 23 November 1883, p. 8.
135 Martin Weiner, 'Convicted Murderers and the Victorian Press: Condemnation vs. Sympathy', *Crimes and Misdemeanours*, 1/2 (2007), 110–25 (pp. 111–12).
136 BRO, D/H14/D2/2/2/513/2.
137 *Carmarthen Journal*, 9 December 1887, p. 2.
138 W. R. Lambert, *Drink and Sobriety in Victorian Wales, c.1820–1895* (Cardiff, 1983), p. 156.
139 *Carmarthen Journal*, 9 December 1887, p. 2.
140 *Carmarthen Journal*, 2 March 1888, p. 3.
141 John Charles Bucknill, MD, 'An Address on the Law of Murder in its Medical Aspects', *The British Medical Journal*, 2/726 (28 November 1874), 667–72 (p. 667).
142 Geo. F. Blandford, 'A Discussion on the Plea of Insanity in Criminal Cases', 588.
143 Busfield, *Men, Women and Madness*, pp. 149–50.
144 *Western Mail*, 27 February 1888, p. 3.
145 *Carmarthen Journal*, 2 March 1888, p. 3.
146 Shepherd, 'One of the Best Fathers', 20.
147 *Carmarthen Journal*, 2 March 1888, p. 3.
148 F. Whitwell, 'The Law on Insanity', *The British Medical Journal,* 2/934 (1878), 784.

149 Edward C. Mann, MD, 'Mental Responsibility and the Diagnosis of Insanity in Criminal Cases', *Journal of Psychological Medicine and Mental Pathology* (5 October 1879), 225–34 (p. 233).
150 BRO, Schedule A, D/H14/D2/2/1/1323/3.
151 *Carmarthen Journal*, 2 March 1888, p. 3.
152 Daniel J. R. Grey, 'Discourses of Infanticide in England, 1880–1922' (unpublished PhD thesis, Roehampton University, London, 2008), 256.
153 Baker, 'Female Criminal Lunatics', 27.
154 *South Wales Echo*, 27 February 1888, p. 4.
155 *Western Mail*, 5 March 1888, p. 3.
156 BRO, Schedule A, D/H14/D2/2/1/1323/3.
157 Return of Judicial Statistics of England and Wales, 1898 (Part I. Police; Criminal Proceedings; Prisons), 19.
158 R. M. Jackson, 'A Note on Broadmoor Patients', *The Cambridge Law Journal*, 11/1 (1951), 61.
159 BRO, Warrant was for removal of a Criminal Lunatic ordered to be detained during Her Majesty's pleasure from Prison to Broadmoor, D/H14/D2/2/1/1323/1.
160 BRO, Warrant of Removal from Prison to Asylum (Unconvicted Prisoner), D/H14/2/2/513/1.
161 BRO, Case Notes, D/H14/D2/1/1/15.
162 Richard Brayn, Superintendent State Criminal Lunatic Asylum, Broadmoor, 'A Brief Outline of the Arrangements for the Care and Supervision of the Criminal Insane in England during the Present Century', *Journal of Mental Science*, 47 (1901), 250–60 (p. 256).
163 Andrews, 'The boundaries of Her Majesty's Pleasure', p. 235.
164 BRO, Letter from M David to Dr Orange, 16 October 1874, D/H14/D2/2/2/269/6.
165 BRO, Letter from Rev. W. Davies, Vicar of Pyle, to Dr Orange, 17 October 1876, D/H14/D2/2/2/269/9.
166 BRO, Letter from J. C. Pritchard to Dr Orange, 15 February 1877, D/H14/D2/2/2/269/10.
167 BRO, Medical Assessment, D/H14/D2/2/2/269/19.
168 BRO, Letter to Dr Orange, D/H14/D2/2/2/269/17.
169 BRO, letter to Dr Orange, D/H14/D2/2/2/269/17.
170 BRO, Letter to Dr Orange, D/H14/D2/2/2/269/25.
171 BRO, Warrant for Re-admission, D/H14/D2/2/2/269/28.
172 Brayn, 'A Brief Outline', 256.
173 BRO, Annual Report as to the condition and circumstances of a Criminal Lunatic, D/H14/D2/2/2/269/30.
174 BRO, Inquest, D/H14/D2/2/2.
175 BRO, Medical Assessment, D/H14/02/2/2/290/9.
176 BRO, Correspondence between Whitehall and Broadmoor, 13 January 1880, D/H14/02/2/2/290/10.
177 Andrews, 'The boundaries of Her Majesty's pleasure', p. 239.
178 McCleod, 'An Address on Puerperal Insanity', 242.
179 Clarke, 'The Forms of Mental Disorder', 69.
180 Census Return, 1881, Llanelly, Carmarthenshire, RG11/5374, https://www.findmypast.co.uk, accessed 30/10/2010.

181 Census Return, 1891, Swansea, RG12 4473, https://www.findmypast.co.uk, accessed 30/10/2010.

182 *Western Mail,* 20 June 1895, p. 6.

183 *Western Mail*, 27 February 1888, p. 3.

184 Annual Report as to the condition and circumstances of a Criminal Lunatic, D/H14/D2/2/1/1323/14 (BRO).

Chapter Five

'The burden is so great for them that they do violent deeds'[1]: Infanticide

In 1881 Susan Mogford, from Cardiff, was indicted at South Wales Assizes for the wilful murder of her newborn illegitimate child after disposing of it in a canal. The details of the case reported in the press reveal distressing circumstances, and the case is one of the few in which the mother was sentenced to death for murder. On the night in question the young woman was seen on the canal side emptying a bucket into the water. The witness realised that it was a baby and rescued it from the water. Following her arrest, Susan Mogford was cautioned by the police that she need not say anything unless she chose to do so. Despite the caution she confessed and said, 'I wish I had drowned myself. I did have a baby, but I thought it best to drown it, as I had no means of keeping it.'[2] The defence counsel pointed out in court that the young woman 'had been left an orphan young in life', and had been seduced while 'alone and friendless'. By the time the infant was born, Susan Mogford had no money, no home; she was living in a deplorable condition; and it was contended in court that she was in such a state as to be unaccountable for her actions. The defence counsel argued that 'the girl could not be found guilty of murder as the child recovered after being taken from the water, death resulting from a subsequent phase of its condition'. However, despite the counsel's appeal, Susan Mogford was convicted of wilful murder, although the jury 'strongly recommended her to mercy on account of her extreme destitution'. The judge assumed the black cap and pronounced that 'you be taken hence to the place from which you came, and thence to a place of execution, and that you be there hung by the neck until you are dead. And may the Lord have mercy on your soul.'[3]

There is no doubt that infanticide is an emotive issue, but cases such as Susan Mogford's reveal much more about the complexities of the crime and that it should not be considered as an indiscriminate act of violence. Attitudes towards infanticide varied between sympathy on the one hand for the typically perceived seduced and abandoned young woman, and condemnation on the other for the failure of a mother to perform her natural duty to protect and care for the child. Many women gave birth in secret; therefore, the law at the time in respect of newborn child murder was difficult to enforce because it had to be proven an infant had experienced a separate existence entirely apart from its mother following the birth to constitute the offence. Establishing proof of a live birth and a separate existence was problematic, regardless of medical testimony in some cases. For that reason, the courts often reverted to the lesser charge of concealment of birth, in spite of obvious violence to the infant's body in cases of infanticide. This chapter addresses the important question of motive: why did one woman choose to acknowledge her pregnancy and raise an illegitimate child, coping with ever-present hardship, and another woman in the same circumstances conceal the birth and kill her newborn child? Although the options for single mothers were bleak (the workhouse, the humiliating procedure to prove the child's paternity, abandonment, abortion or the baby farmer), women made varying decisions based on their circumstances at that point in time. Anne-Marie Kilday and Katherine Watson highlight the fact that 'Little has been written about the reactions to child murder by blood-relatives, near neighbours, or members of the local community in which the crime took place.'[4] It was evident in a number of cases under scrutiny in this chapter that the reactions of relatives and neighbours differed in that some exposed the perpetrators to the authorities, while others acted in order to protect women from possible prosecution. However, in some cases close family members were actually involved in the crime and charged as accomplices alongside the mother.

Susan Mogford's dire situation was characteristic of cases regularly presented before the courts and routinely reported by the press. Hence, scrutiny of local press reports of court proceedings presents the opportunity to explore the motives for the crime and to uncover women's real-life experiences and, therefore, increase our understanding of infanticide in Welsh communities. Newspapers feature as a significant source since they provide a snapshot of Welsh society at a given place and moment in time based on eyewitness accounts and community responses to the crime. The press reports expose the reasons why women committed the offence in many cases and they also help us to understand how social attitudes, economic hardship and politics had a considerable bearing on the crime. Certainly, historians recognise the importance of press reporting on criminal cases because, as Mark Jackson points out, 'newspapers offer an incisive historical entry' into the study of infanticide.[5] Similarly, Nicola Goc found that 'through close reading of news we can see that news texts are multilayered and far richer and more complex than they may at first appear'.[6] Indeed, newspapers offered an interesting forum for debates concerning infanticide and punishment, particularly in capital cases. Consideration is also given to the manner in which infanticide cases were reported in the press, as this often had much to do with engendering public sympathy for offenders. Furthermore, the press were extremely influential in gaining support for numerous campaigns to secure reprieves for mothers convicted of killing their infants. The authorities also obtained newspaper cuttings uncovering additional information reported by members of the community which was not put forward as evidence in court.

Infanticide cases reveal a distinct lack, if not a complete absence in the majority of cases, of the putative father's involvement, even though commentators and feminist campaigners of the day frequently condemned a man's irresponsible behaviour via campaigns, newspapers, periodicals and medical journals. Organised feminist groups actively lobbied the government for comprehensive reform of the Bastardy Laws in an attempt to reduce cases of illegitimacy, infanticide and infant mortality. Not surprisingly, as feminists campaigned to protect young women and girls, the groups questioned the extent of men's control over women's bodies, both medically and legally. This authority was challenged when feminists drew parallels with the coerced medical examinations of women suspected of infanticide with the enforced searches of women under the Contagious Diseases Acts 1864, 1866 and 1869. Feminists had long campaigned for the abolition of the mandatory death penalty for mothers who killed their infants and repeatedly demanded law reform, but it was only lifted with the introduction of the Infanticide Act in 1922. The new act made provision for a separate offence of manslaughter to be brought against the mother, instead of murder.

This removed the mandatory death penalty that had long been a source of complaint, since no woman who had been found guilty of murdering her newborn infant had been executed since Rebecca Smith in 1849.[7] Yet the convicted women were subjected to the anguish of not knowing whether a petition for a reprieve to the Home Secretary would be granted or not.

The chapter is based on close scrutiny of seventy randomly selected cases of concealment of birth and newborn child murder reported in the press. The first part of the chapter addresses the social and economic causes of infanticide. Individual cases reflect social and religious issues, while others point towards government legislation as a cause of the economic hardship endured by many single women who found themselves pregnant out of wedlock. Referring to newspaper reports of criminal trials, coroners' inquests, periodicals and contemporary journals, the second part of the chapter explores the legal consequences for those women charged or convicted of concealment of birth and newborn child murder. It discusses the criminal act, the gathering of police evidence at the time of the suspect's arrest, the authority's decision to prosecute and reasons why some offenders were acquitted or convicted of the crime. Infanticide was committed predominantly by single women; therefore, owing to the nature of the crime, the issue of gender is present throughout. As gender is of particular relevance, this chapter also explores the activities of the feminist movement from the 1860s onwards. By the 1920s, after decades of feminist activism, a number of women had gained prominent positions in both the fields of politics and criminal justice; so the final part of the chapter considers the influence of the feminist movement on the introduction of the Infanticide Act in 1922.

'I had no means of keeping it'[8]: Social and economic causes of infanticide

Many single women were dismissed once their pregnancies became known to employers, and not surprisingly, without familial support or paternity payments, this often resulted in homelessness or admission to the workhouse. With no employer's reference, it also proved difficult for a woman to find another situation once she had 'lost her character'. John Gillis explains why domestic servants were particularly vulnerable to pregnancies out of wedlock.

He maintains that 'The answer lies in their efforts to combine customs of courtship and marriage appropriate to women of their class backgrounds with the standards of conduct expected of them by their employers.' While away from home, servants were often under strict supervision by their employers. Therefore, unlike women who practised rural Welsh courting customs such as 'bundling', Gillis points out that for many servants, 'it was rare for them to meet men in the traditional setting of courtship, namely dances, hiring fairs and festivals or at home and among friends'.[9] Indeed, Gillis found that the conditions of employment for servants 'dictated a peculiarly private kind of liaison'. Couples met 'by appointment' on their days off work, and courtship was 'necessarily furtive and clandestine'.[10]

One apparent reason for the correlation between servants, illegitimacy and infanticide was due to the fact that domestic service was the most common form of employment for girls and women during this period. Paternity cases discussed in Chapter One provide evidence that the lowly status of young female servants, such as Hannah Jones from New Quay, within the household hierarchy meant that they were susceptible to unscrupulous men for a number of reasons, including overfamiliarity with fellow male servants, or sexual harassment and abuse from members of the household. However, paternity cases involving young women like Mary Jane Mathias[11] and Sarah Davies,[12] for example, also prove that unwanted pregnancies were frequently a result of courtship, broken relationships or seduction that had taken place under the promise of marriage. Servants who worked further afield left their families and support networks behind, which, under certain circumstances, might have left them isolated. Apart from the support of fellow servants, a number of women and young girls were vulnerable and naive; therefore, when confronted with an unwanted pregnancy, many lacked the ability to deal with the situation alone. Servants who concealed their pregnancy and killed the child at birth were also at greater risk of discovery, particularly for those who lived in. Under these conditions, servants had fewer places to conceal the bodies and tended to hide them in similar places, such as the privy or in a box in their bedroom, although it was reported in 1874 that Dinah Thomas, from Haverfordwest, hid her dead infant in a clock case in the kitchen.[13] Disposal of bodies appeared to be less challenging for women who lived in poorer urban areas, because there were more opportunities to conceal dead infants in the deprived districts of towns and cities. This explains why more infant bodies were discovered in dock areas or waterways and why the offenders were never apprehended.

In the absence of any statement from the perpetrator, it is difficult to establish the exact motive for the crime, especially as the reputed father was rarely mentioned. Even so, the available evidence indicates that fear of economic hardship, social ostracism and the prevailing religious attitudes towards illegitimacy, underpinned by double standards of sexual morality, played a significant role. That is not to say that women did not deliberately commit wilful murder. Jessica Sheetz-Nguyen questioned the historical agency of women and explored the degree to which they made choices based on personal limitations. Sheetz-Nguyen maintains that 'A woman based her actions, regarding pregnancy and childcare, on internal emotional limits, her value system, and external opportunities.'[14] At what stage women made the conscious decision to conceal the birth is unknown, although Katherine Watson argues that 'Their reactions to societal norms that made their pregnancies so problematic caused them to view the child as a burden to be disposed of, presumably under the influence of a significant degree of psychological dissociation.'[15] Clearly some women denied their pregnancy and suppressed any maternal feelings in order to avert exposure and dismissal by their employer. This may have been the case for Catherine James, a farm servant from Johnstown, Carmarthen. In 1884 she gave birth prematurely during the night, having repeatedly denied to her master and fellow servants that she was pregnant, even when she was in labour. The same morning, after giving birth, Catherine James regained sufficient physical and mental strength to milk the cows and proceeded to cut up swedes in the field afterwards.[16]

Research into modern-day cases of denied or concealed pregnancy reveals both medical and social perspectives to help explain the thought processes and experiences of women in the past. Kathryn Stammers and Nicola Long account for denial of pregnancy as 'a woman's subjective lack of awareness of being pregnant or when a male partner contests or disputes the pregnancy'. Pregnancy can be unrecognisable to first-time mothers because they are unfamiliar with the symptoms. In some cases symptoms are absent and, therefore, not detected by relatives.[17] Angela Jenkins *et al* make clear that a woman's fears can be so overwhelming that this defence mechanism can drive them to deny their pregnancy and hamper their ability to form an attachment to the foetus and prepare for the birth. Consequently, these associated risks lead to 'emotional disturbance, lack of antenatal care, precipitous delivery (often into the toilet bowl) and neonaticide'. Research indicates that 'men's doubts, denials or disputes of pregnancy are generally based on the credibility of the woman, questioning her moral or drinking behaviour, infidelity and spiteful intentions'.[18] There is no doubt that current research can draw parallels with the experiences of women from the past, as they denied or deliberately concealed their pregnancies.

Employers often dismissed servants if they were pregnant outside wedlock because, as Sheetz-Nguyen points out, 'her presence could blight the household's reputation'. To continue her employment 'could create a highly disturbing scenario, upsetting the lady of the house, and casting suspicion on all males, including husband, brother, son or other male servants'.[19] In view of the prevailing attitudes, it is not surprising to find that women concealed their pregnancies from employers out of necessity, rather than deception, in order to keep their posts. Anne-Marie Kilday found that unmarried women developed 'personal strategies' to hide their pregnancies, and 'used prolonged subterfuge of one kind or another to maximise their chances of self-preservation'.[20] This pattern of behaviour is evident in many cases referred to in this chapter, as servants left their current posts and usually found new employment during the last two months or so of their pregnancy; therefore, their current shape and size were unfamiliar to the new household. Shani D'Cruze and Louise A. Jackson take into account that the signs of pregnancy could be interpreted as symptoms for other conditions, whereby weight gain could be 'explained as "dropsy", or a birth or miscarriage as some sort of "flux"'.[21]

Other women in the household frequently challenged pregnant servants about their condition. In 1884 Kate Hickey, from County Cork in Ireland, gave birth two months after she began work as a cook for her new employer at Tenby. Other members of the household were suspicious of her condition, although she denied it when challenged by her fellow servant, even after the onset of labour. A fellow servant, also from County Cork, stated in her evidence in court that 'Among Irish girls illegitimacy was looked upon more seriously than was the case in this country.'[22] Ireland's attitude to illegitimacy might have had a considerable bearing on why Kate Hickey chose to seek employment in Pembrokeshire rather than remain in Ireland.[23]

Women undoubtedly went to great lengths to conceal their pregnancies. However, without evidence from the women themselves, it is difficult to establish whether unwanted pregnancies were a result of seduction under the promise of marriage, broken relationships or sexual harassment and abuse. Jill Barber's study of the sexual harassment of female servants in west Wales revealed a disparity between incidences and court cases. Barber points out that 'Most victims suffered in silence, and where complaints of sexual abuse were made, many were withdrawn before they reached the courts.'[24] Likewise, Françoise Barret-Ducrocq maintains that servants were often left vulnerable not only to their masters, but also to their male guests 'whose social position gave them a large measure of impunity. Through shame or deference, and through fear of getting the sack, very few maids dared complain to their mistresses.'[25] Young women and girls were vulnerable and had little recourse to seek legal representation; in the vast majority of cases they remained undefended in court and were usually left traumatised by the whole experience. With so few resources and fearful of the consequences, it seems that many victims were reluctant to lodge complaints of sexual assault against their abusers.

'I did not know what to do'[26]: The legal consequences of infanticide

Infanticidal mothers were deemed to be at odds with their natural instinct to protect and nurture their children. This rendered the crime distinct from other murders; hence, it was felt at the time that women were more deserving of pity than punishment. The relaxation of attitudes towards this particular crime had developed over three centuries. In the seventeenth century women who were accused of murdering their newborn infants were tried under the statute of 1624, An Act to Prevent the Destroying and Murthering of Bastard Children, introduced to limit the number of illegitimate children born to 'lewd' women. It was assumed at the time that if a woman concealed the infant's death she was guilty of murder, although, as D'Cruze and Jackson point out, the law appeared to take little account of the possibility of stillbirth.[27] The onus was on a woman to prove her innocence, rather than for the court to prove her guilt. In 1803, the statute of 1624 was repealed and replaced with the Lord Ellenborough Offences Against the Person Act. The 1803 Act allowed for a separate charge of concealment of birth, which brought with it a lesser sentence of up to two years' imprisonment. This was an alternative to the indictment of wilful murder, which was punishable by death if convicted of the charge.

In August 1805 Justice Hardinge complained that the Lord Ellenborough Act was too lenient by referring to two Welsh infanticide cases that occurred in April 1805. One woman, who had been charged with the murder of her infant, was acquitted and convicted of the alternative indictment of concealment of birth and imprisoned for two years. Justice Hardinge commented, '*Imprisoned* – (I blush for the law in stating it) – *for two years*! – the severest punishment left us for that offence, which is the root and principal of these murders.'[28] The two women lived in close proximity on the border of two counties. Even though Justice Hardinge mentioned no names or locations, the other woman referred to was almost certainly Mary Morgan, aged seventeen, from Radnorshire.[29] She committed the same offence in a similar manner, was convicted of murder and sentenced to death by Justice Hardinge. The young woman was executed, and her body was 'dissected and anatomized'.[30]

The change in the law in 1803 required evidence to prove a live- or still-birth, and a woman was deemed to be innocent until proven guilty. Justice Hardinge argued that 'The difficultly of reaching it by legal proof is increased fifty-fold by a new Act of Parliament, passed upon grounds of policy, which I dare not, as a judge, arraign, but which I am not able to fathom.'[31] Historian Mark Jackson maintains that:

> By authorizing a return to common law, and by establishing an official requirement for evidence about live- and still-birth, the 1803 Act was simply endorsing the evidential rules and procedures, including the routine admission of medical testimony, that had been adopted in both coroners' and trial courts since the middle of the eighteenth century.[32]

Also in April 1805, at Haverfordwest Assizes, a mother and daughter were indicted for the murder of the young woman's illegitimate child; 'but as no proof could be adduced that the infant was born alive, the old woman was acquitted, and the daughter sentenced to two years solitary confinement for concealing the birth'.[33] Another case in April 1805, again at Haverfordwest Assizes, was that of Jane Davies, who was acquitted of the murder of her illegitimate child but convicted of concealment of birth and sentenced to two years' imprisonment.[34]

Between 1730 and the introduction of the 1803 Act, it was clear that juries were reluctant to convict, since offenders were either acquitted of murder or no true bill was found; therefore no criminal trial took place. The records of the Courts of Great Sessions in Wales revealed that three women were sentenced to death in Carmarthenshire during the period 1730–1803, although Ann Walter from Llangyndeyrn was reprieved, while Susan David from Llangynner was pardoned and transported for life. Elinor Hadley, from Carmarthen, however, was shown no mercy. In Pembrokeshire, Grace Morgan, from Roch, was sentenced to death, pardoned and also transported for life. The records indicated that no offenders in Cardiganshire or Glamorganshire were convicted of the charges brought against them. Even after the introduction of the Lord Ellenborough Act in 1803, the tendency of juries to acquit remained, or they found the offender guilty of concealment of birth instead of wilful murder. Alternatively, the grand jury returned no true bill.[35]

The next major piece of legislation following the Lord Ellenborough Act was introduced more than a century later in the form of the Infanticide Act in 1922. The new law meant that the charge brought against an infanticidal mother could be one of manslaughter rather than murder, and the mandatory death penalty was finally removed. The 1922 Infanticide Act referred to newly born infants, but it did not define the age. Therefore, the Act was amended in 1938 to provide for the age definition and is still in force in England and Wales at present. The 1938 Act states that:

> Where a woman by any wilful act or omission on the part of the mother which caused the death of her child under the age of twelve months, while the balance of her mind was disturbed by reason of her not having fully recovered

> from the effect of giving birth or by reason of the effect of lactation consequent upon the birth of the child, then, notwithstanding that the circumstances were such that but for the Act the offence would have amounted to murder she shall be guilty of a felony, to wit infanticide, and may for such offence be dealt with and punished as if she had been guilty of the offence of manslaughter of the child.[36]

The lenient attitudes held by judges and juries in cases of newborn child murder were due in part to the difficulties of proving a live birth. Nineteenth-century physician Dr William Burke Ryan argued that the state of the law concerning punishment accounted for the unwillingness of juries to convict on the capital charge. He contended that 'Even when the evidence is very strong, and the offence of a very aggravated character, the severe penalty attached to conviction sways the minds of the juries; and it is a rare thing indeed that a conviction takes place on the capital charge.'[37]

Condemnation for the part of the reputed father was another reason why some juries sympathised with the mother. S. G. O. commented in *The Times* that 'the jury are men; being men, the jury lean to the condoning of one who stands at the bar accused of a crime with which, without man's guilt in the first instance, she would not have been charged'.[38] Echoing the same sentiment in 1912, crime writer Hargrave L. Adam, the author of *Women and Crime*, maintained that:

> The man who gets a woman into trouble and then deserts her is among the most despicable of mankind, and ought to be punished as a criminal. His act does, in fact, frequently lead to crime. He should, therefore, be brought within the scope of the Statute Book.[39]

The fact that the life of a newborn illegitimate infant was considered less than that of a legitimate child might account for leniency, and partly explains why the law treated infanticidal mothers differently. Karen Clarke argues that 'In order to be swayed by the plight of the mother, the plight of the infant had to be regarded as relatively unimportant,' and that 'this could only happen if the illegitimate infant was not seen as a person'.[40]

During a debate of the Royal Commission on Capital Punishment, it was put forward that the moment of breath entering the body at birth was the point at which the child became a living soul. However, S. H. Walpole argued that this did not 'make it a rational being'. He understood that the real definition of murder was 'the unlawful taking away of the life of a rational being from malice express or implied'.[41] The *British Mothers' Journal and Domestic Magazine* contended that 'the danger to society at large is not so great, or at least not so immediate, from the murder of an infant an hour old as from the murder of an adult. Society therefore refuses to punish the one crime as severely as it punishes the other.' It was suggested that capital punishment for infanticidal mothers should be abolished completely because it would be far more appropriate to sentence women to life imprisonment for the crime instead, and also proof that the infant had once drawn breath was evidence enough on which to convict.[42] S. G. O. argued that 'If infant life has not the ordinary value of human life, let the law say so. If it has that proportion of such value which should make it worthy of protection, make that protection a reality.'[43] Cases prove that the majority of infanticide victims were illegitimate, therefore as a 'child of no one', or *filius nullius*, this lowly status explains why an unwanted infant's life was worth considerably less than that of a legitimate child in the general public's perception.

Evidence indicates that the police were keen to prosecute in cases of concealment of birth and newborn child murder. The offending women were charged with the wilful murder of infants in a number of cases, yet in court the Grand Jury ignored the bill and found a true bill for the lesser charge of concealment of birth instead. Under these circumstances, one form of defence against the charge of concealment of birth was to show that preparations had been made for the birth by the provision of baby clothes, therefore proving that there was no intention of concealment. In one case Annie Bevan, from Laleston near Bridgend, denied the charge of concealment of birth because she had prepared clothes for the child.[44] Another form of defence was to have a witness present at the birth, although this was unlikely to be the case given the nature of the crime. When seventeen-year-old Mary Morris, from Llanelli, was charged with concealment of birth, Miss Isaacs, a prosecution witness, admitted that the girl had called to her several times during the night. The defence claimed that Mary Morris had never attempted to conceal the birth since calling for assistance negated concealment. Moreover, the defence pointed out that Mary Morris had been 'far more sinned against than sinning'.[45]

In cases of concealment, disposal of the infant's body was crucial, and women often assumed that they had successfully concealed the pregnancy and birth without suspicion. Yet, other members of the household and those living within the surrounding community were often well aware of the woman's condition. Servants were more likely to give birth in their bedroom and, when questioned, would claim to be suffering from an ailment at the onset of labour. When women failed in their covert attempts at disposal, the finger of suspicion was immediately pointed in the direction of the suspect upon discovery of an infant's body. Kilday found that the 'intricate surveillance networks that existed in communities' meant that women were seldom on their own, and it was not obvious 'whether the presence of these networks affected attitudes to new-born child murder when it was discovered, or whether that was more connected with the way in which the crime was committed'.[46] The presence of networks in Welsh communities certainly affected the promptness of a woman's arrest, where she concealed the birth, and the method chosen to dispose of the body.

The most common form of defence put forward by the offender in cases of concealment was to claim that the infant was stillborn. When Maud Benson was charged in 1906 with concealment of birth, her behaviour was characteristic in that she had begun new employment approximately three months before she gave birth. It was reported that the young woman had repeatedly denied her pregnancy when questioned by her mistress, claiming that 'she had been in this condition for the past eighteen months suffering from results of a cold'. Maud Benson was reportedly under surveillance because 'people in Canton were saying that she was in the family way'. With the onset of labour, her mistress could see that she was in pain, but Maud said that it was just inflammation of the bowel and left the house an hour later, allegedly to visit the doctor and then go to stay with her sister for a few days. That same evening, at 10.30 p.m., Maud returned to the house and told her master that she was now alright. At this point, he noticed a change in her appearance. The following morning, the body of a newborn infant was found in a lane close by and Maud was immediately suspected of wrongdoing. The young woman was arrested and taken to the workhouse infirmary. In her statement Maud Benson said, 'I had much pain, and the child was born. I was alone at the time, and afterwards I walked around until it was time to go back in about 10.30 p.m. I left the child in the lane.' The post-mortem indicated that the infant had lived, but death was caused by strangulation. The prosecution pointed out in court that Maud Benson had previously given birth to an illegitimate child in the workhouse in December 1903, and that 'she should know what her proper duty as a mother was'.[47] Despite the evidence against her, the judge directed the jury towards an acquittal. He contended that:

> the child was deposited in the road and not hidden away at all, while the offence was defined by law as concealment of birth by secretly disposing of the body. As the defendant simply left the child in the highway, an act which people must condemn, she had not committed an offence in law.[48]

Maud Benson had previously given birth in the workhouse; therefore, it appears that the decision to conceal the birth was based on her previous experience. Women had options, and on this occasion Maud seemed to be in control of the situation, because the repeated denials, the excuses and the appropriate disposal of the infant in a place not hidden from view meant that she clearly avoided punishment, even though there was conclusive medical testimony to prove that the infant had been strangled.

The suspicious behaviour of pregnant women, while under surveillance by others, meant that few managed to evade the law. A form of surveillance naturally existed in close-knit rural communities; hence, any suspicious behaviour on the woman's part quickly gave rise to gossip. However, it was possible for offenders in rural communities to get away with murder. Evidence shows that it was feasible in some instances to conceal the birth, dispose of the body and avoid arrest. This was the case in 1877 when the body of a dead infant was found in a ditch at Pensarn, Carmarthen. Attempts to locate the mother failed, which prompted the coroner to complain that as the population of Carmarthen and district was not so numerous, the child's mother should have been traced.[49] Towns and cities provided the cover necessary to conceal a birth in urban districts; although, in rural areas, while fields and outbuildings offered immediate cover, discovery was far more likely. A considerable number of dead infants were discovered in urban areas, such as Swansea, where bodies of newborn infants were found under bridges, in back streets and by the waterside. In such cases, the coroner returned an open verdict of 'found dead'.

The disposal of dead infants in rivers, particularly with fast-flowing currents, meant that the bodies were swept away far beyond the point from where they were thrown in. In 1881 two dead infants were discovered in the River Teify in the same neighbourhood, a month apart, but the police were unable to apprehend the perpetrators. As part of the investigation, the Lampeter Board of Guardians wrote to the Chief Constable of Carmarthenshire suggesting that he should apply to the Secretary of State to ask for a reward to be offered for information that would lead to the detection of the perpetrators. Even though the chief constable offered his support to the guardians, he declined to make the application himself. The guardians responded with some strong comments concerning his conduct.[50] Similarly, in 1883, a dead infant was discovered on the banks of the River Aeron between Aberaeron and Lampeter. The infant's body had been swept away by a flood and was covered in more than two feet of sand. In this case the coroner's inquest recorded a verdict of 'found dead'.[51] The disposal of infants in quarries, pits, mines, dock areas, waterways and rivers tends to suggest that in some cases accomplices may have been responsible for concealing the bodies, as these places would have been inaccessible to mothers immediately after the birth. For example, in the case concerning Margaret Jones, from Llanelli, her sister admitted disposing of the infant's body in a clay pit.[52]

It is interesting to note that Michelle Oberman's study of neonaticide cases in Chicago, 1870–1930, found that out of 136 cases 115 were unsolved. In fact, Oberman found that other sources revealed that 115 cases may be an underestimate of the number of unidentified infants found dead. The Chicago Police Department discovered between fifty-one and seventy-nine infant bodies each year during 1906–1920.[53]

Unsolved cases proved that it was possible for perpetrators to elude the authorities. However, as Ann Higginbotham found, many accused women failed to plan for disposal of the infant's body, which meant that they were not the 'cunning murderesses portrayed in some Victorian accounts; their cases reveal instead their fear and confusion and perhaps an unconscious desire for discovery'.[54] This might explain why some women immediately confessed to the crime when questioned, rather than continue to protest their innocence. It is also possible that, after the trauma of childbirth, exposure might well have come as a relief to some women. In the majority of cases referred to in this chapter, the bodies of infants were either found in boxes in servants' rooms, secreted in water tanks or in privies. Christine L. Krueger maintains that disposing of the body in a privy was an effective form of defence in court. Krueger found that 'Judges and juries were willing to accept the defendant's claims that she was unaware of her pregnancy, and indeed what had passed from her into the privy was a foetus, or that the baby had dropped from her and drowned before she could do anything to save it.'[55] From another perspective, Margaret Arnot questions whether young women at the time had the physiological understanding to know that they were pregnant until the onset of labour.[56] This might have been the case in 1899 when assistant teacher Annie Davies informed the court that she did not realise that she was pregnant until just before the child was born. Annie said, 'I used to suffer from indigestion', and that she did not know what she was suffering from at the time.[57] In some cases close family members and fellow servants also testified that they were unaware of a woman's pregnancy. For instance, it was reported in 1918 that Hilda Male's mother claimed that she was not aware of her daughter's pregnancy, even though they slept together. She noticed that Hilda was 'not all right and concluded that she was consumptive'.[58]

Naturally, most women protested their innocence when questioned by the authorities. In fact, an admission of guilt was only relevant to the outcome of the court proceedings in a small number of cases. This was evident in 1887 when twenty-year-old servant Caroline Randall, from Pembroke, described by the press as well-educated, pleaded guilty to the charge of concealment of birth. The infant was discovered in Caroline's box in her bedroom. The post-mortem revealed that the infant had been born alive, although it bore no marks of violence, and had probably died due to the effects and circumstances of the birth.[59] The judge stated that he had taken into consideration the agonising pain Caroline Randall had endured, and sentenced her to one month in prison without hard labour.[60] In the majority of cases in court, young women had given birth for the first time; therefore, many would have had little knowledge of the procedure of childbirth or were physically incapable of managing alone.

In an extraordinary case in 1894, and seemingly determined to conceal her pregnancy, twenty-two-year-old servant Jane Rees was in labour while preparing and serving the mid-day meal for her employer. On the day in question, the young servant was called during the meal but she failed to respond to the bell. Jane was found collapsed in the kitchen in a pool of blood suffering from a convulsion, but she died from haemorrhage before the doctor arrived. The dead baby was discovered in a bucket close by. The post-mortem in this case revealed that the baby had been born alive. Jane had been with her employer at Swansea for fifteen months and had always conducted herself in a very respectable manner, although she had repeatedly denied her pregnancy when questioned by her mistress. It was reported that Jane had 'borne her pain with such extraordinary fortitude that she had not uttered a single cry to apprise her mistress of her agony'. Jane Rees had denied her pregnancy; even though the press reported that she was known to have had a sweetheart who had been away at sea for nine months. Apparently, she had been anxiously awaiting his return home for the past few weeks.[61] There are a few cases of concealment of birth concerning women who appeared to have been in a relationship at the time of the offence.

The obvious leniency shown to offenders by the courts was evident in the case of Mrs Mary Jane Perrin, from Llandow. In 1900 she was charged with concealment of birth after the mutilated remains of a newborn infant were discovered in a well on the farm where the woman was employed. The *Western Mail* reported that Mrs Perrin was married to a subcontractor with a three-year-old child, and she apparently came from a very respectable family. The doctor testified that the infant was known to have had a separate existence, but from a preliminary examination he was unable to determine how long it have been alive, although 'the child must have lived at least three days'.[62] The *Cardiff Times* commented that twenty-six-year-old Mrs Perrin was supposed to be half-witted, and alleged that her husband, who was a navvy, had deserted her and a warrant had been issued for his arrest.[63] Mrs Perrin was later charged with concealment of birth at Bridgend Police Court. After a long hearing with several witnesses called, the case broke down completely for the prosecution; Mrs Perrin was discharged.[64] The fact that Mrs Perrin's husband had deserted her suggests that the infant was illegitimate, although it could be the case that she killed the infant because he had absconded. Again, the medical testimony was somewhat vague as to whether the infant had been born alive or not. Based on the available evidence, Mrs Perrin was discharged for what appears to have been an extremely violent crime.

Mrs Perrin's apparent use of violence seems to be consistent with Kilday's findings that some women were malicious in their intent to kill their infant. Women who had been abandoned while pregnant 'chose to take out their anger on the new-born child, perhaps explaining the ultra-violent tendencies in evidence amongst some of the women accused of this crime'.[65] Kilday found that in known cases of infanticide in Wales recorded during the pre-modern period 1700–1830, strangulation was the most common method used to kill newborn infants. However, the methods associated with cases of infanticide during the same period in England and Scotland were more evenly distributed between wounding, battery, neglect, suffocation and strangulation. The number of infants killed by the acts of drowning and deliberate smothering was considerably less across England, Scotland and Wales. Kilday maintains that married women were more inclined to commit infanticide by deliberate neglect because it was more or less undetectable.[66] In the majority of cases that form the basis of this chapter, the methods associated with infanticide were strangulation and suffocation. Recorded cases of wounding were significantly less.

An illustrative case of a violent child murder was that concerning nineteen-year-old Amelia Stephenson, who killed her newborn with a pair of scissors in 1884. It was reported that Amelia gave birth and killed the infant in her bedroom, which happened to be situated next to her father's room. She then buried the body in the garden. Before the incident took place, the girl's father had suspected her pregnancy, and based on his suspicions, his wife took her to see the doctor. Amelia was thought to have been about four to five months pregnant, although the doctor could not confirm it at that stage. Family members usually protected the offender from the authorities, yet in this case Amelia's sister, Mrs Tovey, forced an admission of guilt and later reported her to the police. Under duress Amelia confessed to her sister and said, 'I cut its throat with a pair of scissors and buried it in the back.' Mrs Tovey recovered the infant's body from the garden, and also retrieved a pair of bloodstained scissors found in her bedroom, which she handed to the police.[67] In expressing his concern the coroner was sure that the jury felt sympathy for the young woman's father and her family, in what was a most painful case.[68] The coroner's inquest found Amelia Stephenson guilty of wilful murder and committed her to trial at the assizes. Amelia Stephenson was charged at the South Wales Assizes with feloniously killing and murdering her newborn infant. The judge pointed out that as Mrs Emma Tovey had charged her sister with being confined, this made the case peculiarly sad.[69] The defence argued that Amelia Stephenson's statement was not admissible since her sister had extorted it by a threat. However, the judge held that the statement was admissible. The prosecution pointed out that:

> The English law in respect of child murder was highly technical, he might almost say merciful. If the child had not really had a separate existence entirely apart from its mother its death would not constitute the offence; but if the child was fully born and had a separate existence the prisoner would be guilty of murder. If they felt that the circumstances left any reasonable doubt upon their minds that the unfortunate girl, who was so much to be pitied, was not guilty of the crime of murder they then might instead of entirely acquitting her, find her guilty of concealment of birth, as there was a count to this effect in this indictment.

Despite her alleged admission of guilt and the evidence stacked against her, Amelia Stephenson was acquitted of murder. She was convicted on the lesser charge of concealment of birth and sentenced to eighteen months' imprisonment with hard labour.[70]

The identity of the reputed father of Amelia Stephenson's child, Alfred Webber, was discovered not in court, but by chance in the press after the trial. Daniel Grey found that it seemed standard practice with English newspapers not to report any further on infanticide cases, unless related to public campaigns for the reprieves of convicted murderers.[71] This practice was generally the same with Welsh newspapers; although in this particular case both the *Western Mail* and the *Cardiff Times* reported on Alfred Webber's death. According to a letter received by Alfred Webber's father just after the trial, he had met with an accident in March that same year. Apparently, while shooting in the bush with another young man, Alfred Webber was accidently shot and died two days later.[72] It was reported that he had left Cardiff for Queensland during the previous November when Amelia Stephenson was six months pregnant. The timing of his departure might well have coincided with knowledge of her pregnancy, or if Alfred Webber already knew, perhaps it gave him the opportunity to make arrangements to leave the country.

The use of newspapers in this way provides a wider social context which helps us to understand why some women committed newborn child murder. Evidently, the local community believed that Alfred Webber was the reputed father, yet there appears to be no mention of him in the trial press reports. Without the publication of this additional information regarding Alfred Webber's death, it might have been assumed that Amelia Stephenson had been seduced by her employer, or by an older man. It was fortunate that the press named the reputed father, because a search of the 1881 Census Return revealed a little more about the young man. In 1881, three years before her trial, eighteen-year-old Alfred Webber was recorded as a plasterer.[73] Amelia Stephenson, then aged sixteen, was a dressmaker living with her father, a baker.[74] It is unknown whether they were a courting couple, but if that was the case then Alfred Webber's disappearance probably contributed to her killing the child.

Putative fathers were rarely mentioned in infanticide cases, let alone appeared in court, while the young woman was named and shamed in court and in the press. The case of a young servant proved how difficult it was to bring the putative father to court, even as a witness. In 1892 Anne Williams was charged at Carmarthenshire Assizes with concealment of birth and secretly burying her dead infant in the parish of Llandingat, Llandovery. She had been turned away by her employer once her condition was known. It was reported that Anne Williams was taken ill while walking to Lampeter and was forced to turn into a field where she gave birth. She claimed to have remained there for two days and two nights. Anne Williams was undefended in court, and in answer to the charge she said, 'I was with the father there; I did not do it myself.' As the police sergeant gave evidence, Anne Williams spoke to him (in Welsh) and said, 'Didn't I tell you it was the father of the child who did it?' 'Didn't I ask you to bring the father up for trial?' The sergeant stated that the accused had given the name of the father and claimed that it was he who had buried the child. The sergeant knew the man mentioned but declared he could prove that the putative father was not with Anne Williams on the day in question. Anne Williams was convicted of concealment of birth; however, the jury recommended mercy to be used in her sentencing. The judge informed the court that 'Her master had given her a good character' and that he was prepared to take her back into his service.[75] The judge stated that, 'as long as you behave yourself, nothing will be further heard of it'. It was reported that there was cheering in the court, which was promptly suppressed.[76]

The fact that Anne Williams's employer had turned her away in the first instance was likely one contributory factor to account for her actions. Anne Williams was adamant in court that the father was present at the birth, yet it is not clear to what extent the man was questioned by the police over his alleged involvement in the child's death, or the reliability of his alibi. Kilday argues that 'collusion of this sort was largely ignored by the authorities and contemporary commentators, as the courts were unsure about how to deal with accomplices to the crime of infanticide'.[77] The judge in Anne Williams's case commented that, 'It might be true what had been said with regard to the father of the child. There was, unfortunately, in cases of this kind, somebody in the background who led women to bear the pains and penalties.'[78] Cliona Rattigan found that the Irish police investigating infanticide cases seemed to have little interest in the infants' fathers. Rattigan points out that 'men who fathered children outside wedlock were not regarded as "real" fathers by the Irish authorities unless they married the child's mother'.[79]

The reputed fathers of infant victims were seldom reported in the press, but not all men shunned their responsibilities. The following cases provide examples of how named fathers were reprimanded by the trial judges as the cause of the women's downfall. When Annie Bevan, from Laleston, was charged with concealment of birth in 1893, the father of the child, a man named Gould, married her before her court appearance. The judge said, 'The man who was the author of this woman's shame and trouble had stood by her, and had married her before her case came before the Magistrates.'[80] In this case Gould, who was employed as a gardener, and Annie Bevan were fellow employees.[81] The judge at the trial of Eliza Maud Chambers had a few words to say to the father of the infant victim. In 1908 at the West Wales Assizes, held at Carmarthen, housemaid Eliza Chambers was charged with the manslaughter of her infant at birth. The post-mortem indicated that the infant had died from strangulation and injuries to the head that could not have been caused by accident. Eliza Chambers was in service at Williamston, Burton in Pembrokeshire. It was reported that she was engaged to be married to Isaac Hook, an underkeeper, who was also employed at Williamston. When Eliza Chambers was acquitted the judge said, 'I hope that this will be a lesson to you and I hope that the man who was the cause of it will make you an honest wife. It is his duty, and I am told that he has said he would.'[82] In another case a fifteen-year-old girl, Mary Ann Jones, died after giving birth prematurely. The twenty-year-old father, Enoch Simpson, was present at the inquest. He claimed that he had met with Mary Ann Jones three or four times but had not used violence against her. The jury returned the verdict and requested that the coroner censure Simpson, which he did. The coroner said, 'It was sad to think that there were such cads about. They could not call him a man – he was only a youth – but his actions showed that he was not worthy of the name of a man.'[83] In this instance the father was present at the coroner's inquest, and it is also interesting to note how the jury perceived his actions.

Few women confessed to killing their newborn infants, but for those who did so, it was usually when placed under arrest. At that point, women were understandably scared and began to comprehend the consequences of their actions. Mary Peterson Mahoney and Susan Mogford confessed to killing their newborn infants. However, the judge criticised the police handling of Mary Mahoney's case because it had a detrimental effect on the outcome of her trial. In 1876, at the South Wales Assizes, eighteen-year-old servant Mary Peterson Mahoney was charged with wilfully murdering her newborn infant at her place of work at Whitchurch. Although she pleaded not guilty to the indictment, she had already incriminated herself when she was arrested by admitting that she had killed the child. The manner in which the police cautioned her and then questioned her over a pickaxe used to kill the infant was disputed by the judge, causing him to condemn their conduct.

Traumatised by the experience and under duress, Mary Mahoney said, 'I killed the child with the coal pick, and buried it in the small coal. I did not know what to do.' Mary Mahoney's admission of guilt placed her defence counsel in a difficult position because she had already incriminated herself.

It was reported that Mary Mahoney's defence counsel was funded by some gentlemen who sympathised with her 'melancholy circumstances', and felt that her interests should be watched over, while the jury, which consisted of 'twelve good men', held her fate in their hands. Mary Mahoney was convicted of wilful murder and sentenced to death.[84] Her case was widely publicised in the press to generate public support and therefore petition the Home Secretary to grant a reprieve. The young woman's petition for clemency was in the charge of Reverend J. Akroyd, and was signed extensively by the High Sheriff, several magistrates of the county, members of the Cardiff Board of Guardians and other influential individuals, plus 2,500 signatures.[85]

Reputed fathers remained invisible in court from the outset even in high-profile cases such as Mary Mahoney's, despite a significant degree of male support from different sections of society. Nineteenth-century historian C. A. Fyffe stated that had Mary Mahoney 'been an educated woman instead of a poor creature of weak intellect, unable to read and write, the black cap would not have assumed that terrible aspect which it did in her case'.[86] The *Western Mail* pointed out that 'If Mahoney should prove sane she will be sent to one of the convict establishments, and on proof of good behaviour, be released at the end of three or five years; if insane, she will probably be detained permanently at Broadmoor Asylum.'[87] A woman's intellect was examined in court in some cases, but the question of insanity was seldom mentioned. Mary Mahoney's sentence was commuted to fifteen years' penal servitude.[88]

The press were influential in engendering public sympathy and often portrayed infanticidal mothers as victims of cunning seducers. Elaine Farrell found that Irish newspapers 'did not regularly present the woman accused of infant murder as a demonic, evil figure'. Indeed, Farrell's findings were also replicated in the Welsh press. Farrell maintains that 'The most popular image construct portrayed a "desperate woman" who had been forced by circumstances outside of her control to murder her infant.'[89] In contrast, the Welsh press presented an image based on a woman's vulnerability, femininity and, in some cases, her youthfulness. Mary Mahoney was described by her defence counsel as 'almost a child herself'.[90] The younger women and girls were deemed to be sexually inexperienced and, therefore, easily intimidated, which emphasised their susceptibility to sexual abuse. Even though Susan Mogford was twenty-five, her defence counsel exposed her vulnerability by pointing out that she had been orphaned at a young age, and seduced while destitute.[91] Daniel Grey points out that 'the requisite displays of emotion in court' also fitted into the '"appropriate" standards of feminine behaviour'.[92] This was evident when the *Western Mail* reported that during the hearing, Mary Mahoney 'burst into tears at intervals, and incessantly rocked herself to and fro in an agony of grief'.[93] Farrell also found that the Irish press reported positively on the offender's physical appearance. The Welsh press were less inclined to report on a woman's physical appearance; however, the issue of an offender's respectability was more readily referred to. It was reported that Amelia Stephenson was of the most respectable character and, as in most similar cases, the person who had brought her all the misery 'had got off, except for the pangs of guilty conscience, scot free'.[94]

Miss Gertrude Jenner of Wenvoe was a feminist campaigner and philanthropist acting as a 'friend' to many young girls and women on trial for concealment of birth and wilful murder. Apart from providing support, she raised funds for defence counsels to act in a number of cases, corresponded with the Home Office and campaigned on behalf of Miriam Jones and Susan Mogford. In September 1887, after six years' imprisonment, Susan Mogford was released from Fulham convict prison into the care of Miss Jenner. It was reported that Susan's behaviour in prison had earned her £4 good conduct money. Miss Jenner stated that she was going to be adopted by the family, who were also willing to take in Miriam Jones and her child. Susan Mogford was referred to as Miss Jenner's protégé because while in prison she learned to read and write and was regularly visited by voluntary lady workers in preparation for her release. Young servant Miriam Jones was convicted of attempted murder and sentenced to eight years' imprisonment in 1887, which was the same year of Susan Mogford's release. Therefore, Miss Jenner announced that she would now be concentrating her attention and petitioning on behalf of Miriam Jones.[95] Amelia Stephenson[96] and Blanche Young[97] were also supported by Miss Jenner following their arrests. The avid campaigner raised funds for Beatrice Hall's defence counsel; otherwise she would have remained undefended.[98]

Newborn child murder was committed predominantly by single women, although married women also committed the crime, often due to deprivation, and did so while the husbands were absent. Even so, married women usually had no reason to conceal the birth. Unless, of course, infants were conceived as a result of an extramarital affair, in which case there were often few alternatives for some women. In 1871 Hannah Evans, a married mother of three, was living at Canton, Cardiff. Her husband was reported to be in America, and she was planning her departure to join him there. This was an unusual case because Hannah Evans was charged with concealment of birth, although the infant was reported to have been four weeks old when it died. When arrested at her mother's home at Merthyr, she stated, 'People have said that I was pregnant; but they were wrong.' Despite her protestation, she soon confessed that the infant was sick and had died during the train journey to visit her mother and sister, who knew nothing of the child's existence. The landlady also corroborated the midwife's evidence; it was reported that the infant was sick the day the mother travelled to Merthyr. Two surgeons examined the infant's body and maintained that it was well-nourished, but neither could establish the cause of death. Even though the infant was four weeks old, Hannah Evans was charged at Glamorgan Assizes with endeavouring to conceal the birth of her child. As the judge pointed out, this was not a normal concealment, because she had been attended by a midwife during the birth and infant clothing had also been provided in preparation. Hannah Evans was unrepresented in court, and when asked if she had anything to say in her defence, she said, 'I beg your pardon my lord. I am only a poor servant, without money. Please let one of your lordship's gentlemen assist me through my case.'[99] The judge contended that 'she made a secret disposition of the body that was concealment within the meaning of the law'.[100] He stated that:

> There are circumstances of grave suspicion surrounding the case. I shall not act upon those suspicions, but still I must

> distinguish between it and one of ordinary concealment. You had the fullest opportunity of informing your mother and sister of the child's death. Instead of doing this, you disposed of the body of the child under circumstances which leave grave doubt in my mind as to whether the child actually died [a natural death] or not. You might have stood there under a graver charge if further evidence had been given.[101]

Hannah Evans was convicted and sentenced to twelve months in prison with hard labour. Her actions were unusual since the midwife and her landlady were present at the birth; therefore, she would have had to explain the child's whereabouts to others on her return from Merthyr, unless, of course, she had no intention of returning to her lodgings. The evidence suggests that the baby might have died naturally, and that Hannah Evans panicked because she did not want her family to know about the child. However, the fact that she concealed the infant's body also suggests that the child was illegitimate and, therefore, could not travel to America with her.

Cases pertaining to the suspicious deaths of legitimate children prove that absent husbands made life difficult for married mothers as they struggled to feed and clothe their children, but the case concerning Margaret Vincent, from Neath, amounted to criminal neglect. In 1878 she was charged with wilfully killing and slaying her twenty-two-month-old daughter Alice Vincent. The infant died of starvation, allegedly weighing just 8 lbs, whereas a child of her age should have weighed at least 26 lbs. It was reported that the woman's seven children were so neglected and hungry that they used to pick up crumbs thrown out for the chickens. Margaret Vincent's husband was in California and regularly sent payments home; although, in his absence she was often seen with another man. The woman was convicted and sentenced to nine months in prison with hard labour. Margaret Vincent had already been in prison for three months at that point, and during that time had given birth to twins, although one child had died.[102]

Women who concealed the birth of their child sometimes acted with the assistance of accomplices. In such cases, offenders were charged under the Offences Against the Person Act 1861, which included anyone, man or woman, who was involved in a concealment of birth. This was the case in 1885 when Hannah Marshall, from Briton Ferry, and her parents, John and Ann Marshall, were charged with concealment of birth. Apparently, rumours had been circulating locally that Hannah Marshall was pregnant. The police acted on the information when a dead infant was discovered in the vicinity of the Marshall's home. As expected, this gave rise to gossip because the alleged father of the illegitimate child was a close relative, although the press reported that 'it was not deemed desirable that the public should become acquainted with the circumstance'.[103] In spite of that objection, the same newspaper reported later that the reputed father was her brother-in-law, who was well known in Briton Ferry and respectably connected. It was alleged at the Glamorgan Assizes that the infant was stillborn and that the placenta had been concealed in the back garden.[104] This was Hannah Marshall's second illegitimate child. The first child had been successfully affiliated to a married man named Menda. The defence argued that no concealment of birth had taken place, even though the dead infant was secreted in a wheelbarrow, covered with ashes and buried in the family grave at the cemetery.[105] The judge remarked on the painful nature of the case and stated that, as far as he could discern, there was no evidence against the daughter; therefore, Hannah Marshall should be acquitted of the charge. He asked the jury to say whether there had been such a concealment to bring the accused within the law. The jury acquitted all three individuals.[106] The press reported that Hannah Marshall was the daughter of respectable parents, and much sympathy was extended to her father. Interestingly, even though John Marshall was charged with concealment of birth, and he could well have been found guilty of the offence, much sympathy was extended to him; yet there appeared to be no mention of his wife or indeed his daughter in this display of concern. John Marshall, reported by the press to be a respectable man, was charged with an offence usually committed by single women. However, he had been brought to this level by his daughter; therefore, according to the judge, he was deserving of sympathy.

An illustrative case concerning a family member was that of seventeen-year-old Margaret Jenkins, from Neyland, Pembrokeshire, who was indicted in 1879 with concealing the birth of her illegitimate child and burning the body. Her grandmother, a midwife, also named Margaret Jenkins, was charged with being an accessory to the crime.[107] The girl, Margaret Jenkins, was employed by Captain T. Perrin until she was accused of being 'in the family way'. Not surprisingly, she denied the accusation and immediately left her post. As discussed previously, the majority of infants' bodies were concealed in a privy, boxes or other suitable places of cover, but it was unusual in reported cases for an infant's body to have been disposed of by burning. When Margaret Jenkins's grandmother could smell burning flesh, the girl told her that 'it was the b------ child, and that she had a great mind to burn herself'.[108] In this case the accusation made by Margaret Jenkins's employer, followed by her denial and subsequent disappearance for seven weeks, instigated local gossip and confrontation with a neighbour. The community's response to Margaret Jenkins's suspicious behaviour indicates that local inhabitants knew her well. When arrested, a large crowd followed the two individuals to the lock-up, no doubt to express condemnation. Both Margaret Jenkins and her grandmother were committed for trial at the Swansea Assizes. It was reported that the young girl 'appeared to feel her position acutely, but her grandmother behaved with great levity'.[109] Margaret Jenkins was sentenced to eight months in prison with hard labour, while her grandmother was imprisoned for twelve months.[110] The grandmother, as an accessory to the concealment, received the longest prison term, even though it was Margaret Jenkins who actually killed the infant and attempted to dispose of the body.

Another case concerning an accomplice was that of thirty-six-year-old Margaret Stephens and her stepbrother Enos Davies, from Cilgerran, Pembrokeshire. Both were charged at South Wales Assizes in 1887 with complicity in the murder of her newborn infant. In this case the Grand Jury rejected a bill of indictment (a true bill) on the capital charge and amended it to a charge of concealment of birth instead. Local surveillance prompted the police to question the two suspects. Both Enos Davies and Margaret Stephens denied the accusation, although it was admitted later that the body of the baby had been placed in a coal bucket. The infant had allegedly been born alive. It was reported that Margaret

Stephens said to the police, 'I hope they will not hang me'. Not surprisingly, upon their arrest, the response and realisation that they could be hanged was a fear also expressed by other women in the same situation. Margaret also said, 'I hope you won't do your worst by me, for, indeed, I am not the one who killed the child. I had a child on the hearth and went to bed, leaving it with Enos. I heard it cry once. Enos put it in the culm.' In court, the defence argued that there was no evidence against Enos Davies. The judge sentenced the man to four months in prison and stated that 'he had behaved very cruelly to the woman in the time of her need by leaving her absolutely without assistance, the result being the death of the child and its subsequent concealment'. As the biological mother, the judge probably considered Margaret Stephens the less guilty of the two and sentenced her to one month in prison, without hard labour.[111] There was insufficient evidence to indicate the identity of the child's father or the motive for the crime. In order to protect the mother, and to maintain secrecy, family members sometimes found themselves involved in cases of infanticide. In this case both Margaret Stephens and Enos Davies were involved, yet when indicted each claimed that the other person had committed the crime. Enos Davies was handed down the harsher sentence because he was accused of not assisting his stepsister in her time of need.

There were calls, particularly from women within the feminist movement, to indict the child's father as well as the mother in infanticide cases. Then again, this begs the question whether the mother would have received less sympathy from the all-male juries if the father was also indicted, since each would incriminate the other. If the actions of the mother were blamed on her feminine weakness, at the mercy of her biological make-up, then in all probability she would have received the lesser sentence of the two. Hence, the father would have needed to form a strong defence in order to save himself from possible punishment. In fact, such cases might well have replicated the same patterns of behaviour exhibited by reputed fathers when defending themselves in paternity cases. Therefore, in doubtful cases, it could be argued that the risk was potentially far greater to the mother if the father was also indicted than if she was the only person on trial for the crime.

Infanticide and the feminist movement

There is little evidence regarding reputed fathers in the majority of infanticide cases, but where the alleged identities of reputed fathers were known, for instance in the cases of Amelia Stephenson, Eliza Maud Chambers, Annie Bevan and Jane Rees, the men were from the same social class. Paternity cases prove that inter-class seduction took place, but it is difficult to establish how many infanticide cases were the results of inter-class seduction, or indeed sexual abuse. The susceptibility to inter-class seduction was one issue addressed by the women's campaign group, the Committee for Amending the Law in Points wherein it is Injurious to Women (CALPIW), formed in 1871. While the group was influential in the infant life protection movement during the 1870s, the CALPIW also campaigned for better protection of women and young girls. The CALPIW argued that:

> There being no associations for the rescue and reformation of fallen men, we cannot speak positively as to the social position and education of the seducers; but we know that whatever may be the truth as regards the whole number of seductions, where seduction is followed by desertion and those are the instances in which there is reason to apprehend infanticide – the betrayers are often better born, better bred, better taught than the betrayed.[112]

The CALPIW reported that young girls were most at risk of seduction from the age of twelve years, which increased every year until the age of sixteen but then began to decline until the age of nineteen years.[113] Where it has been possible to ascertain the ages of women referred to in this chapter, the majority were in their twenties. The vulnerability of this particular age group was not confined to Wales and England, because Elaine Farrell and Rachel Ginnis Fuchs found that cases concerning women in their twenties were also an issue in Ireland and France.[114]

Feminists were angered by the double standards of sexual morality, gender and class bias, issues that were clearly reflected in the Contagious Diseases Acts. In towns where military barracks were present, the police were sanctioned to arrest women suspected of being common prostitutes as a method of disease control.

A woman was subjected to an intrusive medical examination following arrest and forced by a magistrate to comply if she refused, which was clearly a violation. Prostitution, as an issue relating to infanticide, does not appear to be mentioned in cases under review in this chapter; however, it is alluded to in some paternity applications and abortion cases. Mary Lyndon Shanley maintains that:

> the reason some women became prostitutes was the result of economic pressures created by women's exclusion from remunerative occupations. Men closed women out of most jobs, seduced those made desperate by poverty, and then condemned the 'fallen woman' to the life of a social outcast.[115]

In fact, lack of well-paid employment was one of the main contributory factors in many cases of paternity, baby farming, abortion and child murder.

Tensions ran high at a public meeting at Swansea in connection with the Society for the Promotion of the Repeal of the Contagious Diseases Acts 1864, 1868 and 1869. Mrs Josephine Butler, a leading feminist campaigner and secretary of the Ladies Association, was also present at the meeting. In his address to the audience, Mr Stuart pointed out that the Acts were 'unjust, unconstitutional, immoral, and not calculated to effect the end for which they were framed'. Mr Stuart posed the questions:

> How would men like to be treated in a similar manner to that in which a certain class of women were to be treated under these Acts? How would men, who were engaged in any business, like to have policemen looking after them, with power – if they suspected that their books were not right – to bring them up before a magistrate?

Indeed, this was a weak analogy on his part. Moreover, Mr Stuart's first question to the audience was clearly explicit. T. D. Griffiths put forward the other side of the argument concerning repeal of the Acts. He held that 'if the defects really existed it was a good reason why they should be remedied, but it was not a good reason for abrogating the Acts altogether'. Josephine Butler argued in her speech that, 'Other laws were said to be a "terror to evil-doers, and a praise to those who did well;" but these laws, on the contrary, were a praise and an advantage to the shameless evil-doer, and a constant terror to those who did well.'[116]

The feminist movement also drew parallels between the enforced searches of women under the Contagious Diseases Acts with those suspected of infanticide.[117] Daniel Grey discusses the case of Fanny Goss as part of his research into coerced medical examinations and suspected infanticide. The case caused considerable interest amongst feminist groups because Fanny Goss committed suicide rather than undergo an enforced medical examination. Fanny Goss, a single woman, was the sister of Reverend Goss. The discovery of a newborn infant in the rectory grounds prompted the authorities to suspect Fanny Goss and the maid. The coroner issued a warrant requesting that both women agree to a medical examination to establish the dead infant's mother. Fanny Goss refused to be examined, locked herself in her bedroom and committed suicide.[118] Grey found that one anonymous coroner argued in *The Times* that either the legal principle that nobody could be forced to incriminate themselves held true, in which case such a warrant was 'waste paper', or most coroners were unaware of the powerful tool for gathering evidence against an accused person. Grey points out that the circumstances surrounding the Goss case raised the question of whether a coroner had the authority to force a woman suspected of infanticide to submit to a medical examination.[119]

Medical examinations on suspects formed part of the police investigations in a number of cases. Once arrested some women confessed to having given birth, but maintained in their defence that the infants were stillborn. In contrast, others emphatically denied the accusation and, therefore, had to undergo an intrusive medical examination as part of the police enquiries. Women reluctantly agreed, although some refused to give their consent because they would knowingly incriminate themselves. The authorities argued that it was the most appropriate way to establish if a suspect had given birth or not. At the time such examinations were viewed as another form of the violation of women's bodies, in a similar way to the enforced examinations under the Contagious Diseases Acts. Following the discovery of a dead infant, Annie Bevan refused to be medically examined by the surgeon, insisting that she was just feverish, although she eventually gave her consent.[120] At that point Annie Bevan was in a difficult position since a refusal was construed by the authorities as proof of her culpability, yet once examined there was no question of her guilt; therefore, she incriminated herself by consenting to the examination.

One particular case concerning the medical examination of a suspect was brought to the attention of the Home Secretary, and it was also discussed in both the House of Commons and the House of Lords. Nineteen-year-old Catherine Morgan, from Lampeter, was employed as a domestic servant at Stoke Newington. During this period many young girls and women left close-knit Welsh communities to seek employment, especially in London where there was a considerable influx of Welsh people. In 1888 Catherine Morgan was charged at the Old Bailey with concealment of birth. It was reported that Catherine's mistress had accused her of giving birth one morning, which was firmly denied, and she left her place of work to go to her uncle's home nearby. Later that same night, the police went to the uncle's home and found Catherine in bed with her clothes on. She was taken to the police station late at night where, after some hesitation, she consented to a medical examination. Catherine later admitted that she had given birth to a stillborn infant, which she had hidden in a cask in the cellar. The fact that Catherine spoke Welsh as her first language meant that her experience was far more distressing because her understanding of English was imperfect. Justice Hawkins asked the sergeant in court why he arrested the girl and had her examined in the middle of the night. The sergeant reported that he had been acting on orders because the girl had escaped in the morning. He also confirmed that he had not had a warrant for Catherine's arrest. The judge pointed out that as Catherine Morgan had female relatives in the neighbourhood, someone should have been sent for, or the examination should have been deferred until the following morning. The judge stated that, 'All this might have been avoided if a little more humanity had been exercised', and that 'in his opinion if she had been found guilty she would have had ample punishment in what she had undergone'.[121] Catherine Morgan was acquitted of the charge and instantly dismissed.

While this appeared to be just another typical case of concealment of birth perpetrated by a young domestic servant, it was actually discussed in the House of Commons the following day. Mr Matthews, the Home Secretary, was asked whether his attention had been drawn to the comments made by Justice Hawkins. The Home Secretary was informed that the police had received information which would probably have resulted in Catherine Morgan being charged with child murder. For this reason, the inspector in charge of the inquiry gave orders for her arrest. The police feared that Catherine Morgan might commit suicide or escape and, therefore, they felt it was their duty to lose no time in arresting her.[122] The actions of the police were also criticised in the House of Lords. Indeed, Lord Coleridge supported the criticism made by Justice Hawkins. He commented that 'A body of men engaged in the pursuit of crime were naturally sometimes overzealous', which meant that their evidence could possibly be called into question.[123] The Lord Chancellor admitted that the police failed occasionally, but he maintained that it would be difficult to find 'a finer or more respectable body of men'. Likewise, Lord Herschell praised the general good conduct of the police in London, and throughout the country, although he believed that there was a 'natural temptation to men in the position of the police which might lead them sometimes to exaggerate'.[124]

Medical proof that a woman had given birth did not necessarily preclude her from being acquitted by a jury. This was the case for Margaret Jones from Llanelli. Following the discovery of a dead infant in a reservoir and several local inquiries, the police charged Margaret Jones with concealment of birth. The coroner instructed that she undergo a medical examination. In this case the doctor gave Margaret Jones the option of refusing, but she agreed to the examination and the doctor confirmed that she had recently given birth. It was reported that her sister had admitted to throwing the infant into a clay pit, which she claimed was at Margaret Jones's request. Based on the evidence, Margaret Jones was charged in August 1869 with concealment of birth and committed to take her trial at Carmarthenshire Spring Assizes.[125] The judge informed Margaret Jones's sister, who had disposed of the child, not to incriminate herself. Her sister admitted in court that Margaret Jones had given birth, because that had previously been established by the doctor, but she declined to say what had become of the infant, even though at the Petty Sessions she had admitted throwing the infant into the pit. Despite the incriminating evidence, the judge stated that there was no case against the accused. Hence, the jury acquitted Margaret Jones and she was discharged from court.[126] This particular case proved that even with police evidence, medical testimony and obvious wrongdoing on the part of the offender, it was possible for the accused to be acquitted of the crime.

It was certainly not uncommon to find that many women were acquitted of the charges of concealment of birth even in the face of indisputable evidence. Another similar case concerned twenty-nine-year-old widow and mother-of-two Ellen Donoghue.[127] It was reported in 1869 that a dead infant was discovered at Llanddarog wrapped in a carpet and buried in a field adjoining the house where she was lodging. A witness had allegedly seen Ellen ill in bed the day before the discovery, and she had also disappeared on the day that the body of an infant was found. Furthermore, a medical examination confirmed that she had recently given birth. The surgeon stated that the infant had been born prematurely and had not breathed. Ellen Donoghue was subsequently charged with concealment of birth and committed to trial at the Carmarthenshire Assizes.[128] The leniency shown towards the offender in court was blatantly obvious in this case. The judge addressed the Grand Jury and remarked that, 'the evidence is clear, and you will not, therefore, have much difficulty in this case'. However, the Grand Jury returned no true bill (they directed that evidence was not strong enough to hold the suspect for trial). Therefore, the case was not heard and Ellen Donoghue was discharged.[129] Richard Ireland questioned why there was reluctance to prosecute in Ellen Donoghue's case. He maintains it was significant 'that it was the Grand Jury who received the praise for the conduct of the population they oversaw when the legal audit of morality was played out at Assize'. Ireland also maintains that in this case there was every chance that 'the prosecution was doomed to failure', and that to put an early end to proceedings would prevent the embarrassment of an acquittal 'after the evidence had been adduced in court'.[130] Both Margaret Jones and Ellen Donoghue were treated with leniency by the Carmarthenshire juries, despite incriminating evidence against them.

Even though the courts frequently dismissed such cases, the police were keen to prosecute. The particular case discussed below illustrates this point and relates to the discovery of the body of an infant in an old colliery boiler at Pontardulais. It was reported that several young women in the neighbourhood were suspected; however, the evidence pointed to domestic servant Esther Rees. At Swansea Police Court Esther Rees, described as a 'respectable-looking single woman', was charged with concealment of birth, although she denied the charge. Esther Rees's employer, a tailor, consented to two police constables searching her room, where they found bloodstained clothes, but he stated that 'she had nothing to do with those marks'. Under the circumstances Esther Rees had to undergo a medical examination, although it proved inconclusive because, rather oddly, she 'appeared to have either had a child or a tumour' two or three weeks previously. The surgeon could not be sure 'as other circumstances might produce exactly the same conditions as he noted'.[131] Another surgeon, Timothy S. Jones, was called to provide evidence, but he appeared to have been drunk, and due to his condition, it was not possible to question him.[132] The case was dismissed due to insufficient evidence. In Esther Rees's case the medical evidence moved in her favour, rather than against her. In fact, the evidence suggests that it was fortunate for her that Timothy S. Jones was called to provide evidence while in a drunken state. This was the same Timothy S. Jones who was later sentenced to life imprisonment for the death of Lily Challenger in 1896 (discussed in Chapter Three) after he performed an illegal operation on her. Jones admitted, on his arrest at the time, that he had a drink problem. Indeed, it is interesting to note that just two weeks after Esther Rees's case, he was a complainant in a court case following an altercation, in which the defendant alleged that Jones was drunk at the time.[133]

There is clear evidence that the acquittal rate for concealment of birth and infanticide was considerable, but this had much to do with the onerous task of convicting a woman for wilful murder when it was difficult to prove that the infant had been born alive and had attained a separate existence. Then again, juries tended to acquit women, even on the lesser charge of concealment of birth, in spite of conclusive evidence. Therefore, while the acquittal rate remained high, many women were getting away with murder. In 1866 the issue of the mandatory death penalty for infanticide was discussed by the Royal Commission on Capital Punishment. S. H. Walpole commented that 'The fact of the convictions not being numerous now only confirms what I say, namely, that the public opinion would go along with the alteration of the law, which separated infanticide from the classification of the crime of murder.'[134] In 1902 John Baker, deputy superintendent at Broadmoor Lunatic Asylum, argued from a medical perspective that some form of legislature was needed other than the charge of murder for infanticide, so that 'the sentence might be apportioned according to the degree of guilt and the measure of responsibility'.[135] Lord Alverstone introduced the Child Murder (Record of Sentence of Death) Bill in 1909 for its second reading in the House of Lords in an attempt to remove the mandatory death penalty in cases of infanticide. There was mounting concern that the passing of the death sentence on mothers convicted of infanticide was becoming a mockery because it was doubtful that the execution would be carried out.[136] The Lord Chief Justice proposed that the death sentence should be recorded in secret, rather than in open court, but the punishment would remain unless the Sovereign intervened. However, the Lord Chancellor argued that the same influences over witnesses and juries would still continue. The only difference would be that 'the sad pageant of passing the death sentence in open court would be dispensed with'.[137] Mr George Greenwood submitted the Law of Murder Amendment Bill in 1910, again to address the sentencing of mothers who committed infanticide.[138] Irrespective of all efforts, any petitions to amend the law relating to infanticide stalled until 1921, which also coincided with the high-profile case of twenty-one-year-old Edith Roberts.[139]

It was reported that Edith Roberts, from Hinckley in Leicester, was a factory worker with an exemplary character and the daughter of respectable parents. In June 1921 at Leicester Assizes, she was charged with the murder of her newborn infant. Edith Roberts had concealed the birth of her child and hidden the body in a box in her room, which was discovered by her mother three days later. The child had been suffocated by a camisole that had been placed over its mouth. Edith Roberts's defence counsel, G. W. Powers, caused controversy because he challenged female jurors as they were sworn in and then had the women removed in order to gain sympathy from the resulting all-male jury. Powers claimed that 'He had simply wanted a fair jury, and he did not think that women were fair to their own sex.' Edith Roberts was convicted on the charge of murder and sentenced to death; although the sentence was later commuted to penal servitude.[140]

On 25 July 1921, Edith Roberts's case was heard at the Court of Criminal Appeal, where the young woman applied for leave of appeal against the conviction and sentence. It was suggested that Justice Avory had misdirected the jury at Edith Roberts's original trial. There were two grounds for appeal. Firstly, the judge had made unfair comments, and secondly, he did not 'leave to the jury the issue which was raised on the evidence that the crime, if any, was manslaughter and not murder'. The Lord Chief Justice contended that there was no evidence to prove Edith Roberts was 'incapable of forming the intention to kill her child', and that there were no grounds for leave of appeal; hence, her case was dismissed.[141] Edith Roberts had created a great deal of sympathy on a national scale, while an extensive petition of 30,000 signatures was presented to the Home Office in favour of remission of her sentence. The petition worked in her favour, because Edith Roberts was released from prison exactly twelve months later on 7 June 1922.[142]

Just days after passing the death sentence upon Edith Roberts, Mr H. McLaren asked whether the Home Secretary 'can see his way to introduce into the House of Commons a Bill giving discretionary powers to the judge to pass a sentence other than death'. Mr Shortt responded by referring to the Bill, which had been agreed by the Lord Chancellor, the Lord Chief Justice and the Attorney General in 1910. Shortt believed that if a Bill was introduced along those lines, and it proved to be uncontroversial, it might be passed.[143] In February 1922, Mr Arthur Henderson introduced the Child Murder (Trial) Bill to 'Provide that a woman charged with the murder of her infant may, under certain conditions, be convicted of manslaughter.'[144] Finally, the introduction of the Infanticide Act in 1922 removed the mandatory death penalty and made a provision for a separate offence of manslaughter rather than wilful murder. The new Act also made an allowance for the fact that the balance of a woman's mind was disturbed as a result of giving birth.

The Infanticide Act in 1922 was a significant piece of legislation. Tony Ward maintains that it was the 'complex interweaving of law, medical knowledge and lay values and beliefs which gave rise to the infanticide legislation'.[145] From a gendered perspective, Grey argues that feminist activists contributed to the campaign to reform the infanticide law in 1922, and that it is essential to consider the influence of 'women's policy networks' and the new roles open to women after 1920. Grey points out that the introduction of the Representation of the People Act in 1918 permitted women over thirty to vote, and the Sex Disqualification (Removal) Act in 1919 meant that women were able to act as lay magistrates and serve as jurors. Therefore, women were in a stronger position to effect change as voters and political activists and to perform new roles in the administration of criminal justice.[146] Similarly, Anne Logan maintains that the involvement of feminist activists in the introduction of the Infanticide Act was 'a direct result of feminist pressure, which was arguably particularly effective so soon after women's partial enfranchisement and entry to the magistracy'.[147]

No mother had been executed for killing her own child since 1849, yet by 1922 a number of women had been sentenced to death and endured the agonising wait for a reprieve from the Home Secretary. The publicity associated with Edith Roberts's case brought reform of the law to the government's attention again in 1921. Her case had attracted considerable public attention generated by the press and tireless efforts on the part of feminist campaigners to secure her release. Goc maintains that the press represented Edith Roberts as 'fragile and contrite' and 'regarded as a victim of an outdated and unjust system, creating the social and political climate for change'.[148] Throughout the period 1870–1922, feminists had been active campaigners in amending the laws on infanticide and infant life protection, bastardy laws, baby farming, abortion, coerced medical examinations and the protection of young women and girls. By the 1920s, women were finally in a position to bring about reform as voters, campaigners and participants in the administration of justice. It could be argued that if feminist campaigners had been appointed to positions of power in order to effect change, cases of illegitimacy and infanticide might well have decreased because women would have addressed the causes of the crime in the first instance.

Conclusion

The majority of single women who found themselves pregnant out of wedlock had some form of coping mechanism and probably based their decisions on social and economic constraints. Michelle Oberman points out that 'Infanticide is not a random, unpredictable crime. Instead, it is deeply embedded in, and responsive to the societies in which it occurs.'[149] This chapter confirms Oberman's findings, because it has located women and their accomplices, suspected or accused of concealment of birth and child murder, in a particular place and time to set the crime in its social context within Welsh communities. A broad pattern emerged whereby cases were often similar in the way that women and young girls reacted to unwanted pregnancies. Women considered the options available and chose what they considered to be the most appropriate way to deal with their predicament. It was evident that many women were challenged over their suspected pregnancies, not just by employers and fellow servants but by their own families, yet their desire for secrecy remained. The overwhelming urge for single women to be rid of the child was exacerbated by the fact that reputed fathers were not subjected to the same level of social ostracism and economic hardship; men tended to continue their lives largely unaffected by an unwanted child.

Scrutiny of seventy cases of concealment of birth and infanticide reveals that only two young women, namely Mary Peterson Mahoney and Susan Mogford, were convicted of murder and condemned to death. The few men referred to in infanticide cases were known to be accomplices to the crime. Given the nature of the crime, it is impossible to identify how many men were complicit in the act whereby infants were killed and their bodies remained undiscovered, or the bodies were found yet the mothers were never apprehended; or, indeed, men who actively participated in the crime but remained nameless. Social commentators, infant welfare campaigners and feminist activists complained that reputed fathers should be indicted more frequently in infanticide cases. Then again, the indictment of putative fathers could have hindered a woman's ability to engender the same degree of sympathy in court. The wronged woman, allegedly seduced and abandoned, would no longer occupy a vulnerable position in front of juries and judges because both parents might seek to blame each other. In the case of Anne Williams, who claimed to the police and in court that the father had buried the infant, she still received sympathy from both the jury and judge because the father was not indicted. Anne Williams was discharged from court with a warning from the judge to 'behave herself' in future.[150] Enos Davies and Margaret Stephens also blamed each other when indicted for wilful murder, although the charge was reduced to one of concealment of birth.[151] Attempts to apportion blame were obvious in the abortion case concerning Mrs Anna Lloyd and her co-conspirators. Yet the pleas from Leslie James and abortionist Elizabeth Thomas to the authorities to incriminate their alleged accomplices fell on deaf ears, which was hardly surprising given that the individuals had remained on the right side of the law.

The degree of leniency shown by Welsh juries was evident, even in the face of obvious wrongdoing, violence and medical evidence, although this appeared to have much to do with the condemnatory attitudes concerning reputed fathers. Indeed, some jurymen might have sat uncomfortably in such a position. As Richard Ireland points out in the case of rural communities, 'the farmers who sat on the juries were the very people who would fire their servant girls if they became pregnant, thereby inducing the commission of the offence'.[152] The reluctance of juries to see young women punished was evident in the case concerning young servant girl Miriam Jones. Mr Law, from Neath, who was one of the twelve jurymen in her case, stated in a letter that he would sign any petition if it would help the poor girl. Mr Law claimed that 'the jury never for one moment anticipated the imposition of so heavy a punishment and, had the judge taken their view, the prisoner would have had no more than six months imprisonment'.[153]

The removal of the mandatory death penalty for mothers who committed infanticide was discussed in 1866, although five decades had lapsed before the Infanticide Act was finally introduced in 1922. The Infanticide Act considered infanticide from a medical perspective by taking into account the balance of the mother's mind during childbirth. However, it could be argued that the final push for legislation in 1922 was attributed in part to the efforts of feminist campaigners and to the women who were finally in a position to participate in criminal justice.

Notes

1 Dr A. Wiltshire, Report from the Select Committee on the Protection of Infant Life (1871), PP (HMSO, London), p. 27.

2 *Western Mail*, 8 June 1881, p. 3.

3 *Western Mail*, 5 August 1881, p. 3.

4 Anne-Marie Kilday and Katherine D. Watson, 'Infanticide, religion and community in the British Isles, 1720–1920: 'Introduction'', *Family and Community History,* 11/2 (2008), 84–9 (p. 85).

5 Mark Jackson, 'Fiction in the Archives: Sources for the Social History of Infanticide', *The Journal of British Records*, XXVII (October 2002), 173–85 (p. 177).

6 Nicola Goc, *Women, Infanticide and the Press, 1822–1922: News Narratives in England and Australia* (Oxfordshire, 2013), p. 171.

7 Katherine D. Watson, 'Religion, Community and the Infanticidal Mother: Evidence from 1840s Rural Wiltshire', *Family and Community History*, 11/2 (2008), 119–30.

8 *Western Mail*, 8 June 1881, p. 3.

9 John R. Gillis, 'Servants, Sexual Relations, and the Risk of Illegitimacy in London, 1801–1900', *Feminist Studies*, 5/1 (1979), 142–73, (p. 157).
10 Gillis, 'Servants, Sexual Relations, and the Risk of Illegitimacy', 158.
11 *Western Mail*, 31 January 1871, p. 2.
12 *Western Mail*, 18 October 1876, p. 6.
13 *South Wales Daily News*, 7 August 1874, p. 3.
14 Jessica A. Sheetz-Nguyen, *Victorian Women, Unwed Mothers and the London Foundling Hospital* (London, 2012), p. 136.
15 Watson, 'Religion, Community and the Infanticidal Mother', 125.
16 *Western Mail*, 12 December 1884, p. 3.
17 Kathryn Stammers and Nicola Long, 'Not your average birth: considering the possibility of denied or concealed pregnancy', *BMJ Case Reports* (29 May 2014), doi: 10.1136/brc-2014-204800, 1.
18 A. Jenkins, S. Millar, J. Robins, 'Denial of pregnancy – a literature review and discussion of ethical and legal issues', *Journal of the Royal Society of Medicine*, 104/7 (2011), 286–7.
19 Sheetz-Nguyen, *Victorian Women*, p. 138.
20 Anne-Marie Kilday, *A History of Infanticide: c.1600 to the Present* (Basingstoke, 2013), p. 58.
21 Shani D'Cruze and Louise A. Jackson, *Women, Crime and Justice in England since 1600* (Basingstoke, 2009), pp. 76–7.
22 *Western Mail*, 2 June 1894, p. 6.
23 Elaine Farrell, *'A most diabolical deed': Infanticide and Irish Society, 1850–1900* (Manchester, 2013); Cliona Rattigan, *'What Else Could I Do?' Single Mothers and Infanticide, 1900–1950* (Dublin, 2012).
24 Jill Barber, '"Stolen Goods": The Sexual Harassment of Female Servants in West Wales during the Nineteenth Century', *Rural History*, 4 (1993), 123–36 (p. 123).
25 Françoise Barret-Ducrocq, *Love in the Time of Victoria* (London, 1991), p. 48.
26 *Western Mail*, 14 December 1876, p. 5.
27 D'Cruze and Jackson, *Women, Crime and Justice*, p. 79.
28 *The Cambrian*, 31 August 1805, p. 3.
29 For discussion see Kilday, *A History of Infanticide*, pp. 125–31.
30 *The Cambrian*, 27 April 1805, p. 4.
31 *The Cambrian*, 31 August 1805, p. 3.
32 Mark Jackson, 'Suspicious infant deaths: the statute of 1624 and medical evidence at coroners' inquests', in Michael Clark and Catherine Crawford (eds), *Legal Medicine in History* (Cambridge, 1994), pp. 64–88 (p. 82).
33 *The Cambrian*, 27 April 1805, p. 3.
34 *The Cambrian*, 7 September 1805, p. 3.
35 National Library of Wales, Crime and Punishment, https://crimeandpunishment.library.wales, accessed 15/11/2019.
36 Infanticide Act, 1938 (1 & 2 Geo. 6 c. 36).
37 William Burke Ryan, *Infanticide: Its Law, Prevalence, Prevention, and History* (London, 1862), p. 15.
38 S. G. O., 'Infanticide', *The Times*, 5 August 1865, p. 6, *Times* Digital Archive, https://www.gale.com, accessed 23/02/2007.

39 H. L. Adam, *Women and Crime* (London, 1912), p. 181.
40 Karen Clarke, 'Infanticide, Illegitimacy and the Medical Profession in Nineteenth-Century England', *Social History of Medicine* (1979), 11–14 (p. 12).
41 *Royal Commission on Capital Punishment* (1866), PP, 21 (HMSO, London), p. 59.
42 *British Mothers' Journal and Domestic Magazine*, 1 October 1862, 222.
43 S. G. O., 'Infanticide', p. 6.
44 *Western Mail*, 22 March 1893, p. 6.
45 *Western Mail*, 6 September 1871, p. 4.
46 Kilday, *A History of Infanticide*, p. 76.
47 *Cardiff Times*, 17 November 1906, p. 10.
48 *Cardiff Times*, 24 November 1906, p. 7.
49 *Western Mail*, 8 February 1877, p. 4.
50 *Western Mail*, 21 February 1881, p. 3.
51 *Western Mail*, 16 March 1883, p. 4.
52 *Western Mail*, 20 August 1869, p. 4.
53 Michelle Oberman, 'Understanding Infanticide in Context: Mothers Who Kill, 1870–1930 and Today', *The Journal of Criminal Law and Criminology*, 92 (2002), 707–38 (pp. 716–17).
54 Ann R. Higginbotham, '"Sin of the Age": Infanticide and Illegitimacy in Victorian London', *Victorian Studies*, 32/3 (1989), 319–37 (p. 326).
55 Christine L. Krueger, 'Literary Defenses and Medical Prosecutions: Representing Infanticide in Nineteenth-Century Britain', *Victorian Studies*, 40/2 (1997), 285–6.
56 Margaret Arnot, 'Understanding women committing newborn child murder in Victorian England', in Shani D'Cruze (ed.), *Everyday Violence in Britain, 1850–1950: Gender and Class* (Essex, 2000), pp. 56–70 (p. 62).
57 *Haverfordwest & Milford Haven Telegraph*, 11 October 1899, p. 3.
58 *Haverfordwest & Milford Haven Telegraph*, 29 May 1918, p. 4.
59 *Pembrokeshire Herald & General Advertiser*, 15 April 1887, p. 2.
60 *Western Mail*, 3 May 1887, p. 4.
61 *Western Mail*, 5 December 1894, p. 5.
62 *Western Mail*, 7 May 1900, p. 6.
63 *Cardiff Times*, 12 May 1900, p. 6.
64 *Western Mail*, 14 May 1900, p. 4.
65 Kilday, *A History of Infanticide*, p. 166.
66 Kilday, *A History of Infanticide*, pp. 96–7.
67 *Western Mail*, 5 May 1884, p. 4.
68 *Western Mail*, 21 February 1884, p. 3.
69 *Western Mail*, 2 May 1884, p. 4.
70 *Western Mail*, 5 May 1884, p. 4.
71 Daniel J. R. Grey, 'Discourses of Infanticide in England, 1880–1922' (unpublished PhD thesis, Roehampton University, London, 2008), 41.
72 *Cardiff Times*, 17 May 1884, p. 2.
73 Census Return, 1881, Roath, Cardiff, RG11 5286, www.findmypast.co.uk, accessed 20/01/2015.
74 Census Return, 1881, Roath.
75 *Western Mail*, 18 July 1892, p. 7.
76 *Carmarthen Journal*, 1 July 1892, p. 8.

77 Kilday, *A History of Infanticide*, p. 67.
78 *Western Mail*, 18 July 1892, p. 7.
79 Rattigan, *'What Else Could I Do?'* p. 162.
80 *Western Mail*, 22 March 1893, p. 6.
81 *South Wales Daily News*, 6 February 1893, p. 8.
82 *Pembrokeshire Herald and General Advertiser*, 27 November 1908, p. 2.
83 *Evening Express*, 18 January 1902, p. 2.
84 *Western Mail*, 14 December 1876, p. 5.
85 *Western Mail*, 20 December 1876, p. 5
86 *Western Mail*, 5 June 1877, p. 2.
87 *Western Mail*, 20 December 1876, p. 5.
88 *Western Mail*, 21 December 1876, p. 4.
89 Farrell, *'A most diabolical deed'*, p. 183.
90 *Western Mail*, 14 December 1876, p. 5.
91 *Western Mail*, 5 August 1881, p. 3.
92 Daniel J. R. Grey, "Agonised Weeping': Representing femininity, emotion and infanticide in Edwardian newspapers', *Media History* (2015), DOI: 10.1080/13688804.2015.1047332, 8.
93 *Western Mail*, 14 December 1876, p. 5.
94 *Western Mail*, 5 May 1884, p. 4.
95 *South Wales Daily News*, 12 November 1887, p. 3.
96 *Western Mail*, 22 February 1884, p. 3.
97 *Western Mail*, 1 August 1899, p. 6.
98 *Western Mail*, 21 March 1899, p. 5.
99 *Western Mail*, 10 March 1871, p. 2.
100 *Cardiff Times*, 11 March 1871, p. 7.
101 *Western Mail*, 10 March 1871, p. 2.
102 *Western Mail*, 6 November 1878, p. 3.
103 *Western Mail*, 29 May 1885, p. 3.
104 *Western Mail*, 30 May 1885, p. 3.
105 *Western Mail*, 29 May 1885, p. 3.
106 *Western Mail*, 7 August 1885, p. 2.
107 *Western Mail*, 27 January 1879, p. 3.
108 *Western Mail*, 17 January 1879, p. 3.
109 *Western Mail*, 27 January 1879, p. 3.
110 *Pembrokeshire Herald and General Advertiser*, 2 May 1879, p. 2.
111 *Western Mail*, 3 May 1887, p. 4.
112 Committee for Amending the Points in Law wherein it is Injurious to Women (CALPIW), *Infant Mortality: Its Causes and Remedies* (Manchester, 1871), p. 20.
113 CALPIW, *Infant Mortality*, p. 13.
114 Farrell, *'A most diabolical deed'*, p. 37; Rachel Ginnis Fuchs, 'Crimes against Children in Nineteenth-Century France: Child Abuse', *Law and Human Behaviour*, 6, 3/4 (1982), 237–59 (p. 242).
115 Mary Lyndon Shanley, *Feminism, Marriage, and the Law in Victorian England* (New Jersey, 1993), p. 86.
116 *The Cambrian*, 31 January 1873, p. 5.

117 Daniel J. R. Grey, "'What woman is safe...?' coerced medical examinations, suspected infanticide, and the response of the women's movement in Britain, 1871–1881', *Women's History Review*, 22/3 (2013), 403–21.
118 Grey, 'What woman is safe...?' 405–6.
119 Grey, 'What woman is safe...?' 404.
120 *Western Mail*, 3 January 1893, p. 8.
121 *Western Mail*, 6 August 1888, p. 4.
122 Parl. Deb. (series 3) HC vol. 329, cols. 1842–3 (7 August 1888).
123 Parl. Deb. (series 3) HL vol. 330, col. 58 (9 August 1888).
124 Parl. Deb. (series 3) HL vol. 330, col. 59 (9 August 1888).
125 *Western Mail*, 20 August 1869, p. 4.
126 *Western Mail*, 11 March 1870, p. 2.
127 Carmarthenshire Archives, Felons' Register Carmarthen Gaol, ACC 4916, No. 1306.
128 *The Welshman*, 4 June 1869, p. 5.
129 *Western Mail*, 16 July 1869, p. 4.
130 Richard W. Ireland, 'Putting oneself on whose country? Carmarthenshire juries in the mid-nineteenth-century', in T. G. Watkin (ed.) *Legal Wales: Its Past, Its Future* (Cardiff, Welsh History Society, 2001), pp. 63–87 (pp. 81–2).
131 *Western Mail*, 10 October 1887, p. 3.
132 *Cardiff Times*, 15 October 1887, p. 6.
133 *South Wales Daily News*, 3 November 1887, p. 2.
134 *Royal Commission on Capital Punishment*, p. 59.
135 John Baker, MD, Deputy Superintendent, State Asylum, Broadmoor, 'Female Criminal Lunatics: A Sketch', *Journal of Mental Science*, 200 (1902), 13–25 (p. 19).
136 Hansard, HL vol. 1, col. 722 (4 May 1909).
137 Hansard, HL vol. 1, col. 725 (4 May 1909).
138 A Bill to classify Murders and to amend the Law with regard to Suicide and Infanticide (1910).
139 For discussion see Goc, *Women, Infanticide and the Press*, pp. 145–69; Daniel J. R. Grey, 'Women's Policy Networks and the Infanticide Act 1922', *Twentieth-Century British History*, 21 (2010), 441–63.
140 *Manchester Guardian*, 7 June 1922, p. 12.
141 'Court of Criminal Appeal', *The Times*, 26 July 1921, p. 4, *Times* Digital Archive, 1785–1985, https://www.gale.com, accessed 31/05/2018.
142 *Manchester Guardian*, 7 June 1922, p. 12.
143 Hansard, HC vol. 143, WA, col. 925 (20 June 1921).
144 Child Murder (Trial). A bill to provide that a woman charged with the murder of her infant may, under certain conditions, be convicted of manslaughter (1922).
145 Tony Ward, 'The sad subject of infanticide: Law, medicine and child murder, 1860–1938', *Social & Legal Studies*, 8, 163 (1999), 163–80 (p. 164).
146 Grey, 'Women's Policy Networks', 442.
147 Anne Logan, *Feminism and Criminal Justice: A Historical Perspective* (Basingstoke, 2008), p. 130.
148 Goc, *Women, Infanticide and the Press*, p. 151.
149 Oberman, 'Understanding Infanticide in Context', 737.
150 *Western Mail*, 18 July 1892, p. 7.

151 *Western Mail*, 3 May 1887, p. 4.
152 Richard W. Ireland, *Land of White Gloves? A history of crime and punishment in Wales* (Oxfordshire, 2016), p. 70.
153 *Western Mail*, 17 August 1887, p. 3.

Conclusion

In 1834 Mr Walcott held that a rise in cases of infanticide, infant abandonment and abortion would be unlikely because the introduction of the New Poor Law and the Bastardy Clause would reduce the illegitimacy rate.[1] However, the clause had an adverse effect, as the number of cases failed to diminish while the new laws hardened social attitudes regarding single mothers and their illegitimate children. The abandonment of pregnant women left them with stark choices, particularly if they had no support networks to alleviate the social and economic hardships of unmarried motherhood. The Welsh rural custom of 'bundling' encouraged intimacy, yet the Bastardy Clause provided putative fathers with the opportunity to evade the responsibility of fatherhood. This freedom was aided by industrialisation and emigration since the prospect for men to gain employment further afield was greater than ever before, thus eliminating the need to remain under the watchful eye of the local authorities.

Religious beliefs and social values possibly influenced the thoughts and emotions of many women who killed their newborn babies, particularly in Welsh communities where religion had a considerable bearing on daily life. Ministers of the gospel regularly preached from the pulpits against the sins of immorality, while some preachers abused their position to either influence or possibly sexually harass women, exposing the religious hypocrisy and sexual double standards during this period. Despite the constraints, prevailing religious attitudes did not prevent courting couples from engaging in sexual relationships, although this could have had more to do with the well-established Welsh courting practices than a deliberate flouting of religious teachings. It was more likely that a woman feared religious condemnation if she found herself pregnant and abandoned by the child's father. As a consequence of his actions, her reputation was often tarnished and she was readily labelled a 'fallen woman'.

Given the lowly status of many women under discussion, it is inevitable that the issues of gender and class are visible throughout each chapter. One noticeable feature is the shift in the gender balance between cases of infanticide to those of paternity. On the one hand, a typical case of infanticide witnessed a woman at the mercy of an all-male jury and judge; the reputed father rarely formed any part of the legal proceedings and largely remained invisible. On the other hand, when the reputed father was summoned to answer a case of paternity, he had to face the consequences of his actions, whereby the outcome was generally not in his favour. Men were sometimes subjected to humiliation in court in much the same way as women were, while support from members of the community towards the wronged woman was discernible. Nor did it matter whether the reputed fathers were working-class or middle-class, or what their level of social prominence was within the community. The scrutiny of paternity cases exposes society's prevailing attitudes to both gender and class relationships in south and west Wales during this time.

A collective analysis of cases both of infanticide and paternity is an area of research that has been overlooked by researchers of Welsh women's history, considering the importance of proof of paternity on the life or death of an illegitimate infant. These cases have provided a fascinating glimpse into intimate relationships that cannot be garnered from infanticide cases alone. Evidence concerning the reputed fathers of infanticide victims is negligible. Hence, it is difficult to establish in the majority of cases whether the victims were born as a result of courting couples, inter-class seduction or sexual harassment from employers and other members of the household. In contrast, paternity cases are socially enlightening because they reveal that reputed fathers came from both working- and middle-class backgrounds. Cases also proved that women summoned up the courage to sue for child maintenance regardless of class, albeit with the assistance of the Board of Guardians in some cases. The same female determination is also apparent in cases where women sued for breach of promise of marriage. Indeed, in most cases social class did not influence the manner in which men were treated during court hearings either, especially by those vociferous members of the local community who crammed into the courtrooms to witness the action. However, where the father's identity was known in cases of infanticide, it appeared that the infant victim might well have been born as a result of a relationship. For example, Amelia Stephenson and Alfred Webber might well have been a courting couple.[2] Even Annie Bevan and her fellow servant Gould were married before her trial for concealment of birth.[3] The paternity cases uncovered infants who had been born as a consequence of consenting relationships, such as that of Jane Davies and Reverend Jenkin Rees, or Jane Mathias and George Lifton, whereby the issue of a paternity summons seemed an appropriate course of action.[4] In Hannah Jones's case, press reports revealed that Cardiganshire squire John Jordan Jones had abused his position as her employer, and he was finally held to account for his actions despite exercising his influence in court in an attempt to avoid the social disgrace and financial penalty.[5]

The decades that followed the introduction of the Bastardy Clause witnessed a proliferation in the methods employed to deal with illegitimate children and unwanted pregnancies. Evidence clearly identifies the interaction of a number of individuals and networks operating within local Welsh communities for financial reward. Abortionists, baby farmers and unscrupulous midwives played a significant role in the destruction of infant life; therefore, their practices formed a considerable part of the social and legal discourse concerning suspicious infant deaths and deliberate child murder from the 1870s onwards. The employment of baby farmers involved a financial transaction; hence the practice degenerated into what could be described as 'infanticide for hire' in some cases. Although cases of newborn child murder continued throughout the period 1870–1922, baby farming was an alternative to concealment of birth, and there was obviously less risk to the mother because the responsibility for the life or death of an infant lay with the baby farmer.

Abortion had been practised in some form or other for centuries, but evidence reveals that use of abortifacients and illegal operations increased by the end of the nineteenth century. The increase was not specifically linked to the number of single women who resorted to illegal operations, because half the victims of abortion were reported to be respectable married women, also desperate to terminate pregnancy for other reasons. The criminal cases also expose the reluctance of juries to convict abortionists, and the women themselves, which suggests that the middle classes were far more tolerant of birth control and possibly explains the lack of convictions after 1900. Moreover, given the reluctance to prosecute for the offence, it was preferable for a single woman to resort to abortion rather than allow the pregnancy to go full-term and conceal the birth, because the onus was on the abortionist if legal proceedings ensued. Otherwise the penalty for a woman who committed concealment of birth was imprisonment, or sentence of death if convicted of wilful murder.

An analysis of randomly selected cases of infanticide, baby farming and criminal abortion revealed that just one person was executed for wilful murder, namely baby farmer Leslie James, alias Rhoda Willis. She was not the infant's biological mother, so there were no extenuating circumstances to the murder, unlike in the cases of the young women Mary Peterson Mahoney and Susan Mogford, who were also sentenced to death. Elizabeth Thomas faced execution for performing an alleged illegal operation upon Agnes Lewis, although she was later granted a reprieve. The fact that the jury did not recommend that mercy be used in the sentencing of Leslie James meant that a reprieve in her case was particularly unlikely. Roger Chadwick maintains that foster parents or baby farmers who murdered infants were nearly always sentenced to death without a reprieve, and they represented the main group of offenders involved in infanticide who were hanged.[6] Searching inquiries by Cardiff City police revealed that Leslie James had an unenviable reputation, which led a Home Office official to declare that 'The prisoner is evidently a bad woman.'[7] As Anette Ballinger points out, 'women criminals who not only commit crime but also fail to measure up to "appropriate" standards where motherhood, domesticity, respectability and conduct are concerned, are "doubly bad" women'.[8] Yet, in this case, the Home Office's assessment of Leslie James's character did not take into account that she had previously complied to the prevailing ideology of femininity before her addiction to alcohol sent her spiralling on a downward path to the gallows.

Leslie James's execution is significant because when her case is considered collectively with her contemporaries, who were living and practising in the same geographical area and during the same period, her case takes on another dimension. Leslie James's punishment was disproportionate in comparison to the penalties paid by other baby farmers; this was argued at the time of the trial and in the weeks preceding her execution. The implementation of the law was such that very few offenders who brought about infant deaths were imprisoned, let alone sentenced to death. Baby farmers from the poorer sections of society, such as Mrs White, Mrs Small and Mrs Ward, were responsible for the deaths of a number of infants that were disguised by the effects of poverty and, therefore, difficult to prove. Hence, Leslie James's execution provides the opportunity to reflect upon all individuals in this book who killed infants, even those who remained within the boundaries of the law.

Undoubtedly, infanticide and illegitimacy existed as real issues within Welsh society and affected young women and girls from different backgrounds and under various circumstances. Evidence has shown that pregnant single women adopted different strategies to deal with their predicament. Susceptible young servant girls like Miriam Jones endeavoured to care for their infants after they had been abandoned by the reputed fathers of the children, but evidence suggests that it was a case of survival and subterfuge for a number of women. For instance, domestic servant Maud Benson repeatedly denied her pregnancy to give birth in secret. She then knowingly abandoned her dead infant at a location that allowed the body to be visible to the public. The act did not fall within prosecution for the law of concealment, therefore freeing herself from the burden of an illegitimate child without punishment.[9] Similarly, Ellen Donoghue[10] and Margaret Jones[11] were discharged at Carmarthenshire Assizes because the Grand Jury did not consider the evidence strong enough to hold the suspects for trial and returned no true bill in both cases, despite incriminating evidence against them. There is substantial evidence available to show that the crime of infanticide was not necessarily the result of the actions of sexually deviant women, which was a common perception in the public imagination.

Evidence indicates that married women committed the crime for reasons such as poverty or extra-marital affairs. However, another group of offending mothers killed their children while suffering from 'puerperal insanity' or 'lactational insanity'. To date, there has been no similar research conducted in Wales that considers puerperal-related mental illness as a cause of child murder and detention of the criminally insane at Broadmoor. This form of insanity was not the same as that sometimes argued by the defence in infanticide trials. Given the leniency directed towards single women who killed their infants at birth and the likelihood of acquittal, to claim insanity as a form of defence in some cases would have been unwise for fear of indefinite incarceration at Broadmoor. The inclusion of the Glamorgan Asylum casebooks has proved significant because the records identified women suffering from puerperal-related mental illness who had attempted to murder their children, yet early intervention averted a tragedy. Thomas Clouston, superintendent of the Cumberland and Westmorland Asylum, said 'Short of death, no event is so great a shock to all concerned, for the perfection of the providence for childhood is destroyed by disease, and the strongest affection turns to hatred and becomes a danger.'[12] The Glamorgan Asylum casebooks certainly bear out Clouston's observations. Undoubtedly, early admission of puerperal-related cases proved that the murder of newborns and older infants by their insane mothers was rare. Timely admission was crucial because those women who killed their children while insane often remained traumatised after the tragedy and spent the rest of their lives living in the constant shadow of the crime.

The aim of this book was to locate the perpetrators of child murder, baby farmers and abortionists in a specific locality, and period of time, to provide an overview of the life experiences of Welsh women. Cases proved that women and young girls had to cope with unwanted pregnancies under differing circumstances; therefore, this had a considerable bearing on how they dealt with illegitimate infants, and they based their decisions on the limited options that lay before them. There was an underlying uneasiness with the operation of the justice system during this period; the difficulty of proving the intentional death of infants was also partly responsible for clemency. Uncertainty in such cases led to the charge of concealment of birth over that of murder. The omission of reputed fathers from the criminal courts in infanticide cases evidently led the justice system to deal with women in a far more lenient manner than the law laid down.

There is no doubt whatsoever that infanticide is both a sensitive and disturbing subject, but it does have its place in the history of women and children in Wales. One outcome that can be stated with certainty is that the number of infants born alive and disposed of, while the perpetrators escaped undetected, can never be established. It is also true that the number of women who resorted to abortion, and the number of infants whose lives were deliberately brought to end by baby farmers and buried without suspicion, will never be known.

Notes

1 Report from His Majesty's Commissioners of Inquiry into the Administration and Practical Operation of the Poor Laws, 1834 (HMSO, London), p. 175.

2 *Western Mail,* 5 May 1884, p. 4.

3 *Western Mail*, 6 February 1893, p. 8.

4 *Western Mail,* 28 November 1895, p. 6.

5 *Evening Express,* 29 April 1898, p. 2.

6 Roger Chadwick, *Bureaucratic Mercy: The Home Office and Treatment of Capital Cases in Victorian Britain* (London, 1992), p. 299.

7 TNA, Home Office Minutes regarding First Petition from Leslie James, 31 July 1907, HO 144/861/155336.

8 Anette Ballinger, *Dead Woman Walking: Executed Women in England and Wales 1900–1955* (Aldershot, 2000), p. 52.

9 *Cardiff Times,* 24 November 1906, p. 7.

10 *Western Mail,* 16 July 1869, p. 4.

11 *Western Mail,* 11 March 1870, p. 2.

12 T. Clouston, quoted in Robert Jones, MD, London, Medical Superintendent of London County Asylum, Claybury, ' Puerperal Insanity', *The British Medical Journal,* 1/2149 (1902), 579.

Bibliography

Archival Sources

Berkshire Record Office

Broadmoor Criminal Lunatic Asylum Archives

D/H14/D1/1/1/2, Admission Register 1868–1900.

D/H14/D1/1/2/2, Admission Register 1900–1906.

D/H14/D1/1/3/1, Admission Register 1907–1914.

D/H14/D2/1/2/1, Case Book, Broadmoor Criminal Lunatic Asylum.

D/H14/D2/2/2/269, Case File Catherine David.

D/H14/2/2/513, Case File Mary Morgan.

D/H14/02/2/2/290, Case File Annie Howell.

D/H14/D2/2/1/1323, Case File Henry Jones.

Carmarthenshire Archives

Felons' Register Carmarthen Gaol, ACC 4916.

Glamorgan Archives

Glamorgan County Asylum Case Books.

Case Book, Females, 1874–1876, DHGL/10/43, 1140–1587.

Case Book, Females, 1877–1880, DHGL/10/44, 1588–2069.

Case Book, Females, 1886–1887, DHGL/10/48, 3160–3605.

Case Book, Females, 1895–1896, DHGL/10/55, 5562–5956.

Case Book, Females, 1905–1906, DHGL/10/67, 10100–10495.

Cardiff Borough Police, D/DCONC/C-3/2/1, Finger Print and Photographic Register 1904–1908.

West Glamorgan Archives

Records of Swansea, Brecon and Carmarthen Prisons, D/D PRO/HMP, 1877–1992.

Nominal Registers, Women, 1889–1922 Swansea Prison, D/D PRO/HMP/2/1a-2/7.

Carmarthen Prison Register 1893–1908, D/D/PRO/HMP/10/1.

The National Archives
Home Office Papers
HO 144/861/155336 Leslie James.

Pembrokeshire Archives
Register of Prisoners, Summary Convictions, 1850, PQ/AG 10.

Powys County Archives
Cefnllys Petty Session Court Register, R/PS/LW/RG/15.

Parliamentary Papers

An Act to consolidate and amend the Statute law of England and Ireland relating to Offences Against the Person 24 & 25, c. 100 (1861).

A Bill for the better Protection of Infant Life (1871).

An Act to amend the Law relating to the Registration of Births and Deaths in England 37 & 38 Vict., Ch 88 (1874).

Infant Life Protection Act, 1897, 60 & 61 Vict. c. 57.

A Bill to classify Murders and to amend the Law with regard to Suicide and Infanticide (1910).

Child Murder (Trial). A bill to provide that a woman charged with the murder of her infant may, under certain conditions, be convicted of manslaughter (1922).

Infanticide Act, 1938 (1 & 2 Geo. 6 c. 36).

Reports

Report from His Majesty's Commissioners of Inquiry into the Administration and Practical Operation of the Poor Laws (1834), PP (HMSO, London).

Reports of the Commissioners of Inquiry for South Wales (1844), PP, 16 (HMSO, London).

Reports of the Commissioners of Inquiry into the State of Education in Wales (1847), PP, 339 (HMSO, London).

Royal Commission on Capital Punishment (1866), PP, 21 (HMSO, London).

Commission on the Employment of Children, Young Persons, and Women in Agriculture (1867), PP, 13 (HMSO, London).

Report from the Select Committee on Protection of Infant Life (1871), PP (HMSO, London).

Report from the Select Committee on Midwives' Registration (1892), PP (HMSO, London).

Report of Royal Commission on Labour: The Agricultural Labourer (1893), Vol. II, Wales C 36 (HMSO, London).
Report from the Select Committee on Patent Medicines (1914), PP (HMSO, London).

Parliamentary Debates

Parl. Deb. (series 3) HC vol. 329, 1842–3 (7 August 1888).
Parl. Deb. (series 3) HC vol. 351, col. 1678 (23 March 1891).
Parl. Deb. (series 3) HL vol. 330, col. 58 (9 August 1888).
Parl. Deb. (series 3) HL vol. 330, col. 59 (9 August 1888).

Hansard

Hansard, HL vol. 1, col. 722 (4 May 1909).
Hansard, HL vol. 1, col. 725 (4 May 1909).
Hansard, HC vol. 143, WA, col. 925 (20 June 1921).

Reports of the Registrar General

Sixth Annual Report of the Registrar-General (1842) BPP 1844 XIX (540).
Seventy-First Annual Report of the Registrar-General (1908) BPP 1909 XI [Cd.4961].

Returns

Return of Judicial Statistics of England and Wales (1898) Part I. Police; Criminal Proceedings; Prisons.
Judicial Statistics, England and Wales, Part 1 Criminal Statistics (1910).

Articles, Pamphlets and Books

Adam, Hargrave L., *Women and Crime* (London, 1911).
Baker, John, 'Epilepsy and Crime', in *British Journal of Psychiatry*, 47 (1901), 260–77.
Baker, John, 'Female Criminal Lunatics: A Sketch', *Journal of Mental Science*, 48/200 (1902), 13–25.
Jackson, R. M., 'A Note on Broadmoor Patients', *The Cambridge Law Journal*, 11/1 (1951), 61.
Bamford, C. B., MD, Assistant Medical Officer, Rainhill Mental Hospital, 'An Analytical Review of A Series Of Cases Of Insanity With Pregnancy', *Journal of Mental Science*, 80 (January 1934), 58–63.

Boyd, Robert, 'Observations on Puerperal Insanity', *Journal of Mental Science*, 16/74 (July 1870), 153–65.

Brayn, R., Superintendent State Criminal Lunatic Asylum, Broadmoor, 'A Brief Outline of the Arrangements for the Care Supervision of the Criminal Insane in England During the Present Century', *Journal of Mental Science*, 47 (April 1901), 250–60.

Briscoe, John F., 'The Responsibility of the Suicide', *British Medical Journal*, 1/2788 (6 June 1914), 1269.

The British Medical Journal, 'Law and Insanity', 1/220 (18 March 1865), 275–8.

The British Medical Journal, 'Legal Tests of Criminal Responsibility', 2/1453 (3 November 1888), 1011–12.

The British Medical Journal, 'Confusional Insanity', 1/1518 (1 February 1890), 250–1.

The British Medical Journal, 'Abortion and Child Murder', 2/1825 (21 December 1895), 1583–4.

The British Medical Journal, 'Self-Induced Instrumental Abortion', 2/1968 (17 September 1898), 841–2.

The British Medical Journal, 'The Traffic in Abortifacients', 1/1987 (14 January 1899), 110–11.

The British Medical Journal, 'The Sale of Abortifacients', 2/2031 (2 December 1899), 1583–4.

The British Medical Journal, 'Pregnancy and Feminism', 2/2772 (14 February 1914), 355.

The British Medical Journal, 'The Duties of Medical Practitioners in Cases of Criminal Abortions', 1/2875 (5 February 1916), 206–7.

The British Medical Journal, 'Puerperal Psychoses', 2/5526 (3 December 1966), 1342–3.

Bucknill, J. C., 'A Lecture on the Relation of Madness to Crime', *The British Medical Journal*, 1/1212 (22 March 1884), 553–5.

Bucknill, John Charles, 'An address on the law of murder and its medical aspects', *The British Medical Journal*, 2/726 (28 November 1874), 667–72.

Campbell, John, 'The Position of the Medical Practitioner Called in to Attend a Case of Procured Abortion', *The British Medical Journal*, 2/3180 (10 December 1921), 985–6.

Churchill, F, 'Puerperal Fever', *The British Medical Journal*, 1/795 (25 March 1876), 380.

Clark, A. C., 'Aetiology, Pathology, and Treatment of Puerperal Insanity', *Journal of Mental Science,* PT 142/33 (1887–88), 169–89.

Clark, A. C., 'Aetiology, Pathology and Treatment of Puerperal Insanity', *Journal of Mental Science,* PT 143/33 (1887–88), 372–9.

Clark, A. C., 'Aetiology, Pathology and Treatment of Puerperal Insanity',*JournalofMentalScience,*PT144/33(1888),487–96.

Clarke, Geoffrey, MD, Senior Assistant Medical Officer, London County Asylum, Banstead, 'The Forms of Mental Disorder occurring in connection with Child-bearing', *The Journal of Mental Science,* 59 (1913), 67–74.

Clarke Hall, W., "The Children Act, 1908," being the Third Edition of the Law Relating to Children containing the Complete Text of "The Children Act, 1908" and Other Statutes Relating to the Protection of Children: *With Notes and Forms* (London, 1909, reproduced Milton Keynes, 2010).

Clouston, T. D., 'What cases should be sent to lunatic asylums? And when?' *The British Medical Journal*, 1/578 (27 January 1872), 96–8.

Committee for Amending the Law in Points wherein it is Injurious to Women, *Infant Mortality: Its Causes and Remedies* (Manchester, 1871), 1–41.

Conolly, John, M.D., 'Description and Treatment of Puerperal Insanity', *Lancet,* 1 (1846), 349–54.

Davies, E.T., 'Self-Induced Instrumental Abortion', *The British Medical Journal*, 2/1968 (17 September 1898), 841–2.

Dickson, J. T., 'A contribution to the study of the so-called puerperal insanity', *Journal of Mental Science*, 16 (1871), 379–90.

Dolan, Thomas M., 'On defective lactation, its causes, and how far it may be influenced by drugs', *The British Medical Journal*, 1/1205 (2 February 1884), 211–12.

Evans, Caradoc, *My People* (1915, reprinted Bridgend, 2014).

Greenwood, James, *The Seven Curses of London* (1869, reprinted Oxford, 1981).

Harris, J. S., MD, Ed., MRCP, London, DPM, Deputy Medical Superintendent, West Park Mental Hospital, Epsom, 'Mental Disorder Associated with Child-Bearing', *The British Medical Journal*, 1/3929 (25 April 1936), 835–7.

Harris-Liston, L., 'Artificial Feeding of the Insane', *The British Medical Journal*, 1/1885 (13 February 1897), 391–2.

Hastings, H., 'Puerperal Mania followed by Insanity', *Medical Times*, 19 (1849), 511.

Herbert, Wm., 'The Forcible Feeding of the Insane', *The British Medical Journal*, 1/1731 (3 March 1894), 462.

Hopwood, J. Stanley, M.B., B.S., Lond., Junior Deputy Medical Superintendent, The State Criminal Lunatic Asylum, Broadmoor, 'Child Murder and Insanity', *Journal of Mental Science* (January 1927), 95–108.

Hyslop, T. B., 'Discussion on post-operative and puerperal disorder', *Proceedings of the Royal Society of Medicine* (8 January 1924), 1–14.

Hytten, F. E., Yorsten, Jessie C., Thomson, A.M., 'Difficulties Associated with Breast-Feeding', *The British Medical Journal*, 1/5066 (8 February 1958), 310–15.

Jackson, R. M., 'A Note on Broadmoor Patients', *The Cambridge Law Journal*, 11/1 (1951), 61.

Jones, Robert, M.D., Lond., Medical Superintendent of the London County Asylum, Claybury, 'Puerperal Insanity', *The British Medical Journal*, 1/2149 (8 March 1902), 579–86.

Jones, Robert, 'The Medical Treatment of Insanity', *The British Medical Journal*, 1/2312 (22 April 1905), 875–8.

Kerr, Norman S., *Female Intemperance* (London, 1880).

Landor, H., 'Cases of Moral Insanity', *The British Medical Journal*, 1/26 (27 June 1857), 542–3.

Leishman, William, M.D., Professor of Midwifery in the University of Glasgow, 'A System of Midwifery, Including the Diseases of Pregnancy and the Puerperal State', *The British Medical Journal*, 1/679 (3 January 1874), 13–14.

Leitch, Archibald, 'The Responsibility of the Suicide', *The British Medical Journal*, 1/2787 (30 May 1914), 1212.

Lombroso, Cesare and Ferrero, Guglielmo, *Criminal Woman, the Prostitute and the Normal Woman,* Trans. Rafter, Nichole Hahn and Gibson, Mary (London, 2004).

Lushington, Guy, *The Law of Affiliation and Bastardy: Comprising the Bastardy Laws Amendment Act, 1872* (London, 1904, reproduced Whitefish, Montana, 2010).

Mann, Edward C., M.D., 'Mental Responsibility and the Diagnosis of Insanity in Criminal Cases', *Journal of Psychological Medicine and Mental Pathology* (5 October 1879), 225–34.

Maudsley, Henry, 'Criminal's Responsibility', *The British Medical Journal*, 1/163 (13 February 1864), 192–3.

Maudsley, Henry, 'Is insanity on the increase?' *The British Medical Journal*, 1/576 (13 January 1872), 36–9.

Maxfield, Francis N., 'The Social Treatment of Unmarried Mothers', *The Psychological Clinic*, 9/7 (1915), 210–17.

McCleod, M. D., 'An Address on Puerperal Insanity', *The British Medical Journal*, 2/1336 (7 August 1886), 236–42.

Mercier, Chas. A., 'A Discussion on the Plea of Insanity in Criminal Cases', *The British Medical Journal*, 2/1966 (3 Sept 1898), 585–8.

Mercier, Charles A., 'The Responsibility of the Suicide', *The British Medical Journal*, 1/2786 (23 May 1914), 1156–7.

Mercier, Charles A., 'The Responsibility of the Suicide', *The British Medical Journal*, 1/2789 (13 June 1914), 1328.

Orange, W., 'The Present Relation of Insanity to the Criminal law of England', *The British Medical Journal*, 2/877 (20 October 1877), 553–4.

Rayner, Henry, 'A Discussion on the Treatment of Melancholia', *The British Medical Journal*, 2/ 1813 (28 Sept 1895), 760–6.

Rigden, Alan, 'Presidential Address Concerning the Insanity of Childbirth', *The British Medical Journal*, 2/2393 (10 Nov 1906), 1253–7.

Robertson, Alexander, 'Influence of Mental Shock in Insanity', *The British Medical Journal*, 1/1545 (10 June 1871), 610.

Robertson, George M., 'Some Medico-Legal and Practical Considerations Relating to Melancholia', *The British Medical Journal*, 1/2623 (8 April 1911), 800–4.

Routh, Amand, 'A Lecture on Ante-Natal Hygiene: Its Influence Upon Infantile Mortality', *The British Medical Journal*, 1/2772 (14 February 1914), 355–63.

Rutherford Hill, J., 'Criminal Abortion', *The British Medical Journal*, 2/1978 (26 November 1898), 1655.

Ryan, William Burke, *Infanticide: Its Law, Prevalence, Prevention, and History* (London, 1862).

Savage, George H., 'Our Duties in Reference to the Signing of Lunacy-Certificates', *The British Medical Journal*, 1/1266 (4 April 1885), 692–3.

Stephens, Joseph, 'The Case of Fatal Attempt to Procure Abortion', *The British Medical Journal*, 2/200 (29 October 1864), 503–5.

Stiles, Henry Reed, *Bundling: Its Origins, Progress, & Decline in America* (Boston, 1872, reproduced Massachusetts, 2004).

Sutherland, Henry, 'On the Artificial Feeding of the Insane', *Journal of Psychological Medicine and Mental Pathology*, 1 (1875), 98–115.

Troup, Sir Edward, *The Home Office* (London and New York, 1926).

Tuke, J. Batty, 'A Plea for the Scientific Study of Insanity', *The British Medical Journal*, 1/1587 (30 May 1891), 1161–6.

Wade, W. F., 'Homicidal Insanity', *The British Medical Journal*, 1/840 (3 Feb 1877), 149.

Waugh, Benjamin, 'Baby Farming', *Contemporary Review*, 57 (May 1890), 700–14.

West, R. U., 'Fatal and other cases of puerperal mania', *Association Medical Journal*, 2 (11 August 1854), 716–18.

White, Ernest, W., Resident Physician and Superintendent City of London Asylum, Dartford, Kent, 'A Note on the Treatment of Puerperal Insanity', *The British Medical Journal*, 1/2197 (7 February 1903), 306.

Whitwell, F., 'The Law on Insanity', *The British Medical Journal*, 2/934 (1878), 784.

Yellowlees, D., Medical Superintendent at the Glamorgan County Asylum, 'Insanity and Intemperance', *British Medical Journal*, 2/666 (4 October 1873), 394–5.

Newspapers, Journals and Periodicals

The Aberdare Leader

Bow Bells

Bristol Mercury & Daily Post

British Mothers' Journal and Domestic Magazine

The Cambria Daily Leader

The Cambrian

Cambrian & Weekly General Advertiser

Cardiff Times

Cardigan Observer and General Advertiser

Carmarthen Journal

Contemporary Review

The Englishwoman's Review

Evening Express

Haverfordwest & Milford Haven Telegraph

John Bull

Llanelly & County Guardian

Manchester Guardian
Merthyr Express
Pall Mall Gazette
Pembrokeshire Herald & General Advertiser
Reynolds's Newspaper
Rhondda Leader
South Wales Daily News
South Wales Daily Post
South Wales Echo
South Wales Weekly Post
The Times
The Weekly Mail
The Welshman
Western Mail

Secondary Sources

Andrews, Jonathan and Digby, Anne (eds), *Sex and Seclusion, Class and Custody: Perspectives on Gender and Class in the History of British and Irish Psychiatry* (Amsterdam, 2004).

Ballinger, Anette, *Dead Woman Walking: Executed Women in England and Wales 1900–1955* (Aldershot, 2000).

Banks, J. A., *Victorian Values* (London, 1981).

Barker, Hannah and Chalus, Elaine (eds), *Women's History: Britain, 1700–1850* (Oxford, 2005).

Bartlett, P. and Wright, D (eds), *Outside the Walls of the Asylum: The History of Care in the Community, 1750–2000* (London, 1999).

Barret-Ducrocq, Françoise, *Love in the Time of Victoria* (London, 1991).

Bingham, Adrian, *Family Newspapers: Sex, Private Life, and the British Popular Press, 1918–1978* (Oxford, 2009).

Brookes, Barbara, *Abortion in England, 1900–1967* (Kent, 1988).

Brooks, C. and Lobban, M (eds), *Communities and Courts in Britain, 1150–1880* (London, 1997).

Broughton, Trev Lynn and Rogers, Helen, *Gender and Fatherhood in the Nineteenth Century* (Basingstoke, 2007).

Busfield, Joan, *Men, Women and Madness: Understanding Gender and Mental Disorder* (Basingstoke, 1996).

Carlen, Pat, *Women, Crime and Poverty* (Oxford, 1988).

Chadwick, Roger, *Bureaucratic Mercy: The Home Office and*

Treatment of Capital Cases in Victorian Britain (London, 1992).

Clark, C. and Crawford, C (eds), *Legal Medicine in History* (Cambridge, 1994).

Cooper, Kathryn J., *Exodus from Cardiganshire: Rural-Urban Migration in Victorian Britain* (Cardiff, 2011).

Cossins, Annie, *Female Criminality: Infanticide, Moral Panics and the Female Body* (Basingstoke, 2015).

Davidoff, Leonore, *Worlds Between: Historical Perspectives on Gender and Class* (Cambridge, 1995).

Davies, John, *A History of Wales* (London, 1994).

Davies, Russell, *Secret Sins: Sex, Violence & Society in Carmarthenshire 1870–1920* (Cardiff, 1996).

Davies, Russell, *Hope and Heartbreak: A Social History of Wales and the Welsh, 1776–1871* (Cardiff, 2005).

Davies, Russell, *People, Places and Passions: Pain and Pleasure: A Social History of Wales and the Welsh, 1870–1945* (Cardiff, 2015).

Davin, Anna, *Growing Up Poor: Home, School, and Street in London 1870–1914* (London, 1996).

D'Cruze, Shani and Jackson, Louise A., *Women, Crime and Justice in England since 1660* (Basingstoke, 2009).

D'Cruze, Shani (ed.), *Everyday Violence in Britain, 1850–1950: Gender and Class* (Essex, 2000).

Digby, Anne, and Stewart, John (eds), *Gender, Health and Welfare* (London and New York, 1996).

Delap, Lucy, Griffen, Ben and Willis, Abigail, *The Politics of Domestic Authority in Britain Since 1800* (Basingstoke, 2009).

Emsley, Clive, *Crime and Society in England 1750–1900* (Harlow, 1990).

Englander, David, *Poverty and Poor Law Reform in Nineteenth-Century Britain, 1834–1914* (London, 1998).

Farrell, Elaine, *'A Most Diabolical Deed': Infanticide and Irish Society, 1850–1900* (Manchester, 2013).

Fisher, Kate, *Birth Control, Sex, and Marriage in Britain, 1918–1960* (Oxford, 2006).

Frost, Ginger S., *Promises Broken: Courtship, Class, and Gender in Victorian England* (London, 1995).

Frost, Ginger S., *Living in Sin, Cohabiting as Husband and Wife in Nineteenth-Century England* (Manchester, 2008).

Gatrell, V. A. C., *The Hanging Tree: Execution and the English People, 1770–1868* (Oxford, 1994).

Gillis, John R., *For Better, For Worse: British Marriages 1600 to the*

Present (Oxford, 1985).

Goc, Nicola, *Women, Infanticide and the Press, 1822–1922: News Narratives in England and Australia* (Oxfordshire, 2016).

Greenwood, Victoria and Young, Jock, *Abortion in Demand* (London, 1976).

Hendrick, Harry, *Children, Childhood and English Society 1880–1990* (Cambridge, 2001).

Hendrick, Harry, *Child Welfare: England, 1872–1989* (London, 1994).

Hopkins, Eric, *Childhood Transformed: Working-Class Children in Nineteenth-Century England* (Manchester, 1994).

Horn, Pamela, *The Rise & Fall of the Victorian Servant* (Sparkford, 2004).

Ireland, Richard W., *Land of White Gloves? A history of crime and punishment in Wales* (Oxfordshire, 2015).

Jackson, Mark (ed.), *Infanticide: Historical Perspectives on Child Murder and Concealment, 1550–2000* (Aldershot, 2002).

Jackson, Mark, *New-born Child Murder: Women, Illegitimacy and the Courts in Eighteenth-Century England* (Manchester, 1996).

Jones, Aled, *Powers of the Press: Newspapers, Power and the Public in Nineteenth-Century England* (Aldershot, 1996).

Jones, David J. V., *Crime in Nineteenth-Century Wales* (Cardiff, 1992).

Jones, Gareth Elwyn, *The Education of a Nation* (Cardiff, 1997).

Jones, Gareth Elwyn, *Modern Wales: A Concise History* (Cambridge, 1999).

Keown, John, *Abortion, doctors and the law: Some aspects of the legal regulation of abortion in England from 1803 to 1982* (Cambridge, 1988).

Kidd, Alan, *State, Society and the Poor in Nineteenth-Century England* (Basingstoke, 1999).

Kilday, Anne-Marie, *A History of Infanticide in Britain: c. 1600 to the Present* (Basingstoke, 2013).

Kilday, Anne-Marie and Nash, David, *Histories of Crime: Britain 1600–2000* (Basingstoke, 2010).

Knight, Rose and Gorton, Antonia, National Abortion Campaign, *Abortion: Where We Stand* (London, 1976).

Laslett, Peter, Oosterveen, Karla, Smith, Richard M (eds), *Bastardy and its Comparative History* (London, 1980).

Logan, Anne, *Feminism and Criminal Justice: A Historical Perspective,*

England and Wales c.1920–70 (Basingstoke, 2008).

Longmate, Norman, *The Workhouse* (London, 1974).

Loudon, Irvine, *Death in Childbirth: An International Study of Maternal Care and Maternal Mortality 1800–1950* (Oxford, 1992).

Malloy, Pat, *And They Blessed Rebecca: An account of the Welsh Toll-gate Riots, 1839–1844* (Llandysul, 1983).

Marland, Hilary, *Dangerous Motherhood: Insanity and Childbirth in Victorian Britain* (Basingstoke, 2004).

Mason, Michael, *The Making of Victorian Sexuality* (Oxford, 1994).

Matus, Jill A., *Unstable Bodies: Victorian Representations of Sexuality and Maternity* (Manchester, 1995).

McLaren, Angus, *Birth Control in Nineteenth-Century England* (London, 1978).

McDonagh, Josephine, C*hild Murder & British Culture 1720–1900* (Cambridge, 2003).

Michael, Pamela, *Care and Treatment of the Mentally Ill in Wales, 1800–2000* (Cardiff, 2003).

Nelson, Claudia & Sumner Holmes, Ann (eds), *Maternal Instincts* (London, 1997).

Pellow, Jill, *The Home Office, 1848–1914: From Clerks to Bureaucrats* (London, 1982).

Pinchbeck, I and Hewitt, M., *Children in English Society: From the Eighteenth Century to the Children Act 1948,* Volume II (London, 1973).

Poovey, Mary, *Uneven Developments: The Ideological Work of Gender in Mid-Victorian England* (London, 1988).

Porter, Roy, *A Social History of Madness: Stories of the Insane* (London, 1989).

Rattigan, Cliona, *'What Else Could I Do?' Single Mothers and Infanticide, 1900–1950* (Dublin, 2012).

Rawlins, Bert J., *The Parish Churches and Nonconformist Chapels of Wales: Their Records and Where to Find Them, Volume One, Cardigan-Carmarthen-Pembroke* (Salt Lake City, 1987).

Roberts, Gwyneth Tyson, *The Language of the Blue Books: Wales and Colonial Prejudice* (Cardiff, 2011).

Rose, Lionel, *Massacre of the Innocents: Infanticide in Great Britain 1800–1939* (London, 1986).

Rose, Sonya O., *What is Gender History?* (Cambridge, 2010).

Ross, Ellen, *Love and Toil: Motherhood in Outcast London,*

1870–1918 (Oxford, 1993).

Rowbotham, Judith and Stevenson, Kim (eds), *Behaving Badly: Social Panic and Moral Outrage: Victorian and Modern Parallels* (Basingstoke, 2003).

Scott, Joan Wallach, *Gender and the Politics of History* (New York, 1988).

Scull, Andrew, *The Most Solitary of Afflictions: Madness and Society in Britain, 1700–1900* (New Haven and London, 1993).

Shanley, Mary Lyndon, *Feminism, Marriage and the Law in Victorian England* (Princeton, 1993).

Sheetz-Nguyen, Jessica A., *Victorian Women, Unwed Mothers and the London Foundling Hospital* (London, 2012).

Showalter, Elaine, *The Female Malady: Women, Madness and English Culture, 1830–1980* (London, 1987).

Smart, Carol, *Women, Crime & Criminology: A Feminist Critique* (London, 1977).

Smith, Roger, *Trial by Medicine: Insanity and Responsibility in Victorian Trials* (Edinburgh, 1981).

Smout, T. C. (ed.), *Victorian Values* (Oxford, 1992).

Stevens, Catrin, *Welsh Courting Customs* (Llandysul, 1993).

Strange, Julie-Marie, *Death, Grief and Poverty in Britain, 1870–1914* (Cambridge, 2005).

Tebbutt, Melanie, *Women's Talk? A Social History of 'Gossip' in Working-Class Neighbourhoods, 1880–1960* (Aldershot, 1995).

Thorn, Jennifer, *Writing British Infanticide: Child-Murder, Gender and Print, 1722–1859* (London, 2003).

Williams, David, *The Rebecca Riots: A Study in Agrarian Discontent* (Cardiff, 2011).

Zedner, Lucia, *Women, Crime, and Custody in Victorian England* (Oxford, 1994).

Zedner, Lucia, *Criminal Justice* (Oxford, 2004).

Chapters in edited collections

Andrews, Jonathan, 'The boundaries of Her Majesty's Pleasure: discharging child-murderers from Broadmoor and Perth Criminal Lunatic Departments, c. 1860–1920', in Mark Jackson (ed.), *Infanticide: Historical Perspectives on Child Murder and Concealment, 1550–2000* (Aldershot, 2002), pp. 216–48.

Arnot, Margaret L., 'The murder of Thomas Sandles: Meanings

of mid-nineteenth-century infanticide', in Mark Jackson (ed.), *Infanticide: Historical Perspectives on Child Murder and Concealment, 1550–2000* (Aldershot, 2002), pp. 149–67.

Arnot, Margaret. L., 'Understanding women committing newborn child murder in Victorian England', in S. D'Cruze (ed.), *Everyday Violence in Britain, 1850–1950: Gender and Class* (Essex, 2000), pp. 56–70.

Digby, Anne, 'The Rural Poor Law', in D. Fraser (ed.), *The New Poor Law in the Nineteenth Century* (Basingstoke, 1976), pp. 149–170.

Grey, Daniel J. R., '"The agony of despair": Pain and the cultural script of infanticide in England and Wales, 1860–1960', in Rob Boddice (ed.), *Pain and Emotion in Modern History* (Basingstoke, 2014), pp. 204–19.

Grey, Daniel J. R., 'Parenting, Infanticide and the State in England and Wales, 1870–1950', in H. Barron, and C. Siebrecht (eds), *Parenting and the State in Britain and Europe, c. 1870–1950: Raising the Nation* (Basingstoke, 2017), pp. 73–92.

Hirst, David and Michael, Pamela, 'Family, community and the lunatic in mid-nineteenth-century North Wales' in P. Bartlett and D. Wright (eds), *Outside the Walls of the Asylum: The History of Care in the Community 1750–2000* (London, 1999), pp. 66–85.

Ireland, R. W., '"Perhaps my mother murdered me": Child death and the law in Victorian Carmarthenshire', in C. Brooks and M. Lobban (eds), *Communities and Courts in Britain, 1150–1880* (London, 1997), pp. 229–44.

Jackson, Mark, 'The trial of Harriet Vooght: continuity and change in the history of infanticide', in Mark Jackson (ed.), *Infanticide: Historical Perspectives on Child Murder and Concealment, 1550–2000* (Aldershot, 2002), pp. 1–17.

Jackson, Mark, 'Suspicious infant deaths: the statute of 1624 and medical evidence at coroners' inquests', in (eds) Michael Clark and Catherine Crawford, *Legal Medicine in History* (Cambridge, 1994), pp. 64–88.

Kilday, Anne-Marie, 'Desperate Measures or Cruel Intentions? Infanticide in Britain since 1600', in Anne-Marie Kilday and David Nash (eds), *Histories of Crime: Britain 1600–2000* (Basingstoke, 2010), pp. 60–79.

Marland, Hilary, 'At home with puerperal mania: the domestic treatment of the insanity of childbirth in the nineteenth century', in P. Bartlett and D. Wright (eds), *Outside the Walls of the Asylum: The History of Care in the Community, 1750–2000* (London, 1999), pp. 45–65.

Marland, Hilary, '"Getting away with murder?" Puerperal insanity, infanticide and the defence plea', in Mark Jackson (ed.), *Infanticide: Historical Perspectives on Child Murder and Concealment, 1550–2000* (Aldershot, 2002), pp. 168–92.

Nash, David and Kilday, Anne-Marie, 'Introduction', in Anne-Marie Kilday and David Nash (eds), *Histories of Crime: Britain 1600–2000* (Basingstoke, 2010), pp. 1–16.

Rabin, Dana, 'Bodies of evidence, States of mind: infanticide, emotion and sensibility in eighteenth-century England', in Mark Jackson (ed.), *Infanticide: Historical Perspectives on Child Murder and Concealment, 1550–2000* (Aldershot, 2002), pp. 73–92.

Suzuki, Akihito, 'Enclosing and disclosing lunatics within the family walls: domestic psychiatric regime and the public sphere in early nineteenth-century England', in P. Bartlett and D. Wright (eds), *Outside the Walls of the Asylum: The History of Care in the Community 1750–2000* (London, 1999), pp. 115–31.

Ward, Tony, 'Legislating for human nature: Legal responses to infanticide, 1860–1938, in Mark Jackson (ed.), *Infanticide: Historical Perspectives on Child Murder and Concealment, 1550–2000* (Aldershot, 2002), pp. 249–69.

Wheelwright, Julie, 'Nothing in between: Modern cases of infanticide', in Mark Jackson (ed.), *Infanticide: Historical Perspectives on Child Murder and Concealment, 1550–2000* (Aldershot, 2002), pp. 270–86.

Wright, David, 'Delusions of gender? Lay identification and clinical diagnosis of insanity in Victorian England', in Jonathan Andrews and Anne Digby (eds), *Sex and Seclusion, Class and Custody: Perspectives and Gender and Class in the History of British and Irish Psychiatry* (Amsterdam, 2004), pp. 149–76.

Journal Articles

Adair, Richard, Melling, Joseph, Forsythe, Bill, 'Migration, family structure and pauper lunacy in Victorian England: admissions to the Devon County Pauper Lunatic Asylum, 1845–1900', *Continuity and Change*, 12/3 (1997), 373–401.

Anderson, Olive, 'Prevention of suicide and parasuicide: what can we learn from history?' *Journal of the Royal Society of Medicine*, 82 (1989), 640–2.

Anderson, Olive, 'Did Suicide Increase with Industrialisation in Victorian England?' *Past & Present*, 86 (1980), 149–73.

Anis-Ur-Rehman, St Clair, David, Platz, Christine, 'Puerperal insanity in the 19th and 20th Centuries', *British Journal of Psychiatry*, 156 (1990), 861–5.

Arnot, Margaret L., 'Infant death, child-care and the state: the baby-farming scandal and the first infant life protection legislation of 1872', *Continuity and Change*, 9/2 (1994), 271–311.

Barber, Jill, "Stolen Goods': The Sexual Harassment of Female Servants in West Wales during the Nineteenth Century', *Rural History*, 4 (1993), 123–36.

Behlmer, George K., 'Deadly Motherhood: Infanticide and Medical Opinion in Mid-Victorian England', *Journal of the History of Medicine*, 34 (1979), 403–27.

Blaug, Mark, 'The Myth of the Old Poor Law and the Making of the New', *Journal of Economic History*, 23/2 (1963), 151–84.

Brockington, Ian, 'Suicide and filicide in postpartum psychosis', *Archives of Women's Mental Health*, 20 (2017), 63–9.

Broder, Sherri, 'Child Care or Child Neglect? Baby Farming in Late-Nineteenth-Century Philadelphia', *Gender and Society*, 2/2 (1988), 128–48.

Busfield, Joan, 'The Female Malady? Men, Women and Madness in Nineteenth-Century Britain', *Sociology*, 28/1 (1994), 259–77.

Campbell, Morag Allan, '"Noisy, restless and incoherent": puerperal insanity at Dundee Lunatic Asylum', *History of Psychiatry*, 28/1 (2017), 44–57.

Chaney, Sarah, '"No 'Sane' Person Would Have Any Idea": Patients' Involvement in Late Nineteenth-Century British Asylum Psychiatry', *Medical History*, 60/1 (2016), 37–53.

Clarke, Karen, 'Infanticide, Illegitimacy, and the Medical Profession in Nineteenth-Century England', *Journal Society for the Social History of Medicine* (1979), 11–14.

Crafts, N. F. R., 'Illegitimacy in England and Wales in 1911', *Population Studies*, 36/2 (1982), 327–31.

Crotty, Homer, D., 'History of Insanity as a Defence to Crime in English Criminal Law', *California Law Review*, 12/2 (1924), 105–23.

Damme, Catherine, 'Infanticide: The Worth of an Infant Under

Law', *Medical History*, 22 (1978), 1–24.

Davies, Kerry, '"Sexing the Mind?" Women, Gender and Madness in Nineteenth-Century Welsh Asylums', *Llafur*, 7/1 (1996), 29–40.

Davies, Russell, '"In a Broken Dream": Some Aspects of Sexual Behaviour and the Dilemmas of the Unmarried Mother in South West Wales, 1887–1914', *Llafur*, III (1983), 24–33.

Davies, Russell, '"Inside the 'House of the Mad": The social context of mental illness, suicide and the pressures of rural life in south west Wales, c. 1860–1920', *Llafur*, IV, 2 (1985), 20–35.

Davin, Anna, 'Imperialism and Motherhood', *History Workshop Journal*, 5 (1978), 9–65.

Dyhouse, Carol, 'Working-class mothers and infant mortality in England, 1895–1914', *Journal of Social History*, 12/2 (1978), 248–67.

Eigen, Joel Peter, 'Lesion of the Will: Medical Resolve and Criminal Responsibility in Victorian Insanity Trials', *Law & Society Review*, 33/2 (1999), 425–59.

Fahrni, Magda, '"Ruffled" Mistresses and "Discontented" Maids: Respectability and the Case of Domestic Service', *Labour/Le Travail*, 39 (1997), 69–97.

Forman Cody, Lisa, 'The Politics of Illegitimacy in an Age of Reform: Women, Reproduction, and Political Economy in England's New Poor Law of 1834', *Journal of Women's History*, 11/4 (2000), 131–56.

Frost, Ginger, 'The Black Lamb of the Black Sheep: Illegitimacy in the English Working Class, 1850–1939', *Journal of Social History*, 37/2 (2003), 293–322.

Frost, Ginger, '"When is a parent not a parent": Custody and illegitimacy in England, 1860–1930', *Journal of the History of Childhood and Youth*, 6/2 (2013), 236–62.

Frost, Ginger, 'Under the Guardians' Supervision: Illegitimacy, Family, and the English Poor Law, 1870–1930', *Journal of Family History*, 38/2 (2013), 122–39.

Frost, Ginger, 'He Could Not Hold His Passions: Domestic Violence and Cohabitation in England (1850–1905)', *Crime, Histories and Societies,* 12, 1 (2008), 25–44.

Fuchs, Rachel Ginnis, 'Crimes against Children in Nineteenth Century France: Child Abuse', *Law and Human Behaviour*, 6, 3/4 (1982), 237–59.

Gillis, John R., 'Servants, Sexual Relations, and the Risk of

Illegitimacy in London, 1801–1900', *Feminist Studies*, 5/1 (1979), 142–73.

Grey, Daniel J. R., '"More ignorant and stupid than wilfully cruel": Homicide trials and "Baby-Farming" in England and Wales in the wake of the Children Act 1908', *Crimes and Misdemeanours*, 3/2 (2009), 60–77.

Grey, Daniel J. R., 'Women's Policy Networks and the Infanticide Act 1922', *Twentieth-Century British History*, 21 (2010), 441–63.

Grey, Daniel J. R., '"Almost unknown amongst the Jews": Jewish women and infanticide in London', *The London Journal*, 37/2 (2012), 122–35.

Grey, Daniel J. R., '"Liable to Very Gross Abuse": Murder, Moral Panic and Cultural Fears over Infant Life Insurance, 1875–1914', *Journal of Victorian Culture* 18/1 (2013), 54–71.

Grey, Daniel J. R., '"What woman is safe...?" coerced medical examinations, suspected infanticide, and the response of the women's movement in Britain, 1871–1881', *Women's History Review*, 22/3 (2013), 403–21.

Grey, Daniel J. R., 'Murder, Mental Illness, and the Question of Nursing "Character" in Early Twentieth-Century England', *History Workshop Journal*, 80 (2015), 183–200.

Grey, Daniel J. R., '"Agonised Weeping": Representing femininity, emotion and infanticide in Edwardian newspapers', *Media History* (2015), DOI: 10.1080/13688804.2015.1047332.

Hagen, Grace, 'Women and Poverty in South-West Wales, 1834–1914', *Llafur* (1997–98), 21–33.

Hager, Tamar, 'Compassion and Indifference: The Attitude of the English Legal System Toward Ellen Harper and Selina Wadge, Who Killed Their Offspring in the 1870s', *Journal of Family History*, 33 (2008), 173–94.

Henriques, U. R. Q., 'Bastardy and the New Poor Law', *Past and Present*, 37 (1967), 103–29.

Higginbotham, Ann R., '"Sin of the Age": Infanticide and Illegitimacy in Victorian London', *Victorian Studies*, 32/3 (1989), 319–37.

Homrighaus, Ruth Ellen, 'Wolves in Women's Clothing: Baby-Farming and the *British Medical Journal*, 1860–1872', *Journal of Family History*, 26/3 (2001), 350–72.

Holtzman, Ellen M., 'The Pursuit of Married Love: Women's

Attitudes Toward Sexuality and Marriage in Great Britain, 1918–1939', *Journal of Social History*, 16/2 (1982), 39–51.

Houston, R. A., 'Explanations for death by suicide in northern Britain during the long eighteenth century', *History of Psychiatry*, 23/1 (2011), 52–64.

Hunt, Aeron, 'Calculations and Concealments: Infanticide in Mid-Nineteenth-Century Britain', *Victorian Literature and Culture*, 34 (2006), 71–94.

Ireland, Richard, W., 'Confinement with Hard Labour: Motherhood and Penal Practice in a Victorian Gaol', *Welsh History Review*, 18/4 (1997), 621–38.

Ireland Richard W., 'Putting oneself on whose country? Carmarthenshire juries in the mid-nineteenth-century', in T. G. Watkin (ed.) *Legal Wales: Its Past, Its Future* (Cardiff, Welsh History Society, 2001), 63–87.

Janson, Asa, 'From Statistics to Diagnostics: Medical Certificates, Melancholia, and "Suicidal Propensities" in Victorian Psychiatry', *Journal of Social History*, 46/3 (2013), 1–14 doi:10.1093/jsh/shs120.

Jackson, Mark, '"Fiction in the Archives?" Sources for the Social History of Infanticide', *Archives*, 27/107 (2002), 173–85.

Jackson, R. M., 'A Note on Broadmoor Patients', *The Cambridge Law Journal*, 11/1 (1951), 57–66.

Jaffery, Nora E., 'Reconceiving Motherhood: Infanticide and Abortion in Colonial Mexico', *Journal of Family History*, 37/1 (2012), 3–22.

Jenkins, A, Millar, S, Robins, J, 'Denial of pregnancy: a literature review and discussion of ethical and legal issues', *Journal of the Royal Society of Medicine*, 104/7 (2011), 286–7.

Johnson Kramer, Kirsten and Watson, William D., 'The Insanities of Reproduction: Medico-Legal Knowledge and the Development of Infanticide Law', *Social & Legal Studies*, 15/2 (2006), 237–55.

Kilday, Anne-Marie and Watson, Katherine D., 'Infanticide, Religion and Community in the British Isles, 1720–1920: Introduction', *Family and Community History*, 11/2 (2008), 84–99.

King, Peter, 'Making Crime News: Newspapers, Violent Crime and Selective Reporting of Old Bailey Trials in the late Eighteenth Century', *Crime, History & Societies*, 13/1 (2009), 91–116.

Knight, P., 'Women and Abortion in Victorian and Edwardian

England', *History Workshop*, 4 (1977), 57–69.

Krieder, Jodie., '"Degraded and Benighted": Gendered Construction of Wales in the Empire, ca. 1847', *North American Journal of Welsh Studies*, 2/1 (2002), 24–35.

Krueger, Christine L., 'Literary Defenses and Medical Prosecutions: Representing Infanticide in Nineteenth-Century Britain', *Victorian Studies*, 40 (1997), 271–94.

Levine-Clark, Marjorie, 'Dysfunctional Domesticity: Female Insanity and Family Relationships among the West Riding Poor in the Mid-Nineteenth Century', *Journal of Family History*, 25 (2000), 341–61.

Loudon, I., 'Puerperal insanity in the 19th century', *Journal of the Royal Society of Medicine*, 81 (1988), 76–9.

Lyle Margaret A., 'Regionality in the late Old Poor Law: The treatment of chargeable bastards from Rural Queries', *The Agricultural History Review*, 53/2 (2005), 141–57.

Mackay, R. D. and Ward, Tony, 'The long-term detention of those found unfit to plead and legally insane', *The British Journal of Criminology*, 34/1 (1994), 30–43.

Marland, Hilary, 'Under the shadow of maternity: birth, death and puerperal insanity in Victorian Britain', *History of Psychiatry*, 23/1 (2012), 78–90.

Marland, Hilary, 'Disappointment and desolation: women, doctors and interpretations of puerperal insanity in the nineteenth century', *History of Psychiatry*, 14/3 (2003), 303–20.

McCandless, Peter, 'Liberty and Lunacy: The Victorians and Wrongful Confinement', *Journal of Social History*, 11/3 (1978), 336–86.

McGowan, Randall, 'Identifying Themes in the Social History of Medicine', *Journal of Modern History*, 63/1 (1991), 81–90.

McLaren, Angus, 'Illegal Operations: Women, Doctors, and Abortion, 1886–1939', *Journal of Social History*, 26/4 (1993), 797–816.

McLaren, Angus, 'Women's Work and Regulation of Family Size: the question of abortion in the nineteenth century', *History Workshop*, 4 (1977), 70–81.

McLaren, Angus, 'Abortion in England, 1890–1914', *Victorian Studies*, 20/4 (1977), 379–400.

McLaren, Angus, 'Contraception and the Working Classes: The

Social Ideology of the English Birth Control Movement in Its Early Years', *Comparative Studies in Society and History*, 18/2 (1976), 236–51.

McLaren, Angus, 'Laughing the Evidence out of Court: The Policing of Gender in the Late Nineteenth Century', *Historical Reflections*, 24/3 (1998), 459–85.

Mooney, Graham, 'Still-Births and the Measurement of Urban Infant Mortality Rates c. 1890–1930', *Local Population Studies*, 53 (1994), 42–52.

Nutt, Thomas, 'Illegitimacy, paternal financial responsibility, and the 1834 Poor Law Commission Report: the myth of the old poor law and the making of the new', *The Economic History Review*, 63/2 (2010), 335–61.

Nelson, Claudia, 'Adoption, Fostering, and the Poor', *Victorian Review*, 39/2 (2013), 57–61.

Oberman, Michelle, 'Understanding Infanticide in Context: Mothers Who Kill, 1870–1930 and Today', *The Journal of Criminal Law and Criminology*, 92 (2002), 707–38.

Poovey, Mary, '"Scenes of an Indelicate Character": The Medical "Treatment" of Victorian Women', *Representations*, 14 (1986), 137–68.

Prior, Pauline M., 'Murder and Madness: Gender and the Insanity Defence in Nineteenth-Century Ireland', *New Hibernia Review*, 9/4 (2005), 19–36.

Prior, Pauline M., 'Prisoner or patient? The official debate on the criminal lunatic in nineteenth-century Ireland', *History of Psychiatry*, 15/2 (2004), 177–92.

Putman, Lara, 'To Study the Fragments/Whole: Microhistory and the Atlantic World', *Journal of Social History* (2006), 615–30.

Reid, Alice, 'Mrs Killer and Dr Crook: Birth Attendants and Birth Outcomes in Early Twentieth-Century Derbyshire', *Medical History*, 56/4 (2012), 511–30.

Riley, James C., '"Did Mothers Begin with an Advantage?" Study of Childbirth and Maternal Health in England and Wales, 1778–1929', *Population Studies*, 57/1 (2003), 5–20.

Roderick, Anne Baltz, '"Only a Newspaper Metaphor": Crime Reports, Class Conflict, and Social Criticism in Two Victorian Newspapers', *Victorian Periodicals Review*, 29/1 (1996), 1–18.

Sauer, R., 'Infanticide and Abortion in Nineteenth-Century Britain', *Population Studies*, 32/1 (1978), 81–93.

Scull, Andrew T., 'Mad-doctors and Magistrates: English

psychiatry's struggle for professional autonomy in the nineteenth century', *European Journal of Sociology*, 17/2 (1976), 279–305.

Shepherd, Anne and Wright, David, 'Madness, Suicide and the Victorian Asylum: Attempted Self-Murder in the Age of Non-Restraint', *Medical History*, 46 (2002), 175–96.

Shepherd, Jade, '"I am not very well I feel nearly mad when I think of you": Male Jealousy, Murder and Broadmoor in Late-Victorian Britain', *Social History of Medicine*, 30/2 (2016), 277–98.

Shepherd, Jade, '"One of the Best Fathers until He Went out of His Mind": Paternal Child-Murder, 1864–1900', *Journal of Victorian Culture*, 18/1 (2013), 17–35.

Shepherd, Jade, '"I am very glad and cheered when I hear the flute": The Treatment of Criminal Lunatics in Late-Victorian Broadmoor', *Medical History*, 60/4 (2016), 473–91.

Showalter, Elaine, 'Victorian Women and Insanity', *Victorian Studies*, 23/2 (1980), 157–81.

Sim, Myre, 'Abortion and the Psychiatrist', *British Medical Journal*, (20 July 1963), 145–8.

Sit, Dorothy, M.D., Rothschild, Anthony J. M.D., Wisner, Katherine L., 'A review of postpartum psychosis', *Journal of Women's Health,* 15/4 (2006), 352–68.

Smith, Cathy, '"Visitation by God": rationalizing death in the Victorian Asylum', *History of Psychiatry*, 23/1 (2011), 104–16.

Smith, Roger, 'The Victorian controversy about the insanity defence', *Journal of the Royal Society of Medicine*, 81 (1988), 70–3.

Stammers, K. and Long, N., 'Not your average birth: considering the possibility of denied or concealed pregnancy', *BMJ Case Reports* (29 May 2014), doi:10.1136/brc-2014-204800, 1–3.

Stearns, Carol Zisowitz and Stearns, Peter N., 'Victorian Sexuality: Can Historians Do It Better?' *Journal of Social History*, 18/4 (1985), 625–34.

Stuebe, Alison M., Grewen, Karen, Pedersen, Cort A., Propper, Cathi, Meltzer-Brody, Samantha, 'Failed Lactation and Perinatal Depression: Common Problems with Shared Neuroendocrine Mechanisms?' *Journal of Women's Health*, 21 (2012), 264–72.

Swain, Shurlee, 'Toward a social geography of baby farming',

History of the Family, 10 (2005), 151–9.

Theriot, Nancy, 'Diagnosing Unnatural Motherhood: Nineteenth-Century Physicians and "Puerperal Insanity"', *American Studies*, 30/2 (1989), 69–88.

Theriot, Nancy M., 'Women's Voices in Nineteenth-Century Medical Discourse: A Step toward Deconstructing Science', *Signs*, 19/1 (1993), 1–31.

Thomson, Michael, 'Abortion Law and Professional Boundaries', *Social & Legal Studies*, 22/2 (2013), 191–210.

Turrell, Rob, '"It's a mystery": the Royal Prerogative of Mercy in England, Canada and South Africa', *History & Societies*, 4/1 (2000), 83–101.

Vaughan, Phillip J., 'Letters and Visits to Long-Stay Broadmoor Patients', *The British Journal of Social Work*, 10/4 (1980), 471–81.

Wannell, Louise., 'Patients' relatives and psychiatric doctors: letter writing in the York Retreat 1875–1910', *Social History of Medicine*, 20/2 (2007), 297–313.

Ward, Tony, 'The Sad Subject of Infanticide: Law, Medicine and Child Murder, 1860–1938', *Social and Legal Studies*, 8 (1999), 163–80.

Ward, Tony, 'Law, Common Sense and the Authority of Science: Expert Witnesses and Criminal Insanity in England, c.1840–1940', *Social & Legal Studies*, 6/3 (1997), 343–62.

Ward, Tony, 'Experts, Juries, and Witch-Hunts from Fitzjames Stephen to Angela Cannings, *Journal of Law and Society*, 31/3 (2004), 369–86.

Watson, Katherine D., 'Women, violent crime and criminal justice in Georgian Wales', *Continuity and Change*, 28/2 (2013), 245–72.

Watson, Katherine D., 'Religion, Community and the Infanticidal Mother: Evidence from 1840s Rural Wiltshire', *Family and Community History* 11/2 (2008), 116–33.

Wheable, P., 'Lone Motherhood: The Unwed Mother in Nineteenth-Century Ringwood', *Local Historian*, 33/4 (2003), 244–54.

Wiener, Carol Z., 'Is a Spinster an Unmarried Woman?', *The American Journal of Legal History*, 20/1 (1976), 27–31.

Wiener, Martin J., 'Judges v Jurors: Courtroom Tensions in Murder Trials and the Law of Criminal Responsibility in Nineteenth-Century England', *Law and History Review*, 17/3 (1999), 467–506.

Wiener, Martin J., 'Convicted Murderers and the Victorian Press:

Condemnation vs. Sympathy', *Crimes and Misdemeanours*, 1/2 (2007), 110–25.

Wood, John Carter, '"Those who have had trouble can sympathise with you": Press Writing, Reader Responses and a Murder Trial in Interwar Britain', *Journal of Social History*, 43/2 (2009), 439–63.

Woods, Robert, 'Working-Class Fertility Decline in Britain', *Past & Present*, 134 (1992), 200–7.

Woodward, N., 'Infanticide in Wales, 1730–1830', *Welsh History Review*, 23 (2007), 94–125.

Wright, David, 'Getting Out of the Asylum: Understanding the Confinement of the Insane in the Nineteenth Century', *Society for the Social History of Medicine*, 10/1 (1997), 137–55.

Unpublished Theses

Grey, Daniel J. R., 'Discourses of Infanticide in England, 1880–1922' (unpublished PhD thesis, Roehampton University, London, 2008).

Homrighaus, Ruth Ellen, 'Baby Farming: The Care of Illegitimate Children in England, 1860–1943' (unpublished PhD thesis, University of North Carolina, Chapel Hill, 2003).

Key Websites

British Library Newspapers https://www.bl.uk

British Medical Journal https://bmj.com/archive

Census Returns https://www.findmypast.co.uk

National Library of Wales, Court of Great Sessions, Wales 1730–1830, https://crimeandpunishment.library.wales

Online Historical Population Reports https://www.histpop.org

Parliamentary Papers https://parlipapers.proquest.com

Pubmed https://www.ncbi.nlm.nih.gov

Times Digital Archive https://www.gale.com

Wales Newspapers Online https://newspapers.library.wales

Index

Author Profile

Shirley Smith gained her Ph.D. in History and Welsh History at Aberystwyth University in 2015.

Publisher Information

Rowanvale Books provides publishing services to independent authors, writers and poets all over the globe. We deliver a personal, honest and efficient service that allows authors to see their work published, while remaining in control of the process and retaining their creativity. By making publishing services available to authors in a cost-effective and ethical way, we at Rowanvale Books hope to ensure that the local, national and international community benefits from a steady stream of good quality literature.

For more information about us, our authors or our publications, please get in touch.

www.rowanvalebooks.com
info@rowanvalebooks.com

www.ingramcontent.com/pod-product-compliance
Ingram Content Group UK Ltd.
Pitfield, Milton Keynes, MK11 3LW, UK
UKHW020441200726
13857UKWH00002B/523

9 781912 655724